He had . . .

- 20/20 vision in both eyes
- a degree in aeronautical engineering
- been an air force pilot for three years
- been involved in aeronautical research for over a year

He saw the objects clearly and described them in full detail!
The official conclusion: "Investigation is not contemplated . . . CASE CLOSED!"

Jacques Vallee, a mathematician and astronomer, is consultant to the "Mars Map" project and a former research associate at McDonald Observatory. His wife, Janine, is a psychologist by training and a data analyst by profession.

Also by Jacques Vallee:

ANATOMY OF A PHENOMENON

CHALLENGE TO SCIENCE

The UFO Enigma

by

Jacques and Janine Vallee

BALLANTINE BOOKS • NEW YORK

The authors acknowledge with gratitude the assistance of Gordon W. Creighton, F.R.G.S., in translating portions of this material from the French.

The extract on pp. 8-13 is reprinted by permission of S. G. Phillips, Inc., from The Truth About Flying Saucers by Aime Michel. Copyright © 1956 by S. G. Phillips, Inc.

Library of Congress Catalog Card Number: 66-25843

SBN 345-24263-7-195

This edition published by arrangement with Henry Regnery Company

First Printing: November, 1974

Printed in the United States of America

BALLANTINE BOOKS
A Division of Random House, Inc.
201 East 50th Street, New York, N.Y. 10022
Simultaneously published by
Ballantine Books, Ltd., Toronto Canada

FOREWORD

WHAT IS THE RESPONSIBILITY OF THE SCIENTIST confronted with observations that seem not only a challenge but sometimes also an affront to science? How does one discharge this responsibility? The UFO phenomenon presents us with such a problem. To most scientists who have no acquaintance with the subject, save that gained from scanning the popular press, it is an "untouchable" area. "Flying saucers" indeed!—the product of immature, imaginative, and even unbalanced minds, the playground of the pseudo-scientist and the quasi-mystic, the haven of the crackpot.

Is this really so? Obviously, if one is to apply the scientific principles we all staunchly defend, one must take the time to look into the subject carefully—to look and to consider. But time is precisely what today's scientists—in some respects the world's busiest people —do not have! Who can take the time to wade through the seeming morass of stories, fanciful tales, chimera, and balderdash when so many pressing things demand the scientist's immediate attention?

As an astronomer, I probably would never have approached the subject had I not been officially asked to do so. Over the past eighteen years I have acted as a scientific consultant to the U.S. Air Force on the subject of unidentified flying objects—UFO's. As a consequence of my work on the voluminous air force files and, to a greater extent, of personal investigation of many puzzling cases and interviews with witnesses of good repute, I have long been aware that the subject of UFO's could not be dismissed as mere nonsense. Nonsense is present, to be sure, and misidentification of otherwise familiar objects that many sincere people report as UFO's. But is there not a "signal" in the "noise," a needle in the haystack? Is it not precisely our role to try to isolate the valid from the nonsensical? By carefully working through tons of pitchblende, Madame Curie isolated a tiny amount of radium—but the significance of that minute quantity was world-shaking.

It is my conclusion (speaking now personally and not in an official capacity) after many years of working through "tons" of reports, that there is a signal, that there is "radium" in the "pitchblende," waiting to be extracted. The authors of this book have come to the same conclusion, by a somewhat different path. Whether the scientifically valid in the entire UFO phenomenon proves to be a physical signal or a psychological one— or even a heretofore unknown phenomenon—it is in every respect a challenge to science.

Perhaps I should have spoken earlier; eighteen years is a long time. But it takes more evidence to get an idea accepted in a revolutionary field, be it biological evolution, relativity, or quantum mechanics, than it does to advance simply another step in an accepted scientific domain. Furthermore, astronomers are among the most conservative of scientists. Perhaps this is because their time scale is so great that they naturally bide their time in proposing or accepting revolutionary ideas, particularly if such ideas are subject to sensational treatment in the press and in the minds of the people.

Nonetheless, I have of late been rebuked, in my correspondence with people whose integrity I respect, with the charge that I failed to call the importance of the air force data on UFO's to the attention of my peers. If any defense is needed, in view of the controversial and explosive nature of the subject, it is that I did indeed on many occasions call guarded attention to the steadily growing mass of reports made by intelligent people from many countries. As early as 1952, before the Optical Society of America, I pointed out the significant nature of some types of UFO reports (article published in the *Journal of the Optical Society of America,* April, 1953). Over and above that, there remains the fact that for years I have personally devoted a portion of my time to this subject, an action that would be unthinkable had I not felt it was worthy of examination. I have long been aware that the UFO phenomenon is a global one and that it has captured the attention of many rational people. Numerous scientists have privately told me of their interest and their willingness to look further into the problem.

Also, as a scientific consultant to the U.S. Air Force, I carry a unique responsibility: any statement I make on the importance of the UFO phenomenon, unless backed by overwhelming evidence, carries the danger of "mobilizing the credulity of the world," as a university colleague of mine so aptly put it. I recognize that responsibility in accepting the invitation of the authors to write the Foreword to this book. It was only my respect for the authors as serious investigators and the continued and growing mass of unexplained UFO reports that prompted me to accept. I have over the years acquired something of a reputation as a "debunker" of UFO reports. If this arose from my honest desire to find a rational natural explanation for the stimuli that give rise to the reports, a procedure very frequently crowned with success, then I must bear with that reputation. If it stems, however, from a belief that I deliberately adopted a Procrustean approach, cutting down or stretching out evidence to make a forced fit, deliberately to "explain away" UFO reports at all cost, then it is a most unwarranted charge.

In my nearly two score years' association with the investigation of the reports, I have yet to write a book on the subject, primarily because there is no physical evidence in support of the phenomenon. Were I to write such a book today, however, I probably would take much the same approach followed by the present authors. The Vallees present a formidable amount of evidence for the global nature of the UFO phenomenon, but despite this they come to no firm conclusion. As they state: "We must realize that the observations we have reviewed . . . have no value in themselves. They are important, and deserve study, only because each one is an illustration of a phenomenon that has manifested itself since May, 1946, in every country in the world." Besides the fact that the reports bear striking similarities to each other, they continue to be made by people of good repute, which makes it imperative that a scientific investigation be undertaken. Because of the global nature of the total phenomenon, this investigation might well be carried out under the auspices of the United Nations. The psychological implications of the UFO phenomenon on world affairs certainly make it worthy of study. It makes no difference, in this respect, what the physical truth of the matter is; it is the impact it has on the minds of people in many nations that makes it potentially important in the psychosociological balance of the world.

My own interest, as an astronomer, in the total phenomenon is, of course, purely scientific. Some readers many well wonder whether this seemingly flamboyant subject is amenable to scientific inquiry. What constitutes scientific evidence in this field? The authors present a convincing argument that the UFO phenomenon can be studied with the advanced methods of inquiry of the physical scientist and of the sociologist and psychologist. In all of these methods the electronic computer figures prominently.

Scientific inquiry becomes possible when the phenomenon under study exhibits patterns and regularities, when it is subject to classification. The authors have shown that a classification system (the start of many branches of science) of UFO phenomena is possible and, indeed, that each type they have identified shows a different diurnal frequency pattern. In particular, their catalogue of five hundred cases should be of interest to scientists. I cannot help drawing a parallel with the first catalogues of celestial radio sources: the great majority of the entries were unidentified optically; only more advanced methods of analysis and observation revealed that some of these were distant radio galaxies and that some were the striking new puzzle, quasi-stellar sources. The present catalogue of UFO cases consists, with very few exceptions, of unidentified items; one wonders whether the parallel with the catalogue of radio sources continues.

Certainly no progress can be made without scientific study. Unfortunately, as the authors point out, scientists, "draped with dignity," have often refused to study the reports. The fact of the matter is that many of my colleagues who have undraped their dignity long enough to take a hard look at the reports have joined the growing ranks of the puzzled scientists: they privately indicate serious interest in the phenomenon but publicly they choose, like the subject itself, to remain unidentified; they are unwilling to expose themselves to the raillery and banter that go with it. It is to them in particular, and to all who foster the true Galilean spirit, that this book will be of greatest value. They grope and seek, examining even those ideas that seem fanciful and strange, for they know how strange and fanciful the term "nuclear energy" would have been to a physicist one hundred years ago. They are ready to accept a new challenge to science.

J. ALLEN HYNEK
*Chairman, Department
of Astronomy, and
Director, Dearborn
Observatory, Northwestern
University*

CONTENTS

INTRODUCTION

THE SUBJECT OF THIS BOOK is the scientific study of the sightings of "flying saucers" or "unidentified flying objects" that have been reported throughout the world.

In order to establish a precise, analytical approach to a subject so long the target of ridicule, we have had to abandon the sensational terminology the press has devised for it. It is not possible, at the present time, to subject the "flying saucer" to scientific study, or even to define it. Yet the fact that since 1946 numerous persons in all countries have made detailed reports of events they regard as strange, mysterious, sometimes even terrifying, deserves attention. While many of the reports can be traced to natural events, we intend to demonstrate that, after the inevitable errors and the obvious hoaxes are eliminated, the reports reveal common characteristics, possess a high degree of internal coherence, and appear to be the result of the witnesses' exposure to a set of unusual circumstances. The unknown cause of these reports is designated throughout this work by the term "UFO phenomenon."

The UFO phenomenon has been the subject of serious official attention only in the United States. The U.S.

Air Force has set up an organization to investigate the reports and certain American scientists acting in an individual capacity have examined the files and reported their opinions and findings. We believe that these studies are open to criticism, for they are based on data on which no attempt at classification has been made, in which significant sightings have remained smothered in a mass of mistakes and misinterpretations, in which the sites of the events have been located only vaguely, and into which the official data-gathering system has introduced obvious selection effects that no one has sought to correct or even to describe.

This book emphasizes the global nature of the phenomenon, showing how the European sightings illuminate the cases observed in America and in other parts of the world. The French observations in particular, dispersed as they are over a small area and revealing an excellent degree of precision, are treated in detail, and the methods developed for studying them are seen to be applicable to the phenomenon as a whole.

Our investigation was based on extensive material; we have drawn from the general files of the U.S. Air Force, from private and official collections in Europe, and from the data we have gathered personally since 1961. We have made it a principle to regard each report as the source of three categories of information: (1) information on the location of the sighting; (2) information on the time of the sighting; and (3) information on the description of the phenomenon.

The information on the location of the sighting is objective: it is independent of the number of witnesses, their age, or their reliability. The time information is also objective, but its study is more complex. The information on the description of the phenomenon is not only difficult to analyze, it is extremely subjective in nature; it involves knowledge of the conditions of the observation, the prevailing meteorological conditions, the instruments at the disposal of the observers, etc., and all the remarks of a physical nature presented: speed, shape, color, dimensions, and general behavior of the objects. For this reason the book is divided, after two introductory chapters designed to give the reader a sufficient understanding of the global and novel nature of the phenomenon, into three main parts. In the first part we begin our analysis of the patterns and general laws behind the observations by examining the spatial information and the topographic distribution of the sightings. In the second part the time information is considered, and the variation in the frequency of sightings is discussed in some detail, with a review of the modern history of the phenomenon illustrated by sightings drawn from the files. Finally, the physical characteristics of the reported objects are analyzed, and the problem of the origin and nature of the UFO phenomenon is posed.

In addition to suggesting new lines of research and improvements in the procedures for reporting and investigating the sightings, we have attempted to evaluate the current interpretations of the phenomenon and to predict what it may hold in store for mankind.

CHALLENGE TO SCIENCE

The UFO Enigma

1

FROM NEW MEXICO
TO NEW ZEALAND

THE CASE OF THE RESEARCH BALLOON

IN ORDER TO DISPEL ANY AURA OF MYSTERY surrounding the subject of this book, let us begin with a few case histories of actual series of observations. Our first document is dated January 16, 1951. It was not reported to the U.S. Air Force until a year later and was carried in the air force files with a one-year error on the date until a new investigation by an air force special agent, dated May 23, 1952, followed by a new interview of two of the witnesses, established the exact date.

The observation took place in Artesia, New Mexico. The manager of the Artesia Municipal Airport, who was among those interviewed, indicated that at the time of the sighting five other men were present. The group had been observing a balloon released by two engineers from General Mills; when the balloon reached an altitude of over one hundred thousand feet, they noticed "some disk-shaped objects in the same vicinity as the balloon." The airport manager said he observed two objects that seemed to be as high or higher than

1

the skyhook balloon (although the report recognizes that there is no way to establish this). Another witness, the manager of an electrical company, believed they were "much higher than the balloon."

The balloon was traveling east. The objects were moving southeast, and at no time were they motionless. They would slow down and speed up: when they left the vicinity of the balloon, they did so at an extreme rate of speed, "covering an arc of approximately 45° in two or three seconds and disappearing from view." They seemed to be two or three times the size of the balloon, which at that altitude was 110 feet in diameter. The reported angular velocity yields a value of the true speed of the objects (assumed to be at the same altitude as the balloon) of from eight to twelve kilometers per second, about the escape velocity at the earth's surface.

It was further reported that the objects scattered and then regrouped close to the balloon. When they departed, they did so in single file. At no time did they pass between the observers and the balloon. The airport manager, who had held that position for five years and had been a pilot for three years, was sure that the objects were not aircraft of any known type. They looked like "round and flat disks," pale gray in color. They left no contrail or any other visible vaporization.

Another witness stated that the objects appeared oblong and that as they departed they traveled at a constant high speed, generally from north to south, through a 50° arc in the sky. One object, he said, followed the other. He did not believe they were aircraft: they seemed to be "twice the size of the balloon, which was at more than one hundred thousand feet." He added that the objects were a dull gray in color and did not reflect the bright sunlight. A third witness stated that they were "definitely not a reflection or a cloud formation"; he described the objects as having a convex surface, being much longer than broad and a dull gray in color, "with a rose tinge as a haze." When first sighted, he said, they seemed to be moving slowly (or else moving away) and then made an abrupt 90° turn and, "leaving a terrific sense of acceleration," went out of view.

One of the men in the group was a General Mills employee assigned to the project as a photographer. At 9:30 that morning he and the pilot for the balloon project had, while tracking the balloon from a research airplane, observed "a round object remaining motionless in the sky in the vicinity of, but a considerable distance above, the drifting balloon."

At 11:00 A.M. the same morning, as he and the pilot joined the group at the Artesia Municipal Airport, he noticed two objects, also described by him as dull in color and at an extremely high altitude, coming toward the balloon from the northwest. They flew "around and above the balloon" and then left toward the northeast. The lapse of time was about forty seconds. The two objects appeared to be round disks, about the size of the disk they had seen earlier in the morning, and traveled in flying formation, one to the side of and slightly behind the other, at a distance of from six to eight times the disk's diameter. As the disks went around the balloon they turned on edge and could not be seen in that position. The pilot and one other witness saw only the departure of the objects; he described them as opaque and off-white in color. He has a degree in aeronautical engineering from the University of Minnesota, was a pilot in the air force for approximately three years, and at the time of the observations had been doing aeronautical research for over a year. His job consisted of tracking research balloons with an airplane, and he had 20/20 vision in both eyes and had never worn glasses.

The air force's conclusion on this case could well serve as an illustration of even greater value than the report itself. It reads: "In that all logical leads have been developed and reported, further investigation is not contemplated. Closed."

THE CASE OF THE CROOKED BOLIDES

Reports such as the above have indeed become commonplace in the private conversations and the public press of recent years. But the reader should not assume on this basis that the phenomenon we are studying is specifically a contemporary one; the evidence for its existence in older times is overwhelming, and it is reviewed in a number of books. We have chosen our second example from these old records.

In the *Comptes Rendus* of the French Academy of Sciences of January 17, 1898, the following article appears:

Meteorology. Observation of a double bolide in Vannes, on January 3, 1898. Note by M. Georget, presented by M. O. Callandreau.

On January 3, as I was returning home about 8:40 P.M., I saw in the northeast, at an elevation of 30° to 40°, a luminous meteor, fairly bright, having the same color as the planet Mars, traveling at a relatively slow rate through the sky. It went away toward the north and disappeared at the horizon at a point that formed an alignment with the stars Zeta and Eta Ursae Majoris, behind the hills situated to the north of Vannes, about eight or ten kilometers away, and about 110 meters higher than the town itself.

It went through a trajectory of 45° in five or six minutes, during which time it steadily lost brightness, as a luminous body would if it went away. About the time of its disappearance, one could see a yellow or reddish flash.

I was able to examine this meteor for a few minutes with a small telescope of 30 mm. (terrestrial telescope of Soulier). It seemed to be formed by two luminous bodies, A and B, situated at approximately the same elevation, the brighter one,

A, being in front. Remarkable peculiarity: the motion of B was affected by sudden oscillations, which lasted about half a second. Four or five oscillations were counted per minute. These objects gave the impression of two balloons linked together.

Callandreau adds the following remark:

The observation made by Commander Georget is very important. It should be compared to another observation made by Schmidt, which was perhaps unique to this date. This astronomer saw, on October 19, 1863, a bolide that was following an exceptionally slow course. He was able to study it through a comet searcher and stated that it was a double object.

Such observations are *not* exceptional. Similar objects have been seen and patiently recorded by astronomers throughout the eighteenth and the nineteenth centuries. Such reports became so numerous in the early twentieth century that Flammarion, the great French astronomer, created a new name for them: *bradytes,* or exceptionally slow meteors. Many excellent observations of such objects are found in Flammarion's journal, *L'Astronomie*. In addition, many astronomical publications in Europe and in the U.S. have gathered similar reports.

In 1908, another French astronomer, Lucien Libert, presented a catalogue of 1,368 meteors observed during the period from November, 1896, to November, 1904, to the Thirty-seventh Session of the French Association for the Advancement of Science, held in Clermont-Ferrand. Among these meteors were especially bright objects that would really deserve the name "bolides," and Libert made a separate presentation to the Society of twenty-five of these remarkable objects. The reader will see that at least five of these were indeed unusual.

First, we should point out that Libert was not a casual observer of the sky. He introduced his communication by stating that since November, 1896, he had observed and recorded meteors at every occasion made possible "by his own health and the state of the weather," and he thanked the Society for granting him a special subvention for the continuation of his astronomical work. He then proceeded calmly with the following statements:

On July 4, 1898, I was in my observatory when suddenly, at 7 hrs. 10 m. 18 s., I saw a luminous body appear above a tree at the northern horizon. It was of a beautiful golden-yellow color and perfectly spherical. Its apparent diameter was one-fourth that of the moon. This object started from the north-northeast, rose slowly in the sky, went through the zenith, then started losing brightness as it went down toward the horizon. It disappeared at elevation 30° above the west-southwest horizon, near Venus, at 7 hrs. 22 m. 44 s. Its duration, therefore, was *twelve minutes, twenty-six seconds*. It is by far the longest duration I have observed. A short time before it disappeared it increased its speed. . . . A fairly strong noise of explosion was heard a few seconds after its disappearance.

On June 29, 1898, at 1 hr. 03 m. A.M., a bolide with very slow motion glided in sixty seconds from Hercules to Ursa Major. Its diameter was 25 seconds of arc, and it was very bright and white in color.

On May 6, 1899, at 8:30 P.M., a magnificent bolide with a very, very slow motion, of yellow color and surrounded with a shower of sparks, appeared in the constellation of the Scale. Night had not completely come and it was difficult to ascertain points of comparison. Only Jupiter and Spica were visible. This bolide had a completely peculiar shape, which I cannot compare to anything better than a tadpole's head. There was a very bright point in front, and a tail with extremely fast movements of undulation.

On June 7, 1899, at 9 hrs. 25 m. 32 s. P.M., a yellow bolide, very slow, of the magnitude of Venus, leaving no trail, went from Ophiuchus to Scorpio in twelve seconds.

On February 9, 1902, at 7 hrs. 40 m. P.M., I observed with MM. Schoux, Marcel Libert and Lucien Briand an extremely remarkable bolide, of the magnitude of Venus. It started from the position of Capella, at a point I estimate to be about five hours of right ascension and +45° declination, and went on a straight line toward β Persei, which it reached in about three seconds. Having reached the vicinity of this star, it suddenly changed direction, followed a sort of loop and went toward Aldebaran with a curved trajectory. When it was about to disappear it split into three or four objects of approximately second magnitude. The whole observation had lasted about twelve seconds. The point of disappearance was about 4 hrs. 50 m. of right ascension and +20° of declination. The bolide left a trail that lasted about one and one-half minutes.

This bolide, a very crooked one indeed, is recorded in Figure 1.

THE CASE OF THE INTERRUPTED DINNER

At 2:03 A.M. on Monday, October 27, 1952, a man having a snack of bread and cream cheese at Marignane Airport interrupted his frugal dinner. The man was Gabriel Gachignard, a customs officer, and his unfinished meal was the starting point for a series of investigations by French officials and policemen and for more discreet inquiries by a group of French scientists. A first investigation was conducted by Jean Latappy. Gachignard told him the following story:

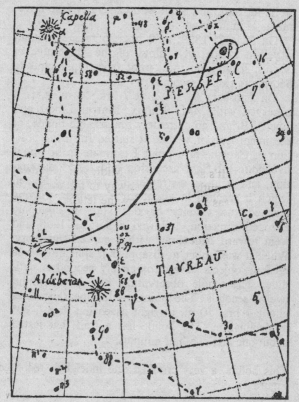

FIG. 1.—The path of the bolide observed by Libert on
July 4, 1898.

"During the night of Sunday 26 to Monday 27
October 1952, about midnight, a light blow of the
mistral cleared the sky, but pretty soon it clouded
over again, as if rain was coming. Toward 2
o'clock I was in the hangar. I had been on duty
since 8 o'clock. I was wide awake, having slept
during the day. I had just bought a snack, some
bread and cream cheese. I went out to eat it on a
bench, in the open air. These benches are on a

cement terrace in front of the hangar. The terrace is separated from the runway where the planes park by some cement troughs with flowers planted in them. I intended, when I had eaten, to go to the control office, to make sure that the mail plane from Algiers was going to land at 2:20, as I had been told. Actually, that was a mistake: that service is suspended on Sunday nights.

"The airfield spread out in front of me in the darkness but I know all the corners of the place by heart and anyway, it is never pitch dark on that big place. It's so clear in the Midi; you can always distinguish outlines. The runway to the hangar behind me was faintly lit up by the letters of the red neon sign, thirty feet long and three feet high, that says 'Marseille.'

"It was not more than three minutes after two—the Nice-Paris mail, scheduled to leave at that time, had just taken off—when suddenly to my left I saw a small light that seemed to be approaching, flying down the runway. It was not very bright, but perfectly visible and clear, even in the darkness. It seemed to be coming at the speed of a jet plane about to land, perhaps 150 miles an hour. At first I thought it was a shooting star and that I was wrong about the distance and the speed; the background of the field was lost in the darkness and I could not see exactly where the sky began.

"However, about half a mile away to the left, at the edge of the runway, there is a building, called the 'Two Barrels' on account of its shape, and I saw the light, which still seemed to be approaching, pass over it at just about 10 meters (30 feet). Its course was absolutely straight, without any oscillation, and came down gradually toward the ground. In a moment it passed in front of me and then I knew that it wasn't any shooting star, that it wasn't any shooting star, that it was something it was something that was really flying.

"All this happened very fast, without my having time to think.

"The light had hardly passed me when it touched the ground and suddenly stopped completely, without slowing down. A dead stop from 150 miles per hour, without transition! It was about 100 yards away from me, on my right. At the exact moment when it touched the grillwork runway, I heard a dull noise, as if it were muffled, not metallic, the noise something makes when you set it flat on the ground. That was the first sound I heard; the approach had been made in total silence.

"Then I realized that the object was not a plane, because it hadn't slowed down or rolled along the ground. Fifteen or twenty seconds had passed since it appeared, and there it was. It wasn't a plane, but it wasn't just a light either, because I had heard a noise. It was something solid. I got up right away and went toward it, partly out of curiosity, of course, but also because it's my job.

"It took me about 30 seconds to cover half the distance, and it was during that time that I discovered that the light belonged to a larger object. The larger object stood out dimly against the lighter background on the small yellow Meteo building. This building hid the landing strip from me; the strip is always well lighted, but unluckily it couldn't light the place where the shape was.

"The object was dark, darker than the shadows around it. What was it made of? I don't have any idea and in spite of all the questions they've asked me about it I can't tell them anything. It could just as well have been made of metal as of cardboard.

"Using the distances and the dimensions of the building behind the objects as landmarks, all we have been able to do is estimate the object's height as three feet and its length as fifteen feet. It had the shape of a football with very pointed ends. The only part of it that was clearly visible were the two ends, because the weak neon light outlined them vaguely, in the shadow. They were very sharp, very tapering. The curve of the object underneath was in complete darkness, which prevented me from seeing whether there were any wheels.

"I couldn't see anything, so I can't tell you anything about them. On the upper curve the same shadows, and I couldn't make out anything there either. The only thing I can be accurate about is this: The light I had seen from the start came from four perfectly square windows, eight to twelve inches on a side. They were placed on a line, and this line wasn't straight but curved, following the upper curve of the cigar, in such a way that the upper edge of the windows seemed to be on a level with the top of the machine.

"The four windows formed a group centered exactly in the middle of the thing, so that the extreme right-hand and left-hand windows were at the same distance from the two pointed ends. But they were in pairs: there was the same distance between the windows of each pair, while the space between the two inner windows was wider. The two outer windows seemed to me slightly inclined.

"Behind these windows a strange light was flickering. It was not steady nor fixed or vivid, but ghostly and soft, almost milky at times. It seemed to go back and forth behind those windows, with changing tints, bluish or greenish, on a pale background. Anyway, it wasn't strong enough to light the dark parts of the object. Its intensity was always the same; it didn't vary when the object was moving. On the other hand, it never stopped 'throbbing,' like the movement of waves. I noticed all this while I was walking towards the object. But suddenly, when I was not more than 50 yards away from it, I saw a shower of sparks, or rather

a sheaf of tiny white glowing particles, spurt out
from under the rear end, on my left. But they did
not give enough light to help me distinguish the
shape of the object any better. This fiery stream
was inclined toward the ground.

"This lasted for only a second, and at the same
time the cigar took off so suddenly, and with such
irresistible force, that I lost my self-control and
retreated instinctively, five or six steps. During
that second I wondered what was going to happen,
whether the machine was going to shoot flames
or run over me! I certainly believed there was
danger. And besides, even if I couldn't see 'them'
clearly, because the machine was in the shadow of
the building, 'they' could see me perfectly, silhou-
etted against the light of the neon sign!

"The shower of sparks and the departure were
accompanied by a slight noise, a kind of swish,
like a sky-rocket. There was no airstream, no
blast, no preliminary downward tilt. It's true, I
was 50 yards away. But in no more than two or
three seconds the object had disappeared, in exactly the opposite direction from its arrival. Just as
the speed of approach had been moderate, the
speed of departure was terrific. There wasn't even
the appearance of acceleration, but it changed
instantly to a frightening speed, impossible to
estimate. The angle of ascent was small; as when
it arrived, the machine went through the space,
thirty or forty yards wide, between the operations
building and the runway-control building. This
passage is in line with the grillwork runway where
it landed.

"After it took off, I could not have followed it
by eye except for the jet of white particles gushing
from the rear, as the windows and their light were
not visible any more from where I was. I could
see that when it flew between the two buildings it
was still very low, lower than their rooftops,
which are about thirty feet up. The next instant

the light disappeared over the lake of Berre, which is at the end of the airport, across the road" (quoted in 26, and used by permission of S. G. Phillips, Inc., original publishers).

The customs officer immediately tried to find another witness who could corroborate his observation. But there was nobody on the runway. Everybody was asleep at the airport building, for there was no traffic at that hour. Finally, at 2:15 A.M., he ran into the Air France agent, a Mr. Dugaunin.

"Good Lord, how pale you are!" Dugaunin exclaimed, before the other had said a word. Gachignard told his story. They telephoned the control tower, but no one had seen anything. The tower hardly watches any area except the main runway where all the planes land and take off. Furthermore, it would appear from Gachignard's narrative that the cigar came and went too low to be seen—lower than the tower itself, perched forty-five feet off the ground.

" 'So I was the only one who saw it; if anyone's around an airport at night, it's bound to be a customs officer.' That was the conclusion of Gachignard's story, as told to Latappy" (quoted in 26).

A French scientist who holds a Ph.D. in physics resumed the investigation in a private capacity when the excitement over the officer's story had subsided. He met Gachignard and cross-examined him on his previous statements, trying to lead him to add details or contradict himself:

I asked him to tell me the Marignane story, the details of which I pretended to know only with great inaccuracy, having only read them in the papers a long time ago. Well, the account given me by this excellent man (whom I submitted to every possible question, trying to trap him into contradiction) coincides exactly with his earlier statements. . . .

It seems that he was blamed for not having fired

at the "object" with his 6.35 revolver. "But," he said, "at fifty meters, I couldn't; besides, I was running toward the thing and then, when I saw the sparks at the rear, I was surprised and it took off at once, with this noise, so fast I became white with fear. . . ."

I asked him what color it was; he said: "It must have been dark, because only the top was visible (it was lighted by the neon sign) and also the two ends, pointed like a ball of rugby. But there were the windows. . . . Well, I say windows because it looked like windows; they were on the top of the object, they went through several colors, green, blue, red, but not clearly; it was translucent, not very bright, anyway, not like our lighting."

And did it damage the ground, when it landed?

"We went there with a flashlight, that very night, to see if the grass had been scratched. We, we didn't see anything. But later 'they' came from Paris with controlling instruments, and they said that the grass was a bit burnt at that place."

Did the lighting of the windows go off when it started?

"No, not at all, I had just time to see them rise, but the next second it was only a little light that ran through the sky and then, nothing."

And the spark, when it took off, can you describe it?

"It was a sort of zig-zag spark; at the rear, under the object, it gave like small lightnings; that is where I got scared. It came from the south and flew away just north, exactly in a northerly course."

How big could it have been?

"This we could figure out precisely, at the distance it was; that came out as 4.50 meters to 5 meters long if I remember right, and it may have been 1.20 meter high, but this I can't tell exactly since the underside was not visible."

Did they believe you when you reported what you had seen?

"My chief did, the newsmen also, but some of the policemen did not believe me, and yet, was it in my interest to make up that story? At the base, they saw it was true, because I was green with fear when I made my report to the control tower. When you're eating, you don't sleep, no?" (260).

So far, the whole story is based on Gachignard's report. He is a serious and solid witness, and there is no reason to doubt his word. But he was alone.

What Gachignard did not know was that, ten kilometers south of the airfield, two children, Xavier Beloeuvre and his sister (aged eleven and ten at the time), were awakened by a high-pitched whistling sound produced by a disk-shaped object, which, they said, flew over their house.

"We looked out of the window," they reported,

and we clearly saw a disk that appeared in perspective, that is, we rather saw it as an ellipse. It was lighted by sources that were not regularly spaced on the disk, but were clearly distinct sources. And since they were elongated all in the same direction, like the tail of a comet, it seemed obvious that the object was spinning. . . . What I saw was going toward Marignane. My position was exactly on the line of travel of an object that would come from the sea toward the airfield. The lights were perfectly constant, of a blue-purple color.

The shape was that of a disk, of such dimension that it appeared larger than the full moon, and it moved very slowly.

Let us note here that a disk five meters in diameter would have had the apparent diameter of the full moon (half a degree) if seen six hundred meters away. The children's description is thus compatible with the dimensions computed in Marignane. Gachignard gave the investigator a rough sketch of the object as he saw it; this is shown in Figure 2.

FIG. 2.—The Marignane object as sketched by Gachignard.

THE CASE OF THE AUTOMATIC CAMERA

The three series of observations studied above have been chosen from several thousand sightings because each illustrates a specific character, or pattern of characters, commonly found in reports of UFO phenomena. The next case is of interest in another respect: not because of what the witnesses described, but because *there were no witnesses.*

Before we comment on this very intriguing case, we will first report on an observation made in Montlucon on April 21, 1957, from 1:45 to 2:30 A.M., by Mrs. Gilberte Ausserre and Mrs. Rolande Prevost. These witnesses saw a yellow, hemispherical object in the sky; its apparent diameter increased to the size of the full moon, and then it vanished, i.e., it suddenly disappeared from the view of the witnesses, and reappeared a few minutes later, at a point situated to the right of the first sighting position. This new period of visibility lasted about five minutes; then the object vanished again for five minutes and came back. It went out completely at 2:30 A.M. From the underside of the object emerged several filaments of a green and purple color spread like a fan as shown on the rough sketch of Figure 3, drawn from the witnesses' account. The brightness was blinding, and the shape reminded one of a *jellyfish*. A French writer has borrowed this expression from the Montlucon report, and the name has become classical in UFO literature (5); for this reason, we shall use the same terminology in the present work. The Montlucon witnesses added that at some of the reappearances the object had lost its "jellyfish" aspect, and was seen as a double-bodied object.

Aime Michel, commenting on the incident at Montlucon, points out that similar observations had been made in 1954 in other parts of France (especially in Lievin, Rue, Marcoing, Armentieres, Milly, Champigny, Corbigny, Montbeliard), but these reports had

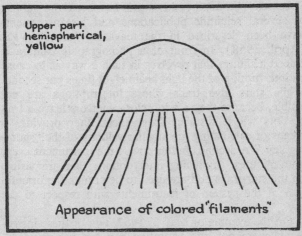

FIG. 3.—Rough sketch of the object seen in Montlucon on April 21, 1957.

drawn absolutely no interest except in the local press, and were swamped by the flood of reports of other types. The permanent character of these reports is therefore difficult to explain on purely psychosociological grounds. We are led to admit the reality of an objective phenomenon with constant and reproducible characters.

The Montlucon case is also invoked in support of the hypothesis that observations of the "jellyfish" object and those of the "double" object should be treated together and studied as a class. In this respect, the record obtained in Forcalquier by an automatic camera deserves special attention. It appears to eliminate any doubt as to the reality of the UFO phenomenon and provides as much information as one could hope to find from a photographic document. It also gives the lie to the contention that "astronomers have no record of the UFO phenomenon," a statement whose falsity will be exposed at several points in this book.

The Forcalquier photographs were taken by a French astronomer, Roger Rigollet, a specialist in meteor studies for the French National Center for Scientific Research (C.N.R.S.); his work has been the subject of several scientific publications and his instruments have been described in the magazine *Science-et-Vie* (April, 1958). In front of a photographic camera is placed a shutter that revolves in such a way as to cause an interruption of the light beam eight times per second. While stars give trails whose interruptions are not visible, because they are too close, meteors leave a trail of dots whose distance from each other provides a means of calculating the angular velocity of the "shooting star." A second shutter covers the instrument every four minutes, producing interruptions that are visible on the star trails and are used to determine the orientation of the system of instruments with respect to the sky.

On the evening of May 3, 1957, two of these instruments were put into operation and left unsupervised. When the recordings were analyzed the next day, they showed two small but definite spots (*see* Plate IV). Detailed examination of the negatives showed the images to be those of real objects, not defects in the emulsion, because the two cameras had recorded the same phenomenon. The shapes of the two spots were different, because one of the cameras was rotating and the other was stationary.

The analysis of the photographs gave the following data: some luminous object had been in the field of the instruments at 22:38 and another object—or the same one—had again given an image at 22:41.

Examination of the negative from the fixed camera showed a luminous protuberance on the underside of the object. Between the two exposures, the object (if it was the same one) must have been dark. The trace left by the unknown source is radically distinct from that of a meteor, a lighted balloon or an airplane.

THE CASE OF THE INTELLIGENT MACHINE

One week prior to the Montlucon incident a most remarkable sighting had been made in Vins-sur-Caramy (Var). It is one of the best-documented cases in the European files; it was extensively investigated by the French police: the gendarmes, the maritime police from Toulon, scientific consultants from Lyons and Paris, and finally the DST, the French equivalent of the American FBI, visited the scene and gathered soil samples, photographed the site and performed multiple analyses. The press did not give much coverage to the case, but here again, private scientific investigations supplemented the published and unpublished findings.

Vins is a small village in the Midi, near Brignoles. Two inhabitants of Vins, a Mrs. Garcin and a Mrs. Rami, were walking on Departmental Road 24, not far from the castle of Vins, which is one kilometer east of the village. Suddenly, a deafening noise startled them and they turned around; they were confronted with an incredible object.

The thing was flying slowly over the intersection of D 24 and the road that goes to Brignoles (Figure 4). It was only a few feet above the ground. The time was 3 P.M.

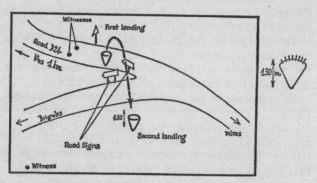

FIG. 4.—The landing at Vins, April 14, 1957, with a rough sketch of the object from a witness' description.

The object was shaped like a top or a cone, with the tapered end down. All descriptions of dimensions agree: it was not more than one and one-half meters high and about one meter in diameter. It had a series of appendages or "antennae," which vibrated rapidly; *in resonance with these vibrations, one of the road signs at the intersection was strongly vibrating*. The metallic sign was the source of the thundering noise that had attracted the witnesses' attention.

Mrs. Rami later declared: "It looked like a big top. On the upper part there were numerous metallic rods that looked like car antennae." Both women screamed as the object touched the ground.

Three hundred meters away, a man working on the hillside also heard the noise, and he thought two cars had just collided on the road. He was Louis Boglio, a municipal council member in Vins. He stated: "I heard a great noise, and I thought there had been a car crash. I ran to the site of what I thought was an accident and

I saw a metallic craft, which made an enormous leap through the air."

The object remained near the ground only a few seconds; it then jumped over a distance of two hundred meters, flying over a second road sign, *which immediately started vibrating like the first one* (Figure 4).

Several remarks can be made concerning this observation. First of all, the witnesses were well known for their reliability: their good faith was established by the official investigation and their personal character was vouched for by local officials, in particular the mayor of Vins. Second, distances and dimensions could be computed accurately from the witnesses' statements. The observation was made in full daylight and the object was very close to the ground, affording points of comparison with background objects. Third, there were independent groups of witnesses: two people in the neighboring village, La Moutonne, reported seeing the object in flight (184).

THE CASE OF THE FRIGHTENED ESKIMOS

We quote below from a report written by a Copenhagen researcher after a series of investigations in the Kangatsiaq district, on the western coast of Greenland, south of Egedesminde:

On October 4, 1957, I was at a small place called Niaqornarssuk, situated in the Arfersiorfik fiord in the Kangatsiaq district. Between 150 and 200 people live there (all Eskimos), out of which 2 or 3 are able to speak Danish. They live on fishing and hunting.

Conversation between the researcher and the natives came to the subject of airplanes and flying craft in general, the passage of an airplane being an exceptional event for the villagers. During this conversation, several interesting facts came to light:

On August 13, 1957, at about 1 P.M. (local time), some children became aware of something coming (perhaps drifting) slowly from the east; the inland ice is in that direction. It was "much higher in the air than airplanes usually go."

I made an inquiry to find out what this meant. They said that it went higher than cumulus but lower than cirrus clouds. As the sky was quite clear and remained so all day, the estimate must have been most uncertain, as they could know nothing about the absolute size of the object. They maintained that it was "rather big," i.e., bigger than an airplane. It must be remembered that the polar atmosphere is particularly transparent.

The question of distance also was difficult. Four people hunting in kayaks about ten kilometers east of Niaqornarssuk also had seen it in the eastern part of the sky. Some say that it was fifty kilometers away, others that it was nearer.

The shape was elliptical. There was some discussion of the possibility that it might be circular when seen directly overhead. This could not be rejected. The image of two deep saucers laid together appeared acceptable. In that case the object must have been lying horizontally in the calm air. B. was inclined to think that this was the case.

Its color was that "of a quite new aluminum pot," and even at full daylight it was shining brightly; perhaps, he suggested, this was the reflection of the sun. In these regions (67°–68° north) the sun sets very late during summer, and at midnight it is still twilight. It could be seen, when the sun was down, that the object kept shining brightly. Moreover, it seemed to emit light from a spot on either side, bluish-green on the left and red on the right. This point was discussed at some length. I asked if the object had been rotating, but the opinion was that it had not, since the colored spots had been constant.

B. saw it about 7 P.M., when he had finished in

the shop. At this time almost everybody had seen it; but there is no evidence that it has been observed elsewhere. He noticed that it was moving very slowly to and fro, like a pendulum suspended in the air. This he measured by means of a wireless antenna. In the evening it rose slowly, and toward midnight it could be seen no more.

Continuing my investigation, I was told by the old Qapak Jeremiassen that between September 24 and 25, about midnight or a little later, he and his wife had been waked up by a strong red light filling the room. They thought their house was on fire, as the shine was "like the glow of English coal" (the Greenlandic coal gives less heat and light). Looking out of the window, they saw a round object passing across the sky from east to west. It was "big" (I did not find out *how* big), and went very quickly. It looked like a circular red disk with a white spot in the middle and a thin white or whitish edge; Qapak's eyes could hardly stand the light. Its height from ground was about two hundred meters, and it passed the place at a distance of six or seven kilometers. This could be seen by comparing with the neighboring islands, which were also lighted. The old couple had been very frightened by the sight and had mentioned it to nobody.

Neither of the two phenomena had given a sound. The two events have been reported nowhere. The Eskimos were highly astonished to learn that similar things are occasionally seen in other parts of the world.

I want to stress that those people, huntsmen as they are, must be credited with an excellent ability of observation.

THE CASE OF THE FRENCH ENGINEERS

The French papers (in particular *France-Soir* and *Le Dauphine Libere* of September 20, 1957) published the observations made by two engineers from Grenoble on September 16, 1957, about 5:15 P.M. The director of an important industrial company was the main witness. One of his assistants, a Mr. B., was with him when they heard the sound of a jet plane. They looked up and, they said:

"We were amazed to see four black craft, which stopped in the sky at a high altitude. They did not have the shape of aircraft or helicopters. They were circular objects that gave the impression that they were swinging in space. I know what balloons are: I experimented with balloons myself. The craft we were observing had nothing in common with these types of balloons.

"Our curiosity reached a peak when one of the objects, all of a sudden, dived vertically at very high speed and then vanished in complete silence. But our emotions were only beginning. There remained three objects clearly visible in the sky. Suddenly, a white object detached itself from one of them and 'floated' for five to seven minutes. Then, abruptly, one of the craft dashed to the west, followed by this 'satellite,' which seemed to catch up with it. Finally, the last two objects went away vertically at an amazing velocity and were lost to sight.

"As we were exchanging our observations, a fifth object of the same circular shape, and coming from the east, crossed the sky at a high rate of speed and was lost to sight in the sky over Saint-Eynard. This was five minutes after the first sighting."

The authors of this report both hold responsible positions in Grenoble and are known to be perfectly trustworthy. They stated that they were "amazed" by what they had seen, which was also observed by several other witnesses.

THE CASE OF THE BLINDING BEAM

The *New Zealand Herald* of October 21, 1957, published an account of an observation made by four inhabitants of the Fiji Islands. The statement was obtained through R. O. Aveling, an official of a local Adventist Church, who himself observed an unusual light in the sky the night of the sighting by the four Fijians. Aveling saw a luminous object, apparently at an altitude of five thousand feet, between the islands Beqa and Viti Levu. At first stationary, this light started sliding slowly through the sky for about five mintues, then vanished entirely, although there were no clouds.

The four Fijians reported having seen an object that came down from the sky near the island of Nawaca, eight miles away from Naboulalu, southwest of Vanua Levu. According to a report by the secretary of the Buanhas province, the incident took place at 3 P.M. The witnesses were two middle-aged couples in a punt with an outboard motor. When they saw the object, they first thought it was an airplane in trouble and decided to go near it.

As the Fijians came closer they found it hovering about twenty feet above the sea. It appeared to be revolving and they said they picked out what looked like a figure of a man standing on the outside of the object. This figure shone a very bright light on the boat—a light so powerful that they were dazzled and felt weak.

When the boat was about five chains from the rotating object, the figure disappeared and the object then rose in a rapid vertical movement and was soon out of sight.

The report emphasizes that all four agree on the details. They live in a fairly isolated area, without access to comic books or other literature on flying saucers.

THE CASE OF THE AUSTRALIAN PROFESSORS

On November 8, 1957, the wire services (Reuters, AFP)—which are here the only available sources—carried information pertaining to an observation made by three astronomers in Mount Stromlo Observatory, of an object brighter than Venus, which crossed the western part of the sky at 5:02 P.M. on November 7:

> Dr. Przybylsky saw the object, which was bright red in color, moved slowly, and remained in view about two minutes.
>
> Its velocity was too small for it to be a meteorite, and the two Soviet satellites had already made their passage. The object in question was also seen by two colleagues of Dr. Przybylsky. No scientist at the Observatory had previously observed such an object.

The press release added that Professor Przybylsky was impatiently awaiting word from other observatories that might have observed the same object. An exceptionally detailed series of observations was made the next day by French astronomers; these were never brought to the attention of scientists.

THE CASE OF THE SPINNING DISK

This incident involves four groups of independent witnesses over an area about forty miles in diameter (Figure 5). The sequence of observations started about 6:45 P.M. on November 8, 1957, when a child, the son of a Mr. Berneyron, a college professor in Orgueil, came home very alarmed and reported the observation of a bright orange object that had hovered briefly and had taken off in a southerly direction. This object had been seen toward the east. The child was able to follow the trajectory of the object with the naked eye and saw

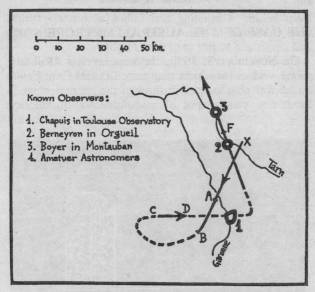

0 10 20 30 40 50 km.

Known Observers:

1. Chapuis in Toulouse Observatory
2. Berneyron in Orgueil
3. Boyer in Montauban
4. Amatuer Astronomers

FIG. 5.—Map of the observations in the Toulouse area,
November 8, 1957.

it describe a loop in the sky; then it was lost in the distance. According to the same report, the object was
circular and supported a dome-like structure. The
underside was a bright red, the top was yellow. The
object seemed to be spinning at a variable rate, and it
left a short yellow trail. The sighting lasted about one
minute.

Having told his experience, the child went out again
and almost immediately saw the phenomenon once
more, this time toward the northwest, at an elevation
of about 70° (these bearings were obtained during the
investigation that followed). The object was traveling
very fast and went rapidly to the horizon.

At the same time, J.-L. Chapuis, of Toulouse Observatory, was studying the sky to determine if the
atmosphere would allow good photoelectric observations. He suddenly saw an oval spot of light emerge

from behind a building and follow a westerly course until it started to rise in the sky, made a sharp loop and continued to rise until out of sight.

Chapuis immediately put into operation a small telescope, and as the object reappeared (point C on Figure 6) he was able to track it through the instrument as "a luminous, yellow spot of magnitude –2 of elliptical

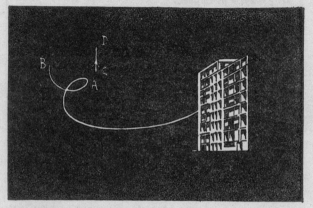

FIG. 6.—Trajectory of the Toulouse object as seen from the observatory.

shape, with absolutely no scintillation, edges very sharply seen against the sky, and leaving a short trail." The instrument used gave a magnification of about thirty.

As the local press reported this observation (with numerous inaccuracies), the paper *La Depeche du Midi* received a letter from Hubert Boyer, an electrician in Montauban (*see* Figure 5), which was published on November 13. Part of this letter is translated here:

First, I was startled by a bright flash similar to a sudden flash of lightning, or an automobile headlight at close range; immediately, I looked up and

I saw the object, whose trajectory crossed the "Rue de la Republique".... I estimated the altitude to be 500 meters.

As the street in question runs northwest-southeast, the object Boyer saw at 6:50 P.M. was following a south-north trajectory.

Finally, other witnesses in that area contacted the Director of Toulouse Observatory, a Dr. Paloque, to report identical observations. These witnesses were members of the French Astronomical Society who were observing from several sites east of Toulouse. They saw a bright object following a long downward course toward the northwest.

This observation is clearly an exceptional one, not only because of the quality of the witnesses, but because two of them (Berneyron and Chapuis) saw the object twice. This intricate series of observations leads to the following analysis:

1. About 6:35 P.M. young Berneyron saw toward the east an object that hovered at close range, then flew toward the south, made a tight loop and was lost to sight.

2. About 6:40 P.M. Chapuis, in Toulouse, saw the object arrive from the north, rise in the sky west of his position, make a tight loop and rise. The total duration of this part of the observation was twenty seconds, as timed by Dr. Bouigue, astronomer at Toulouse Observatory, during the investigation.

3. After the disappearance of the object following the loop (which was seen toward the south by Berneyron, toward the west by Chapuis), the child had time to run home, and the astronomer had time to put into operation his small telescope. But Chapuis saw the object rising straight up from the west, while Berneyron states that it was going away toward the northwest.

4. Amateur astronomers observed a bright object that made a long downward course toward the northwest, thus verifying the child's statements. However,

Chapuis saw the object in the telescope, which was pointing west, and he cannot have been mistaken. The first conclusion is, therefore, that three sections should be considered in the observations: the arrival of the object and the loop were seen by both Berneyron and Chapuis, the rising part (C-D in Figure 6) was seen by Chapuis alone, and the object's departure was followed by the child again and by the amateur astronomers.

5. At 6:50 P.M. Boyer saw the object above Montauban.

This interpretation of the sequence is consistent with the analysis given in a report of limited circulation compiled by the French astronomers:

> Several observations have been made in a fairly large section of the southwest. None of them encompasses the whole phenomenon as it was seen by Mr. Chapuis. [The observation at Orgueil was not known to the authors of this first report.] However, they bring confirmation of the disappearance in B and reappearance in C, the BC direction being the same. Some report an apparent downward trajectory fairly long but toward the northwest. The building that obstructs the view in this direction may have prevented Chapuis from observing it.

With this information it is possible to plot with some accuracy the course of the object, and two comments are appropriate:

1. Since Chapuis' observation lasted about twenty seconds and the child's approximately one minute, the object traveled from X to B (on Figure 5) at a speed of approximately one kilometer per second (3,600 kilometers per hour).

2. When the object was lost to sight in B, it was in the south as seen from Orgueil—about thirty miles away—while Chapuis was looking somewhat south of

west. Therefore it must have been extremely luminous —a fact confirmed by Boyer's statement comparing its brightness to that of lightning and by the child's description of the reappearance of the object "in the midst of a very large flash of lightning."

In summary, the properties of the object, in terms of luminosity and speed, are those of a meteorite. But its low altitude (found by comparison of the lines of sight from the various points), the phenomenon of the loop, and the series of disappearances and reappearances force us to reject this hypothesis. In addition, we must emphasize the consistency of the descriptions of shapes (definitely elliptical), color (orange, red and yellow, red in Montauban) and the trail, seen by the child with the naked eye at the closest approach and also observed by Chapuis in the telescope.

Finally, Chapuis' observation was published in the local papers in such a distorted way that the public would have been unable to find the actual course of the object from the account given by the press; the observations by the amateur astronomers who saw the departure of the object toward the northwest have never been published. They cannot have known of Berneyron's or of Boyer's report at the time. The clarity and consistency of this multiple sighting demand the attention of any objective scientist.

THE CASE OF THE NEW ZEALAND VISITORS

To complete our brief review of the various types of reports with which we are confronted, let us look at a single example of an extreme case, one that offers a detailed description of a "figure." We have already touched on the subject with the report from Fiji, but the witnesses in that case were not very specific in their statements.

As reported in the Nelson, New Zealand, *Evening Mail,* Mrs. Frederick Moreland went out on the morning of July 13, 1959, to milk the cows on her farm near Blenheim. Mr. Moreland works at the Wood-bourne station of the New Zealand Royal Air Force.

Crossing the paddock, Mrs. Moreland suddenly noticed a bright green light among the clouds; it caught her attention because there was no moon. When she had gone half-way across the paddock she saw two large green lights rapidly descending:

"I noticed that I was bathed in a green light and that all the paddock was green, too. It was a horrid sort of colour. My first thought was 'I shouldn't be here' and I made a dive for the trees (a stand of pines on the other side of the three-acre paddock). I stood and watched.

"A saucer-shaped glow with two indented green lights in the bottom descended. The air became very warm. Two rows of jets around the middle shot out orange-coloured flames. They appeared to revolve in opposite directions. The thing was about twenty to thirty feet in diameter. It hovered at about roof height.

"The jets stopped and a light was switched on in what appeared to be a perspex or glass roof or dome, which glowed. The bottom appeared to be of a greyish metal colour. There was a faint hum in the air as it hovered.

"There were two men in it, dressed in fairly close-fitting suits of shiny material. The only thing I can think of to describe it is aluminum foil. Opaque helmets rose from their shoulders. I could not see their faces.

"One of the men stood up and put two hands in front of him as if leaning over to look down-wards. He then sat down and, after a minute or two, the jets started off again and, tilting slightly at first, the thing shot up vertically at great speed and disappeared into the clouds. When it did this it made a soft but high-pitched sound.

"I was so dumbfounded that I stood in the trees

for a moment not knowing what to do. There was a smell of something which resembled pepper in the air. At last I decided to continue getting in and milking the cows.

"While I was milking I kept wondering and felt a bit shaken and puzzled and did not quite know what to do about it. I then went into the house and woke up my husband who did not laugh at me as I had feared, but said, 'Have you rung the police or the Air Department?' I told him I had not and he then telephoned the police."

The witness was visited by the police and by a Royal Air Force representative. An aircraft engineer, D. Thynne, also interviewed her and asked for a detailed sketch of the object. R. Healey, Operations Officer, and F. Simpson, a pilot, also followed the investigation with, as they put it, "open minds." Thynne said that he was "willing to believe that there might be something in it. Most of the people here are interested and have an open mind on it. They don't scoff and are willing to consider it."

Professor I. L. Thomsen, Director of Carter Observatory, expressed interest in Mrs. Moreland's report. He declared:

"This is certainly an unusual report, and different from the ordinary run of reports of strange objects sighted in the sky.

"I had a report on the Blenheim incident sent to me by the Air Force before I left Wellington for Nelson, but have not had time to study it yet.

"I would like to have interviewed the person concerned, preferably as soon as possible after the happenings she has described."

Commenting on flying saucer reports generally, Mr. Thomsen, who has had many brought to his notice, said that he still had not heard of a convincing case for their existence, but he had an open mind on the subject.

This is precisely the attitude the scientist faced with a series of phenomena at once so varied and so surprising must adopt.

We have now reviewed reports from all corners of the world—Europe, New Zealand, the Fiji Islands, the United States, Greenland, Australia. Rather than considering them one at a time, isolated from the sociological and physical context that supports them, let us start our study at the most general level, stripping from them the heavy coat of sensationalism the press has painted and seeking the most general concepts applicable to the disconcerting aspects of the phenomena— for their fantastic character may be only a measure of our ignorance.

2

MORE PIECES FOR
THE PUZZLE

A FRUSTRATING PROBLEM

On August 10, 1964, an American aircraft was parked
on a secondary runway at the Wake Island Airport, in
the middle of the Pacific Ocean, halfway between
Hawaii and the Philippines. The crew was awaiting instructions from the control tower and had nothing to
do but look at the night sky. Then someone noticed
the object. It was just a light, flickering, reddish in
color, and it appeared to approach the runway as if
preparing for a landing. But the traffic controllers
waited in vain for an identifying radio signal.

The unknown source of light seemed to stop above
the airfield, to hover, to retrace its path, to fly randomly for a while, "like a big bird"; finally it went away
toward the northwest. The control tower was definite
in its statements: the thing was not a plane, nor a
meteorological balloon. Birds do not carry lighting
equipment. Conclusion: Unidentified. A new piece for
the puzzle; a new case to be added to the nearly seven
hundred officially recorded "unknowns" in the files of
the U.S. Air Force and the more than five thousand in

the private collections of those who have gathered reports throughout the world.

Did the Wake Island object have physical reality? Was it a product of atmospheric reflection, a mirage, or an unusual deformation of a conventional light source, such as a star or a planet, due perhaps to a temperature inversion? Was it a material object, such as a bird, a flying craft, or a piece of white paper reflecting some light on the ground and carried away by the wind? Or was it a controlled machine, and if so who controlled it? Such problems have intrigued, puzzled, and frustrated scientists for twenty years.

Most reports are fragmentary. Witnesses forget the exact date, do not accurately record the time and the duration. The papers, on top of that, tend to exaggerate details they think "fantastic" and routinely transform quite ordinary shooting stars into "flying saucers." This makes the official files an indispensable source of information; they contain a solid nucleus of data, a series of observations whose authors are known, that have been investigated at some length, sometimes indeed in considerable detail. They are by no means kept secret, but they are not given publicity by the official agencies involved, mainly in order to protect the witnesses from any discomfort that might result from the disclosure of their sightings.

On August 18, 1964, an American military aircraft was flying over the Atlantic Ocean. It had reached a point more than three hundred kilometers east of Dover when suddenly the crew observed a diffuse luminous object straight ahead. As the "thing's" apparent diameter increased, a collision seemed imminent and the pilot abruptly changed the plane's course. The object did not alter its course or its trajectory. It continued on a straight line, passed 150 meters *below* the aircraft, made what appeared to be a right-angle turn, and was lost to sight.

The usual explanations fit such reports only with great difficulty. Some overenthusiastic amateur groups hurriedly label every strange light in the sky "flying saucer." In their publications, such unusual objects are controlled craft, the vehicles of interplanetary or interstellar civilizations that have come to study our planet.

Now, it cannot be denied that modern science— particularly with the recent progress in astronomical knowledge—makes it quite permissible to entertain such theories. The number of planets that enjoy conditions similar to those on earth is estimated to be *several billion* in our galaxy alone. The probability of visitation of our solar system by beings from elsewhere has been computed: it is overwhelming. Such races would be expected to be technically in advance of man, even possibly ahead of us on the intelligence spectrum. Certainly, the idea that unusual aerial phenomena could be the product of an advanced technology cannot be shocking to the scientific mind, which long ago accepted the idea that life must exist throughout the universe; just like any other hypothesis, however, this "extraterrestrial" theory has to be proved to be accepted. In science, there is no such thing as belief at first sight. The physical, tangible, definitive proofs of intelligent control behind the mysterious objects are absolutely lacking.

Of course, it is easy to imagine that the two reports quoted above were caused by a display of superior technology from outer space, but before any far-reaching idea of that sort is proposed all other possibilities, more conventional in nature, must be explored. Could these phenomena be caused by a little-known physical effect or a combination of such effects? If that is the case then, by studying with great care the reports coming from intelligent, articulate and technically competent witnesses, it must be possible to acquire new knowledge about the laws of nature. The potential discoveries in this direction have prompted the U.S. Air Force to gather sightings in a very systematic manner for nearly twenty years. Since a large fraction of the reports come from qualified persons (47), it would be quite unscientific to reject their observations simply because they "sound fantastic"; a mass of valuable information might be lost. The modern scientist, even if he is strongly skeptical of the feasibility of visits from outer space, is generally aware of his responsibilities to society, and ignoring a phenomenon so persistent and so consistent would indeed be taking great chances.

Scientists outside the U.S. have misinterpreted the silence of the American scientific community and the reluctance of the U.S. Air Force to admit that enough sightings were unidentified to warrant a special study as indications that the whole phenomenon has definitely been "explained." As the American public knows, of course, nothing is further from the truth. Not only has the activity of the air force project continued without interruption since 1948, the number of unsolved cases is always on the increase. This variation follows a peculiar law: sometimes, months go by without producing a single report that is both well documented and unexplainable by usual effects; and then a "wave" sweeps the whole country. This was the case in the summer of 1965, during the peak of a large increase in the number of reports that began in May, 1964, and did not subside until early in 1966. The Aerospace Technical Intelligence Center (ATIC), which is located in Wright-Paterson Air Force Base, Dayton, Ohio, and gathers such observations, recorded 17 reports in January, 1964, 25 in February, 18 in March, 41 in April (sharp increase over the previous month), 80 in May, 34 in June, 106 in July, more than 100 again in August, 34 in September, 22 in October. We have plotted on Figure 7 the number of reports that have come to our knowledge (not only from American sources) for this period that seemed to deserve serious study. This graph gives an indication of the sharp variations presented by the phenomenon, when the obvious misinterpretations are rejected from the study.

The authors of this book were fortunate enough to be able to follow some of the investigations that were made into the sightings of this period in the United States.

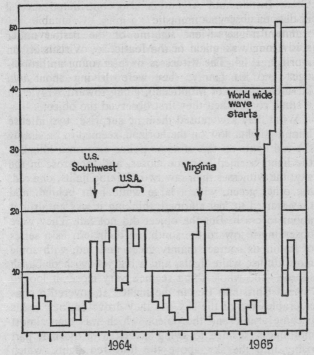

FIG. 7.—Number of "unknowns" in 1964–65.

To researchers already familiar with the European observations of 1954 and 1957, the American sightings of 1964 and 1965 were fascinating.

A HUGE OBJECT WITH MANY LIGHTS

Until the end of March, 1964, the situation on the "UFO front" had been rather calm. Observations had been reported from Africa, Brazil, and particularly Australia in January and February, but most gave insufficient information. Most of the American reports were easily identified as balloons, meteors, aircraft, etc.

Great Britain and Argentina also contributed several ill-defined observations.

The first significant sighting of the period under study here was made near Monticello, Wisconsin, on April 3, 1964. The witnesses were a young anthropologist and his family; they were driving about two kilometers west of Monticello, going toward Argyle on a small road, when they first observed the object.

What they saw caused them no surprise: two intense blinking lights, low on the horizon, seemed to be simply the red lights on top of some police cars on a hill. But the lights seemed to come closer, and they rose in the sky; the witnesses then saw two blinking lights, one red, the other green, with a large white light behind, and they started to feel alarmed, thinking it was an airliner about to crash. But the object did not fall. They were observing it toward the south, on their left, as a series of luminous sources mainly green and red, with some more diffuse white lights, and a big yellowish or bluish source. The whole thing seemed very close; it looked "like a Christmas tree in the night." It covered a considerable area of the sky. As they drove on, new lights became visible and the object, which was then almost motionless, seemed to swing slowly, with the rear part rising into the sky above the four red lights, which seemed to be on a plane (Figure 8). From their relative motion at the closest approach the witnesses estimated that the object was no farther than a few hundred yards away, maybe as close as one hundred yards. It looked like an enormous, solid object supporting a very large number of light sources.

The witnesses slowed down considerably, and at that very moment the object performed its strange maneuver, as if observing them. They turned off their headlights. There was no noise. Very alarmed, but determined to find out what the object was, the witnesses started the car again and turned at the nearest farm entrance, coming back to catch up with the thing. As they approached it (they were now facing east), the object started moving and suddenly took off. They were

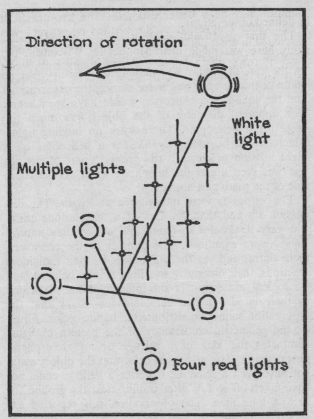

FIG. 8.—A possible model of the Monticello object.

driving at the maximum speed the road permitted, but to no avail: in a few seconds the object had risen very high in the sky and was seen only as a diffuse red glow, way beyond Monticello; in the next instant it vanished completely.

The air force investigation showed that the observation had lasted at least five minutes, taking into account the various maneuvers performed by the witnesses; ten minutes may be a better estimate. The hypothesis of a helicopter (suggested by the vertical maneuver) was discussed in great detail; it had to be rejected for several reasons. First, there was a complete absence of noise. In the car, the radio was playing very softly (but no static or interference was noted during the observation) and the sound of a helicopter would have been heard. The apparent diameter of the object was much too large for a helicopter. There were no landing lights, which would be inconceivable for a helicopter on a night mission so close to the ground (part of the object was seen under the telephone wires on the south side of the road, part above).

The witnesses were interviewed at length. The discussion showed that the idea of a "mysterious craft" was very distasteful to them, and all possible natural causes were examined. The number of the observers, their alarm, and yet the differences in their individual reactions, their obviously excellent mental balance, and the logical succession of the interpretations that came to their minds—police cars, airliner—show that the observation cannot be attributed to hallucination. Finally, the geometric consistency of the pattern of lights eliminates the idea of a mirage or an atmospheric phenomenon. The night was calm and the object could not have been a scientific balloon: a balloon could not have taken off so fast after trailing near the ground for such a long time. The observation was reported exclusively to the military service and the witnesses avoided publicity with great care. Their report is commented upon here for the first time.

THE CLOUD-CIGAR

While months had gone by without bringing a single significant report, only six days after the Monticello case another one was submitted. In Ardmore, Oklahoma, on April 9, 1964, at 8:10 P.M., someone reported a very large object with a great number of cells or "windows," which remained in view about ten seconds and seemed to dissolve in mid-air. Unfortunately, the investigation had little to go on: the witness was alone, and the duration of the sighting was short.

Two days later another observation of a highly unusual character was made. The object and its behavior were, however, typical of a class of aerial phenomena first recognized by Michel in a study of the French cases of 1954. For lack of a better term, Michel called this phenomenon "cloud-cigar." It has been observed in Great Britain, South America, the United States, Australia, Poland, and the Soviet Union. But few descriptions were as detailed as that given by the family of a New York State physiotherapist, who were having a picnic supper on April 11, 1964, at 6:30 P.M. There were four witnesses, and the sighting lasted forty-five minutes. It involved a dark, oblong object, which assumed a vertical position and was seen through binoculars as "almost boiling out," with wisps of smoke actually streaming out of the main body of the black cloud. At one point, this object emitted a flash of light and shot forward at very high velocity, then retraced its path in the same manner. It finally seemed to divide into several smaller objects.

The interesting thing about the reports of April, 1964, was the total lack of publicity: three significant reports came in rapid succession but none of them was published at the time and none of them came to the attention of local groups of UFO amateurs. The case of Monticello had been a near landing. More tangible indications were not long in coming.

LANDING IN NEW MEXICO

An observation made on April 24, 1964, served as the starting point of a series of reports of very unequal value, which were mixed together by the newspapers to give a picture of great confusion. Actually, what happened on that day, at 6:00 P.M., in Socorro,

New Mexico, is known with absolute clarity: some physical craft, shaped like an egg, landed in the desert.

The witness was Lonnie Zamora, a state policeman. He saw an object emitting a bright light rapidly losing altitude above the desert. Alarmed because there was a dynamite shack nearby, he drove into the desert and reached the top of a hill just in time to see a white or silvery object set on four unequal legs in a gully. Two figures of rather small stature ("either large kids or small adults") were standing near it, dressed in white coveralls. Zamora had to go around a hill in order to get a closer view, but when he came within sight of the object again the two figures had disappeared, and the craft took off with a thunderous noise. The policeman had only time to put the car between himself and the object when it rose vertically, stopped in mid-air, and then went away. The sighting had lasted several minutes.

The case is interesting because the conclusion reached by the investigators is definite: Zamora did not lie, nor did he have a hallucination; something landed there. Policemen who answered Zamora's call were the first on the scene and went down into the gully (*see* Plate VIII). Deep marks had been made in the ground, and traces of calcination were evident.

The investigation also revealed that the craft, whatever it was, had not been built by amateurs: it had landed on uneven terrain, firmly set on four legs of unequal length, in such a way as to put its center of gravity in the best position. Such a landing gear, obviously, would be ideal for a lunar module, and it was believed that the object was some secret craft of American construction. Spectroscopic analyses of the calcined areas, however, proved negative, and the mode of propulsion appeared quite different from anything we could produce. In the days that followed, the papers spread the story—with many essential details missing. It was said that Zamora had seen a "flying saucer" and its pilots; the possibility that the craft might have been of terrestrial construction was not even considered.

There has been no satisfactory explanation of the Socorro sighting to date. Its main significance is as the starting point of the recent renewal of interest in the UFO question. The number of detailed reports in this period, however, does not compare to the 1954 or the 1957 waves; what we had was a relatively dense series of localized observations of a phenomenon whose nature and origin were unknown.

On May 15, 1964, a teacher and four other witnesses in Lewistown, Montana, saw a large, circular object flying ahead of their car. Its progression was compared to that of "a cork on water." It was visible for four minutes, then turned to the west and was lost to sight. The wave of 1964 had really started.

THE PENNSYLVANIA "JELLYFISH"

On May 26, 1964, at 10 P.M., a "stationary object with a dome whose inferior edges emitted a whitish light" was observed near Palmerton, Pennsylvania. A smaller object shaped like a disk, maneuvering around the big one, was intermittently visible. Finally it appeared to merge with the main craft, which departed to the east. This report is reminiscent of the "Case of the French Engineers" (p. 23), where a similar phenomenon was described. The object was observed by two Palmerton families. Unfortunately, there was no report to the air force, and we have had to rely on the account published by the press.

If this report were confirmed, it would afford a new illustration of Michel's "jellyfish" phenomenon. Of course, the nature of the object, and the meaning of its behavior, cannot be discussed without questioning the significance of the whole UFO phenomenon, which is the object of this book. At this point we are only trying to gather *reports* for further investigation and to become familiar with the material that seems most generally representative of the phenomena we plan to study.

On June 5, 1964, four witnesses (including three

cadets from the Air Force Academy) were driving toward Texarkana at 2 A.M. when they observed an object, which appeared to be spinning, emitting an orange-reddish light that was not blinding. The four witnesses got out of the car to observe it more easily, then decided to drive closer. For about one minute, the brightness of the object increased steadily; then the object flew away so fast that the eye could not follow it. During this period, reports of "disks," cigar-shaped objects in flight and on the ground, were made in rapid succession. The most interesting cases came from Ohio in June; then a whole series of observations was made in the South.

TWO REMARKABLE OBSERVATIONS

Two excellent observations were made in the area of Toledo, Ohio, on June 12 and 13, 1964. The first one started at 10:15 P.M. and lasted no less than one hour and fifty minutes. During this period, Chief of Police Richard Crawford three times saw a strange blinking object emitting various colors of light, sometimes turning completely dark. Another policeman observed the same object from another location; the two accounts check in every respect. At the time of the best observing conditions, the object was about 750 feet away, and its diameter was estimated as 90 feet (178).

Crawford, who was one mile away from Elmore, at the intersection of Road 51 and Nissen Road, saw the object first. It was motionless, bright, surrounded by a sort of halo about one-half mile in diameter. It was in view for twenty minutes, glowing in silence; but when a spotlight was aimed at it, it went away.

It was seen again at the zenith of the Harris Elmore School half an hour before midnight, at an altitude of about one thousand feet, flying at good speed to the northwest, toward the town of Genoa. It made the noise of a bullet flying by one's ear. Crawford radioed another policeman, Carl Soenichsoen, giving him the approximate position of the object, and asked Soenichsoen to meet him at a certain point. Soenichsoen arrived there first and spotted the object. When Crawford arrived the thing was still there, giving off periodic bursts of light at a frequency close to one per second. Soon it took off again, changed course at high speed, and was lost to sight in a few seconds.

The second Toledo case had only one witness. No official report was submitted, but details were obtained in personal communication with the investigators. The witness was returning from work on June 13 at 9:15 P.M. when he spotted three strange objects above a wheat field. They seemed to be flying slowly away at an altitude of about one thousand feet. They had the size and shape of "helicopter cockpits," as far as could be determined in the dark (the witness first believed they were helicopters). They had a white light and a red glow. When the witness approached them, he heard a low rumble; he tried to follow them by crossing the wheat field. They appeared to stop over a large barn and, as the witness was about 150 yards away, they suddenly started circling the barn at very high speed. The diameter of the circle they were thus following was about the dimension of the building, and they remained above it. When the witness finally reached the barn the objects had gone away.

"FLYING TOPS" IN THE SOUTH

Since it would be highly improbable that the population of Wellford, South Carolina, would have known the details of the observation made at Vins-sur-Caramy in 1957 (*see* the "Case of the Intelligent Machine," p. 19), the genuine character of the following incidents is obvious.

On June 29, 1964, a little before midnight, a man from Wellford was driving on State Route 59, in Georgia, between Gainesville and Lavonia. An amber-colored object flew over the car; it made a leap in the air above the vehicle, came back twice, and seemed to be "observing the headlights" as it jumped ahead of the advancing car. The thing made "as much noise as a million hissing snakes" and left an odor similar to that of embalming fluid. It was about the size of the car, six feet high, and spinning. The outside edges supported strange devices that looked like antennae. A tremendous heat wave was given off by the object, and a yellow light was seen shining through some sort of openings in its lower part.

This strange object followed the witness' car for two miles. When the driver, B. E. Parham, stopped the vehicle and turned off the headlights, the object rose in the sky with a motion of "oscillation" and was lost to view.

A similar sighting was made the following week in Tallulah Falls, Georgia. This time there were numerous witnesses. Nine people, living in three different houses, saw the object and gave a detailed account of it. According to J. Ivester, his television set started behaving peculiarly and soon it became impossible to watch the program. He turned off the set and the family went out for some fresh air. The time was then 9 P.M.; suddenly, they saw an object flying just above tree-top level come within a few hundred yards of the house; it seemed to stop over their neighbor's, Mrs. Russell Mickinan's, garden. It was absolutely silent. Only the lower part was clearly visible; it was bright red. The object was shaped like a cup, and the witnesses could see three lights: red, white, and another red, in a row. The red lights were blinking. When the object rose, these three lights went off (or stopped being visible) while a powerful green light appeared in the lower part, casting an eerie light over the whole countryside. This strange object left an odor compared to that of "brake liquid" or "embalming fluid." No one was able to identify it definitely, but it was immediately noticed by the Habersham County Sheriff, A. J. Chapman, when he arrived a few minutes after the sighting (177, 183).

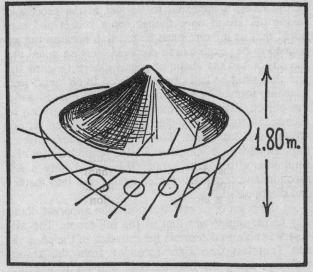

FIG. 9.—Object seen near Lavonia, Georgia, by Parham. Note the similarity with the observation made in Vins, Fig. 4.

ANOTHER "JELLYFISH"

On July 20, 1964, numerous witnesses, including policemen, observed for several hours the evolutions of a number of objects "shaped like umbrellas" flying over Madras, Oregon. The objects sometimes remained motionless, only to dash away at incredible speeds in the next second. They were reddish when stationary and changed color when they accelerated. There are very few details on this observation, which was not officially reported. But earlier the same day two remarkable sightings had been made in Illinois.

The first one took place at 4:45 A.M. on Illinois State Route 101. The witness, a clerk in a state administrative department, was driving east about four miles west of Littleton when he saw an object rising above the tops of the trees; it appeared to be just in the process of taking off. He at once thought of a rocket and even noted that its mixture must be too rich because the jets seemed to be purple-red in color. He further noted that the object had the shape of a half-sphere (Figure 10) and that what he had first considered to be "jets" were in reality formed by a luminous cone that opened under the object, giving the impression that it was rising on flames. It rose still higher in the sky, then turned around and faced him. The object then looked like a dark circle with a luminous ring; it reminded him of a sunflower with yellow petals. This lasted only a few seconds, and the object turned again, rose into the sky and disappeared.

At the point of closest approach, the apparent diameter of the object was that of the full moon. The witness was able to determine the duration of the observation (not less than sixty seconds) from the known markings along the familiar road and his recollection

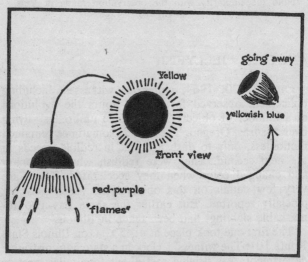

FIG. 10.—Object observed in Illinois, July 20, 1964.
Compare with Fig. 3.

that he was driving at fifty-five miles per hour. He heard no noise. The area from which the object seemed to take off is wild and practically inaccessible. Finally, the behavior of the light emitted by the object is interesting: at first it seemed to be "flames" shooting from the rear of the object, but when the object accelerated, the light became about three times smaller and lost its brightness, changing to a blue-yellowish color at the same time.

Exactly fifteen minutes later, an air force man driving about 8 miles west of Clinton, Iowa, or 120 miles north of the first observation, saw an unusual light in the sky; he stopped the engine of his car and listened, but could not hear any noise coming from the object, which was traveling north-northwest. It remained in view for a full minute, then disappeared. This witness too described a large cone, very bright at the top, more and more diffuse at the base, which blended with the background of the sky.

LANDINGS IN VIRGINIA

After the summer of 1964, UFO activity remained above its 1963 level, but few sightings came to the attention of the public. Most of the incidents received only local publicity, or no publicity at all. The characters of a wave, however, were still present, and the increase in the number of landing reports at the beginning of 1965, one of the important factors in the development of the phenomenon, became—and remains —especially prominent.

In January of 1965 the eastern states of the U.S.A. experienced a flap, the significance of which has seemingly been eclipsed by the remarkable renewal of activity that took place only a few months later

wrote Donald Hanlon in (397). Indeed, about twenty-five observations were made between the end of November, 1964, and the end of January, 1965. These accounts, of varying reliability, were nevertheless of singular interest, as Hanlon perceived, in view of their strong geographical correlation.

The first landing report of this period was made by an industrial worker who said that he observed, at 6:15 P.M. on January 19, two circular flying objects hovering at low altitude over an archery range at Brands Flat, Virginia. The smaller object, about twenty feet in diameter, landed about eighteen yards away from the witness, and three beings, about forty inches tall, emerged. The witness declared that they uttered unintelligible sounds, returned to the craft, and flew away.

This type of report is by no means typical of the American sightings of previous years, and thus deserves special attention. A detailed study of the phenomenon in its physical and sociological aspects will be made later in this book.

This report was followed by many secondary cases, which passed unnoticed. On November 26, 1964, Mrs. F. Rosenburg saw a bright ball of fire close to the ground at midnight. On January 15, at 10:00 P.M., 12, 1965, at 6:30 P.M., a bright yellow object was seen for two minutes by a Mr. and Mrs. Milliner, NASA public relations employees, on Wallops Island, Maryland. Two days later, James Myers, in Norfolk, Virginia, reported seeing a circular object rise from the ground at midnight. On January 15, at 10:00 P.M. Charles Knee, Jr. of Concord, New Hampshire, lost control of his car between Enfield and Wilmot, New Hampshire, as the engine stalled and the lights went off. When he got out of the car he heard a high-pitched sound and saw a bright light cross the sky. On January 23, at 8:45 P.M., two businessmen driving in opposite directions on U.S. Highway 60 near Toano, Virginia, said their cars stopped as they approached a huge cone-shaped object hovering over a nearby field. Two army helicopters were allegedly dispatched from Fort Lee to investigate. On January 25, a policeman and several other people in Marion, Virginia, observed an object

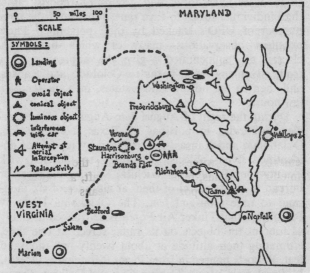

Fig. 11.—Map of eastern United States showing observations reported during period of November, 1964, to January, 1965.

that took off from a wooded area on a hill. Their report indicates that marks were found on the ground.

The Virginia sightings—a series of concentrated rumors and strongly correlated incidents with many details foreign to the witnesses' experience—contain all the characters of the problem; they also present us with a summary of the phenomenon, which was observed on a grand scale a few months later.

THE EXPLOSION

The sudden, massive accumulation of reports noted after July 31, 1965, in the United States and Europe is extremely difficult to record. The sighting accounts that filled the pages of the teletypes at Wright Field were often complete and well documented. Some air force bases even forwarded groups of reports rather than individual forms to save time, because of the large number of UFO's tracked by their personnel. These excellent observations—many of which have been classed as "unidentified"—give the impression of a front advancing from Texas to Colorado and Kansas, and then to the northernmost states, in a matter of a few hours.

During the night of August 1 to August 2, for example, authorities in portions of Texas, New Mexico, Oklahoma, and Kansas were deluged by reports of unidentified flying objects. According to the Sedgwick County sheriff's office at Wichita, Kansas, the weather bureau tracked several of them at altitudes of six thousand to nine thousand feet. The Oklahoma Highway Patrol said that Tinker Air Force Base tracked as many as four of the objects on its radar screen at one time, estimating their altitude at about twenty-two thousand feet. Reports poured in from Pecos, Monahans, Odessa, Midland, Fort Worth, Canyon City and Dalhart, Texas; Chickasha, Shawnee, Cushing, Buymon and Chandler, Oklahoma; and Oxford, Belle Plaine, Winfield, Caldwell, Mulvane and Wichita, Kansas.

Police officers in Oklahoma watched the objects fly in a diamond-shaped formation in the Shawnee area. The witnesses, who were in three different patrol cars, saw the objects for thirty minutes and said they changed color from red to white to blue-green.

Shortly after midnight on August 2 Bob Campbell, a news photographer for station KXWI-TV in Sherman, Texas, who was following police conversations on his shortwave radio, heard the Oklahoma and the Texas Highway Patrols discuss reports of an unidentified flying object, tracked on Oklahoma radar, streaking toward the Texas border. Soon he heard that the object had been spotted by police south of Durant; it was described as a bright blue-white light. Campbell took his 4x5 Speed Graphic camera and drove into town to meet Police Chief Peter McCollum; the two men then searched for the object and found it hovering above a point thirteen miles east of Sherman and one mile east of Bells, on Highway 82. Its edges were clearly defined and it was seen at about 45° elevation in the north-eastern sky. Campbell set up his camera and took four exposures of approximately two minutes each, at three-minute intervals (401).

The negatives of the photographs, which have been examined by the air force's scientific advisers and by experts in astronomical photography, showed star trails, although rather faint ones. From these trails it was determined that the vertical motion of small amplitude noticeable within the large luminous object was genuine, and that the apparent diameter of the object was about two degrees, or four times the apparent diameter of the full moon. The sharpness of the edges of the luminous area and the intensity of the source were further evaluated from several test photographs supplied by Campbell. These were time exposures of the night sky, Venus, and a bright street light at a known distance. They were taken within a few days of the UFO sighting, with the same camera and the same type of film. In spite of the abundant technical material thus accumulated, the Sherman object remains un-identified.

In a puzzling statement, the air force tried to explain the sudden burst of sightings as atmospheric illusions. It was pointed out that a temperature inversion existed over the area during the nights in question and that such a condition would give strong scintillation effects. But the four stars listed by the air force spokesman as the most likely sources of misidentifications were below the horizon at the time of the Oklahoma sightings. Furthermore, the explanation did not take into account the angles of motion and the local character of many of the phenomena attested to by the independence of the groups of observers, which permitted triangulation.

The air force's conclusion was reminiscent of another verdict issued earlier by Project Blue Book, which deserves to be quoted. On May 27, 1965, a civilian living in Economy, Pennsylvania, watched for nearly two minutes, at 9:40 P.M., a large object in the sky. It appeared to be composed of two large spheres, one at each end, with three or four smaller spheres between. The object was distinctly spinning or rotating from left to right. It was also described as tipped at an angle of about fifteen degrees, affording a three-dimensional view. The air force's conclusion was:

> Aircraft. Sighting characteristic of aircraft. No attempt at specific identification. Regarded as possible aircraft sighting. No data presented to indicate object could NOT have been an aircraft.

THE WAVE THAT WOULD NOT DIE

With such disturbing, sometimes shocking accounts of observations on one hand, and the totally unbelievable "explanations" proposed by the official agencies on the other, the phenomenon continued to spread across the country and around the world. From Australia (where the sharp increase of the number of reports had come early in June), from France (where the best-documented report of a landing since 1954 had come to light in the first days of July), from South America (where the mountains and the plateaus—covered with snow—contributed the greatest proportion of sightings, thus disproving the theory that UFO flaps always take place in the summer, the "silly season") came the reports. Many of them contained extremely valuable information, because the quality of the observers was clearly improving; while the reports of 1950 and 1952 generally came from farmers and military personnel who were not in the best observing conditions, the 1965 sightings came, in a surprisingly large number of cases, from scientists and technically trained observers, from policemen equipped with two-way radios, or from engineers. While the "explainers" had not changed their outdated routine, and continued to handle contemptuously the miserable phenomena that dared remain unidentified, their methods started to show definite signs of obsolescence. A rumor was heard in scientific circles that perhaps public opinion in this country and in other countries had been misled concerning the true proportions and nature of the reported phenomena. These rumors found an echo in many editorials, and a steady flow of observations continued to make their appearance.

In September and October, 1965, New Hampshire was the scene of a series of incidents that have been carefully investigated and documented by John Fuller in a series of articles for the *Saturday Review* ("Trade Winds," October 2, 1965, and April 16, 1966) and *Look* magazine (February 22, 1966), as well as in his book *Incident at Exeter*. Fuller wrote in the April 16, 1966, edition of the *Saturday Review:*

> The Exeter case is a good illustration. The incident there . . . happened on September 3, 1965, at about 2 A.M. (it was witnessed first by Navy recruit Norman Muscarello, who threw himself on the ground to avoid being hit by the object) and later at approximately 3 A.M. by Officers Bertrand and Hunt. The object (apparently some hundred feet in diameter, with brilliant pulsating lights, and absolutely silent) zoomed so close to Officer Bertrand that he fell to the ground and drew his service revolver.
>
> The official report to Project Bluebook of the Director of Administrative Services of the Pease Air Force Base at Portsmouth, New Hampshire, concludes with this paragraph: "At this time have been unable to arrive at a probable cause of this sighting. The three observers seem be stable, reliable persons, especially the two patrolmen. I viewed the area and found nothing in the area that could be the probable cause."

The Pentagon spokesman released his "explanation" on October 27. According to the Haverhill, Massachusetts, *Gazette:*

A spokesman said the several reports stemmed from "multiple objects in the area," by which they mean a high-altitude Strategic Air Command exercise out of Westover, Mass. A second important factor was what is called a "weather inversion." . . . The Pentagon spokesman said this natural phenomenon causes "stars and planets to dance and twinkle." The spokesman said: "We believe what the people saw that night were stars and planets in unusual formations."

Here we must pause. Quoting more reports would add nothing. *The boundaries of the unbelievable have been reached, both by accounts describing experiences and phenomena that seem without precedent in scientific history and by explanations that, if taken seriously, would call for a complete overthrow of current scientific concepts.*

No rational person can readily accept the phenomena witnessed over the last twenty years as "visits" from outer space; but neither can a temperature inversion such as might exist in September over New Hampshire cause stars and planets to assume what the Pentagon spokesman, bravely defying forty centuries of scientific knowledge, dares call "unusual formations"!

But we must not lose patience. As scientists, we have a responsibility that far overshadows that of the official spokesmen, and we must realize that the observations reviewed in these two chapters are of no value *in themselves;* they are important and worth studying only because each one illustrates a phenomenon manifested in every country of the world since May, 1946, challenging scientists with a series of problems that have received only partial solutions.

Many of the reports, indeed a very large majority, are of course the result of simple errors on the part of unexperienced witnesses or the misinterpretation of unusual combinations of circumstances surrounding conventional objects. Among the phenomena reviewed here, however, we find not a few cases where ordinary natural causes must be rejected from the list of possible explanations.

Does this constitute evidence that the phenomenon is under intelligent control and possibly extraterrestrial in origin? Certainly not. But can this hypothesis be rejected completely?

It could be rejected *if and only if,* on the basis of a global analysis of well-documented sightings, someone succeeded in proving that the phenomenon, in spite of its unusual appearance, is nothing but a combination of known effects.

It is therefore essential for the scientist who embarks upon the task of explaining the UFO phenomenon to be familiar with the typical phases of UFO behavior (surveyed in Chapter 1) and with current developments in the physical and sociological aspects, reviewed in this chapter. With this background we can dispense with the secondary details of the individual reports and the pathetic efforts of the official explainers and get to the real problem: how to construct methods of scientific research applicable to the phenomenon.

3

IS THERE A SCIENTIFIC APPROACH?

HISTORY OF THE CONTROVERSY

THE DESIGNATIONS "flying saucer," "unidentified flying object," "mysterious object in the sky," "unconventional aerial object," etc. used to label the phenomenon are lamentable, for they all contain within themselves the idea that there is a material object at the source of the observed manifestations. This idea was introduced and propagated by the press long before scientists had a chance to assess the evidence, examine the facts, and establish a coherent system of investigation. It did much to divert the investigators' attention away from a subject whose very terminology seemed to place it more in the domain of sociology, or even psychology, than astronomy or physics.

The initial stage at which the phenomenon could have been the subject of systematic research on a vast scale was rapidly passed. The passions of the public, the frenzy of the press, and the confusion or favor of the governing quarters, political or military, were attached to every attempt to interpret the observations. A journalist or investigator who took any stand at all was deluged by protests, disputes, or denials from groups having no connection with the interests of knowledge and the aims of scientific research.

Official explanations became more and more vague. Soon the investigators could voice their thoughts only in a private capacity, while at the same time exposing themselves to all the risks of journalistic interpretations and abandoning the serenity so necessary to keeping their studies objective.

All serious research outside the areas defined in high places was forbidden. The result has been that the problem has still not been subjected to any research worthy of the name, and the powerful apparatus of modern science has not yet been applied at all to a phenomenon whose existence is officially admitted and whose manifestations are scrupulously recorded by a military agency of the United States government that views it solely as a potential threat to security.

THE VARIOUS TRENDS

The presentation of the phenomenon as a matter of opinion and the limitation of serious research to within the official framework brought about a split in scientific circles; in private discussions two trends, both based on subjective mental reservations whose foundations are debatable, emerged.

The first of these groups, subconsciously irritated by the thought that something other than terrestrial life might be setting out to colonize space, points to the influence of the communications media over modern society's opinions; the control of the media by men unschooled in science; the malleability and inconstancy of the public; and, finally, modern man's appetite for the fantastic, fed by literature and the movies, as factors obstructing attempts to pinpoint the source of the rumor. They tend to attribute the phenomenon entirely to hallucinations, hoaxes, or misinterpretations of natural effects.

Taking as their starting point indications of planetary physics obtained at the extreme limits of present means of observation, and making dangerous extrapolations, this group maintains that evolved life on the planets, and in particular on Mars, is impossible. Starting from even less plausible bases, they proclaim interstellar travel "unthinkable" (149). Finally, they denounce as "contrary to science" the attribution to a material object of the motions observed in connection with the UFO phenomenon, despite the fact that no satisfactory theory of gravity has yet been suggested, and despite the fact that certain fundamental contradictions between the current chief theories in physics have yet not been resolved.

The second of the two groups, far smaller in number, emphasizes, quite rightly, the tenuity of the idea that life is limited to our planet—an idea that, from the psychological point of view, is all too reminiscent of the Middle Ages, when cosmological theories placed the earth at the center of the universe. Science generally refutes such narrow and anthropocentric ideas. Unfortunately, the people belonging to this group are often tempted, solely on this basis, to believe that a material object is at the source of the UFO phenomenon and proceed to guess the ins and outs of the problem without first encompassing their work with the precautions and safeguards necessary for truly objective investigation.

The great majority of the scientifically oriented, whose curiosity has been systematically discouraged, widely reserve judgment, declaring that no solid foundations for any kind of research of value exist.

The situation is very different outside the strict domain of official science. The passions attendant on any enlargement of our vision of the world in the direction of the fantastic—and particularly the possibility of an extraterrestrial solution to the problem we are studying—have favored the development of a whole spectrum of groups and clubs. These organizations have their share of adventurers, magi, and prophets, as well as a large number of persons who, fascinated by the "magical" aspect of modern science, cling to the picture presented by the newspapers and magazines, in which, not without a certain picturesqueness at times, man's profound aspiration toward new spiritual horizons finds expression.

CLASSIFYING THE OBSERVATIONS

The work presented here is based on the idea that the two opposing trends whose views we have cited have both been prejudging the phenomenon's true nature —the one by denying the material reality of an object at the origin and the other by affirming it. The reports have received essentially subjective, non-scientific, and totally contradictory interpretations, to such a degree that numerous cases regarded as certain by one group are roundly discarded by the other.

With such a division of opinion on the question of basic data, the arguments put forward can ultimately be checked only by a patient and systematic study, necessarily voluminous, of the topography of the manifestations, combined with statistical research into their distribution in time. We must concede that there is a "UFO phenomenon," even if the UFO's are not real objects; the sightings appear to be endowed with definite laws in respect to the reported manifestations, the conditions of the sightings, and the secondary features produced. Whatever the physical nature of its component elements, which remains to be seen, this evidence does constitute a phenomenon to which methods of scientific investigation can be applied.

The first question to be settled is the method used to classify the sightings. Although they are reported in different ways, they can be reduced to a limited number of well-defined types whose characteristics recur again and again throughout the whole field of our study, that is, all sightings made around the globe from 1946 until the present.

We have recognized the following types:

Type I: the observation of an "unusual object," spherical, discoidal or more complex in form, on or close to the ground (maximum: tree height). This image may or may not be associated with "traces"—physical effects of a thermal, luminous, or purely mechanical order.

Type I sightings are encountered in every country throughout the history of the phenomenon. An example of a Type I sighting is given in the testimony of an official of the Buenos Aires Province Senate, in Argentina (35). This man was driving along the road from Unusue to Bolivar on August 8, 1958, when his engine suddenly stalled. The dash-board clock stopped, showing 1:27 A.M. The witness got out to find the cause of the breakdown; he wiped the distributor heads and then tried to start the car, but in vain. It was then that he noticed, at a distance of from three hundred to four hundred meters, what he thought was a machine, advancing toward him relatively slowly. He turned off the headlights and watched the object, which was "flattened on the rear part" and emitted a weak phosphorescent light. He reported hearing a soft whistling like the sound of a fan. This sound varied with the different evolutions the object made. The "machine" seemed to have a dome or cockpit emitting a blinding bluish light. Finally, the thing rose at a staggering speed, emitting further whistling noises, and took off toward the south. Returning to his car, the witness found that he was able to start the engine again.

At 5:30 P.M., on May 20, 1959, near Tres Lomas, in La Pampa Province, Argentina, two men out hunting saw at a distance of 150 meters what seemed to be a discoid object resting on the ground. They described it as a machine with the look of an aluminum body, or a surface of silvered metal or even "shining glass that has lost its polish." They estimated its height as between two and two and one-half meters. It seemed to carry a dome with a radius of one meter. After the object departed they said they found the grass flattened.

A study of the French newspapers of the fall of 1954 yields numerous sightings of this type that have not been reported in specialized books or journals. For example, on October 5, witnesses ten kilometers from Beaumont, near Clermont-Ferrand, France, described a "machine" that lost luminosity as it approached them. When it was 150 meters away, they felt a "curious sensation" and were "as if riveted to the spot." They also smelled an odor "like that of nitrobenzine." This sighting took place at 3:45 P.M.

At 11 P.M. the same day, a Mr. and Mrs. Guillemoteau, near La Rochelle, saw a "machine" two or three meters in height, with a diameter of five meters, that rose vertically after hovering for several minutes at an altitude of one meter. Oily marks were said to have been found there in the grass.

Sightings of this type sometimes assume a more dramatic form, provoking violent nervous reactions in the witnesses. On October 16, 1954, at Thin-le-Moutier, France, an object is said to have landed about thirty meters from a woman; the witness fainted and subsequently was reported to have developed a skin disease attributed to exposure to the object. Such sightings are also reported in connection with the American observations of 1957 and 1964–65.

We report these accounts here *merely to illustrate what one can find in the press and the official files;* for the time being we will express no value judgment regarding these statements, the sincerity of those who made them, or the plausibility of the phenomena described.

Type II: the observation of an "unusual object," with vertical cylindrical formation, in the sky, associated with a diffuse cloud. This phenomenon has been given various names, such as "cloud-cigar" and "cloudsphere."

Within the framework of Type II we usually distinguish two categories, II-A and II-B. The first comprises reports of objects answering the above description moving erratically through the sky. The second groups together accounts of a similar nature in which the "object" is stationary and gives rise to secondary phenomena.

The following cases are Type II-A sightings. At Pouilly, near Dole, France, at 6 P.M. on July 18 or 19, 1952, residents of Pouilly and Venarey saw a "spindle, having neither wings nor protuberances, emitting a brief, strong, winking light at regular intervals, and giving rise to a very thick white smoke that rapidly dispersed." The witnesses described this spindle as about thirty meters long, in a vertical position, and accompanied by a loud rumbling noise.

On November 27, 1954, between 4:15 and 4:30 P.M., witnesses in Red Square in Moscow saw "a machine of cylindrical form" moving toward the northwest at an estimated altitude of from two hundred to three hundred meters. The witnesses reported that the thing rose with the speed of a jet, assuming a vertical position.

Examples of Type II-B sightings are furnished by the "cloud-cigars" carefully documented by Michel (6). All these sightings have been checked by us against the original sources. One of the most complete accounts is that of a sighting south of Paris at about 8 P.M. on September 22, 1954. A Mr. Rabot, a butcher in Ponthierry, was driving along road N. 7 when he suddenly caught sight of a red circular object, with what seemed to be luminous smoke escaping from it. The thing appeared to be at a considerable height and was moving about slowly and majestically in all directions. Rabot watched it for several minutes and then got back in his car and returned to Ponthierry, keeping the object in view. In Ponthierry he notified a local official, who saw the thing disappear at great speed among the clouds. At the same moment, a Mrs. Gamundi of Paris, who was returning from Fontainebleu along N. 7, also saw the phenomenon, and she stopped her car to watch it. She described the thing as a cigar surrounded by clouds, red in color, immobile and vertical, and added that it gave out more than half a dozen smaller, disk-shaped objects, which fell out one after the other from the lower part of the "cigar" and flew away. The object finally took off when a commercial aircraft crossed the sky.

Type III: the observation of an "unusual object" of spherical, discoidal or elliptical shape stationary in the sky. Type III-A sightings are those in which the immobility of the object occurs between two periods of motion and is associated with the object's erratic descent to the vicinity of the ground ("dead-leaf" movement).

The sighting in Ales, France, at 11:45 A.M. on October 9, 1954, is to be classed under Type III. Several witnesses, among them a Mr. Taurelle, working at the Riche Hotel, saw a spinning object that hovered in the sky; it soon began moving again, rapidly increased its speed, and was lost to view.

The sighting at Yaounde, Cameroons, on October 28, 1954, by numerous persons living in that town, including the director of the hospital, belongs in this category also. A dog drew the witnesses' attention, by its growling, to an "enormous, motionless disk, brightly lit," low in the sky. This "object" was shaped like a mushroom; it carried underneath it a cylinder dangling in the air.

The report given by Nicetta Edmond and several other persons of a sighting at Anduze, France, on October 2, 1954, provides an example of a Type III-A sighting. According to these witnesses, a "voluminous circle mass which seemed to be revolving and showing alternatively red and blue lights" hovered in the sky; it subsequently descended with a rocking motion.

Certain sightings are difficult to classify under Type III-A, particularly those referring to the observation of a motionless "object" that begins to descend, then becomes stationary again, then rises, and so on. Such phenomena are reported frequently and should be examined in the light of a more complete classification.

Readers interested in developing a "natural history" of the phenomenon on a formal basis will find our extended classification system in Appendix IV. The present informal presentation will suffice for the purposes of our discussion here, however.

An example of a case difficult to classify is the eyewitness account of a Mr. Gauci, dated November 23, 1952. The sighting took place at Belle-Ile, France, on the Locqmaria highway, at a place called "La Butte." The witness described a "luminous ball" of very large apparent diameter (several times the full moon) that seemed at times to become flattened, to lose its orange color and turn whitish. It descended gently, stopped moving, went to the right after a while, and then rose again to its original starting point. It went through this sequence four or five times, and then disappeared toward the southwest.

Type IV: the observation of an "unusual object" moving continuously through the air, regardless of its accelerations, variations in color, or rotations.

The Type IV sightings are obviously the most subject to caution, as they may involve confusion with physical phenomena, among which are all the effects invoked to "explain" the reported manifestations: nonmaterial causes, such as ball lightning, reflections, mirages, distortion of astronomical bodies by atmospheric phenomena; and material causes, such as meteorites, flying devices of human construction, meteorological balloons, birds, debris caught in the wind, and clouds; this latter group now includes artificial satellites of the earth.

Many opinions have been expressed on this subject. H. Haffner, for instance, attributes the "flying saucers" to lightning, while in France Professor E. Schatzmann has stated that numerous types of hallucinations and optical illusions may be at the origin of the accounts (122). In the United States, Professor D. Menzel has similarly devoted himself to the study of the mechanisms of natural conditions that can account for false reports and anomalous radar returns (3, 31).

These studies are extremely valuable, for they make it possible to attribute a considerable number of sightings to recognized conventional conditions. Nevertheless, we believe it legitimate to reconsider the problem in its entirety without seeking *a priori* to assimilate it to conventional conditions. The statistics bearing on Type IV cases will be marred by errors of this kind, but for the sightings belonging to the first three types, especially those classified as Types I, II-B and III-A, the only interpretations possible (other than a still unknown objective cause) are hallucinations and hoaxes.

The method we propose to employ furnishes us with criteria for evaluating the probable error in the different types of sightings and for taking it into account while considering the phenomenon as a whole.

A SYSTEMATIC PROCEDURE

The UFO phenomenon has been the subject of some preliminary analytical work in several countries. This work has been carried out by professional scientists acting in an individual capacity outside both the official investigative commissions and the various groups of amateurs.

These scientists have suggested that, rather than analyze separately each piece of evidence, we should study the manifestations as a whole to determine whether there is a general law regarding the topography of the sightings. The research along these lines by Michel, who was the first to apply analytical methods to the UFO phenomenon, has attracted widespread attention. Michel published his conclusions after a long and very careful examination of the French "wave" of the fall of 1954 (6). These conclusions can be summarized as follows in relation to the classification system introduced above:

1. *The points in question are distributed along straight lines,* whatever the type of sighting with which they are associated.

2. When the sightings for any given day include one or more manifestations of Type II, the geometrical figures associated with the distribution of the alignments form *star-shaped networks;* that is, these alignments have one or several points of convergence.

3. When the point of intersection of two alignments is itself a sighting point, the phenomenon observed at that point is generally of Type III-A.

4. No selective distribution of the various types of sightings or of the chronology of the manifestations along a given line is observed; this would seem to rule out the possibility that the alignments result from series of eyewitness accounts along the path of a single "object."

These points can be verified by an extensive and straightforward analysis of the documents compiled. They use only information on the location of the sightings, which is, as we have seen, the most accessible and most objective aspect.

Accordingly, the first purpose of the present work will be to make a critical examination of these conclusions, that is, a study of the distribution of the sightings along alignments and the arrangement of the lines in star-shaped networks. Whether or not the lines should be entirely attributed to chance can then be discussed in mathematical terms.

A REMARKABLE IDEA

If Michel's conclusions are false—if the appearance of the alignments is pure illusion—the sightings have to be explained individually. If they are correct, they provide a valuable starting point for studying a phenomenon that may be critical, not for only one branch of science, but for the whole vision of the world, and they enable us to judge the witnesses' testimony against solid criteria.

Among the alignments Michel thought he had succeeded in tracing, one in particular catches the attention at first glance. We will take it as an example.

For the single day of September 24, 1954, the French press reported the following sightings, here listed with their classifications: Lantefontaine, Type IV; Le Puy, Type IV; Langeac, Type IV; Tulle, Type IV; Ussel, Type I; Gelles, Type IV; Vichy, Type IV; Lencouacq, Type I; Bayonne, Type III.

At least half these eyewitness accounts would be rejected if studied within the limits of the usual official criteria. The Type IV sightings in particular could be judged insufficiently documented. Moreover, the phenomena reported at Tulle and Lencouacq were seen by only one witness. The Gelles sighting was of a "luminous cigar-shaped machine crossing the sky at a quite high speed and without sound." Must we immediately exclude it as being a meteor?

It is clear that the problem is one of method. To reject a measurement made on a *known and reproducible* physical phenomenon is certainly permissible when a new measurement may improve the accuracy; but to reject a piece of testimony concerning an *unknown* phenomenon deprives us of a certain quantity of information about the phenomenon and implies that the lost quantity is negligible. But how can we tell whether it really is negligible, since the phenomenon is unknown?

What Michel does is this. He draws a straight line from Bayonne to Vichy (*see* Figure 12). This line passes through Lencouacq, Tulle, Ussel and Gelles; of the nine groups of sightings, six are along one and the same straight line. Tracing the straight line from Le Puy to Tulle, we see that it passes through Langeac. No single standard phenomenon (release of a balloon, aircraft flight, etc.) will account for this arrangement. To convince ourselves of this, it is enough to look at the times. The Bayonne and Vichy sightings are dated some time in the afternoon. The Lencouacq sighting falls four hours later. The Gelles sighting is at the beginning of the night. The one at Ussel is still later, and the

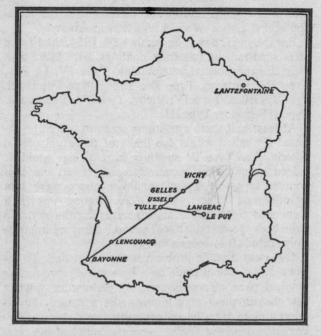

FIG. 12.—The Bayonne-Vichy line (after Michel).

Tulle case is at 11 P.M. Furthermore, the Bayonne sighting involves a triple object, whereas the other reports speak of single phenomena.

The problem that immediately presents itself is the calculation of the probability of such a distribution's occurring by chance.

DISCUSSION ABOUT PROBABILITIES

In recent years Michel's hypothesis has been widely commented on and applied to UFO reports all over the world. O. Fontes, C. Vogt and A. Ribera (*see* Figure

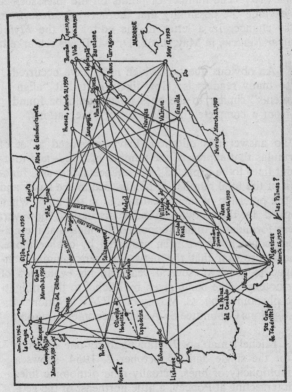

Fig. 13.—The Spanish orthotenic network (after Ribera).

13) have published maps showing "networks" strikingly similar to those found by Michel for reports from Brazil, Argentina, and Spain, respectively. In 1961, one of the authors of this book noticed similar relations between sighting points in North Africa while conducting a search for systematic patterns in African observations (13). The number of points on the lines seemed to exclude the possibility that the network arose from pure chance. In a letter to the editor of the *Flying Saucer Review,* in May, 1962, Dr. M. Davis remarked:

An obvious question which must have occurred to many readers is: How likely is it that "alignments" similar to the ones noted could be found from a completely *random* set of observations?

To answer this question, Davis proposed a set of formulas that expressed the number of three- and four-point lines to be expected from chance alone, as a function of the total number of points used in the study and of the precision of their localization on the map. When applied to the networks under discussion, however, these formulas actually supported the idea that the network could not have been produced by chance alone. The impression that the networks were genuine continued to grow for several years. In his evaluation of "orthoteny" (the name given by Michel to the straight-line phenomenon), C. Maney of NICAP (National Investigations Committee on Aerial Phenomena) wrote:

Michel's map no. 7, utilizing thirty-one sightings for the single date of October 2, 1954, shows a multiplicity of lines, actually nine orthotenic lines intersecting at Poncey, a little northeast of the geographic centre of France. And again, as Michel points out, on the night of October 2 a vast illuminated cigar was observed at the intersection, at Poncey. It would seem to be a plausible interpretation of such unique geometric alignment that a well-organized programme of exploration of features of the area of France were being carried out by some extraterrestrial intelligences (50).

Quite recently, "orthotenic" alignments were researched from sighting points in the U.S. Southwest, within the framework of the investigation conducted by APRO (Aerial Phenomena Research Organization) on the 1964 American wave. In the meantime, the reality of "orthoteny" was questioned on a new basis.

The first challenge came from Professor D. Menzel, who sent the British *Flying Saucer Review** several articles dealing with Michel's theory. The first of these articles appeared in the March-April, 1964, issue and was entitled "Do Flying Saucers Move in Straight Lines?":

> Of all the phenomena adduced by believers to prove that flying saucers really exist, one of the most intriguingly complex is Orthoteny, the occurrence of saucer sightings from places that lie on the same straight line.

The article pointed out the preliminary precautions that should have been taken in a statistical study of this sort. Menzel placed particular emphasis on the difficulty of dealing with such material as UFO events whose dates and locations are sometimes not known with complete accuracy. On the basis of these remarks, he developed a set of new formulas and, applying them to the case of the French sightings discussed by Michel, showed that almost all the lines were questionable, especially those of three points. Even in the light of this new analysis, however, the six-point line Bayonne-Vichy (often referred to as "BAVIC") remained unexplained.

The effectiveness of Menzel's attacks on Michel's hypotheses was somewhat lessened by the nature of his assumptions concerning the investigative method used by those in favor of the straight-line theory:

* *Flying Saucer Review:* 21 Cecil Court, Charing Cross Road, London, W. C. 2, Great Britain.

Let us suppose, for example, that a four-point line has shown up, crossing some map. He would like to get some more sightings to confirm the reality of this line. How easy to write to some friend, to the local newspaper, or to the post-master of several of these towns, requesting information about sightings on a certain date. Sure enough, two replies came in: the four-point line becomes a six-pointer. And the amateur statistician becomes impressed with his predictive powers and in the reality of the line.

That this criticism was superfluous was demonstrated in our own investigation of the significance of the networks. In this study, we started from a completely different basis. The first thing we did, in our efforts to evaluate Michel's theory, was to check the original reports one by one. This investigation revealed that Michel had acted in good faith and that his job of documentation was superb; it also uncovered many confirmations of the sightings he had used in his book, in the form of additional reports unknown to him at the time. Our second task was to compute the alignments exactly, to verify that the points were indeed situated on the lines. Our last investigation was a reevaluation of the role played by chance in the geometry of the networks. The results we found are analyzed in Chapter Four. They caused us some surprise, but, at the same time, they demonstrated that the personal attacks on Michel and his methods were unjustified and out of place, *as are all emotional reactions in the appraisal of a scientific fact.*

THE GREAT-CIRCLE THEORY

The statistical estimates of the type presented by Davis, Menzel and Mebane, estimates based on mathematical formulas alone, cannot furnish a true proof of the existence or nonexistence of significant alignments.

They merely draw attention to the fact that attributing the sightings to chance *a priori* is rash and unscientific, since the elementary statistical criteria that would settle the question once and for all encounter serious resistance.

This fact appears even more distinctly if we make counter proofs by dispersing points at random on a map of France. At the time of the publication of Michel's book, several well-known scientists expressed the opinion that if such counter proofs were made they would show clearly that points taken randomly form alignments just as well. The fact that these counter proofs have never actually been carried out leads us to think that the result was considered a foregone conclusion. The only experiment of this type published before our own work is that by Mebane in his Appendix to the American edition of Michel's book. His results, as well as all our early attempts to study the problem, confirm the tenuity of attributing a six-point alignment, or even a five-point alignment, to mere chance.

The notion of alignment itself is vague and inadequate. Michel, in introducing it, pointed out that as a result of the large number of eyewitness accounts gathered for the 1954 wave, the investigation rapidly moved from a local setting, where an alignment can be shown by means of a map. To the sightings involving French territory were added reports from Great Britain, Italy, Spain, Russia, Poland, etc. On this scale the notion of alignment, which is introduced naturally on the local scale, no longer has any meaning. The problem becomes that of establishing the curve of which the alignment is considered a portion. Finding this curve will enable us to examine the possible connections between the alignments traced across neighboring countries and even perhaps to investigate whether, on a planetary scale, the phenomenon has general laws accessible to our methods of research.

If, having noted an alignment, we plot the sighting points (defined by their longitude and latitude, which must be precisely known) on a graph, a very clear curve appears. The most natural hypothesis then is the one Michel has proposed (12) on the basis of our first calculations: it theorizes that the alignments are local sections of great geodetic circles.

Although the great-circle hypothesis is the simplest hypothesis that can be arrived at, inasmuch as the great circle is the simplest figure on a sphere, it obviously invalidates the methods previously utilized by investigators to represent alignments with simple equipment. It calls for calculations that, while elementary (since they are purely geometrical), are relatively voluminous, and for a body of techniques and technical data never before considered in connection with the UFO problem.

In other words, quite apart from the interest such an intriguing theory as "orthoteny" provokes, it is *the first organized application of the scientific method* to the analysis of unidentified flying objects. Michel's hypotheses provide a splendid avenue of approach to a problem that until now has seemed doomed to irrationality.

4

EXTRACTING THE DATA

FOLLOW THE LINES

THE CONTROVERSY OVER PROBABILITIES that raged in the pages of the serious publications devoted to the UFO problem soon made it clear that the available formulations were only rough approaches to the subject; the surface over which the sightings are distributed can be of irregular shape, and the accuracy of each location is variable. In the majority of the cases (except those of Type I) the location cannot be obtained from direct measurement on the ground. It is consequently necessary to establish a broader method that takes these facts into account. Above all, one must bear in mind that the problem is not that of verifying the existence of *one* alignment or of a few specific alignments, but of finding a general method applicable to the straight-line phenomenon as formulated by Michel.

In order to lay the foundations for this general method (a certain number of sighting points for a given day being known), we propose to determine precisely, by numerical calculation, the parameters of the great circle of the earth that passes through these points and to tabulate this curve so that it can be easily plotted on a planisphere. This problem of spherical geometry has been set out in detail by us in (16). The application of this method enables us to verify that the circle does in fact represent the sightings, to evaluate the degree of accuracy actually attained (by calculating the deviation of each sighting from the mean great circle), and to verify the arrangement of the alignments into networks. Only on the basis of these results can the question of the role played by chance in the networks be discussed profitably.

The period to which our attention will be directed is that for which alignments have been produced: from September 24 to October 15, 1954. It is not within the scope of the present work to investigate whether any other lines can be drawn up on the basis of sightings made before or after this period; our aim is to develop criteria by which to judge whether or not the alignments announced as existing (6) do in fact exist.

We have already mentioned the sightings of September 24, with the Bayonne-Vichy line (Figure 12); another alignment has been produced for September 26 and two for September 27, the latter with two interesting Type I reports (Foussignargues and Premanon) and a Type II (Rixheim). For September 29 there are three more alignments, but the important period is the first two weeks of October. It is organized around three series of reports. These are the accounts of October 2 and October 4 ("Poncey network"), those of October 7 ("Montlevicq network") and those of October 11. A considerable number of sightings correspond to each of these dates, and it seems that these points lie along alignments that intersect precisely, forming "stars." After October 11, the phenomenon began to decrease in France, although alignments are still observed for the distributions of October 12, 14, and 15. The verification of these networks is essential, but first we must know more about the sightings themselves and the information that can be extracted from the reports.

SELECTING SIGNIFICANT REPORTS

The selection of sightings likely to produce useful data in an analysis of the phenomenon is a delicate operation: we can expect much further discussion and argument on this point. If we try to set down on a map the exact location of the sighting points, we at once find two categories of reports for which this operation is difficult. With the first group, the difficulty derives from the incomplete nature of the reports received. Quite often, for example, newspapers give the place of origin of the witnesses, but omit the place where the sighting occurred! In the second group, the eyewitnesses can be placed satisfactorily at the location of the sighting, but the phenomenon itself is vague. Many Type IV sightings, and observations of other types made from aircraft in flight, often have to be excluded from topographical studies for this reason.

We thus find that the sightings that produce reliable data for making these calculations come from Types I, II, and III, which are generally easy to locate when the observer was on the ground.

The Type IV phenomenon, as we have defined it, is difficult to pin down to an exact spot for two reasons: first, because it occurs at such a height that its distance from the witness can only be worked out very roughly; and second, because one of its distinguishing features is continuous motion, from its appearance until its disappearance, so that the coordinates of one point of the trajectory cannot arbitrarily be used.

The phenomena of Types I, II, and III always have a certain spatial extension; but whatever the complexity of the trajectory, they are characterized by a discontinuous kind of behavior, and the discontinuity defines the coordinates of a single point. For the Type I phenomenon, this point is the spot where the "object" is described as "having been resting on the ground," or the exact site of the traces, if they are available (as in the Socorro case). For the Type II phenomena, which are generally visible over a fairly large area because of the size and brightness of the image, the point we use is defined by the release of "secondary objects," if this is available from the reports. For the Type III phenomena, the pendulum motion and the sudden stop are precise, well-defined discontinuities from which coordinates can be determined.

THE FIRST CATALOGUE

The numerous calculations we required to verify the laws predicted by Michel called for a reliable list of sightings giving coordinates, dates and types, as free from selection effects as possible. Unfortunately, no such catalogue was available in UFO literature. Every writer on this subject, it seems, has his own theories to prove; each focuses his attention on reports that provide convenient illustration of his ideas. Thus most books give an incomplete picture. Few compilations exist, and these are sadly lacking in useful information. Every source must be followed and carefully checked.

We have therefore been obliged to use the codification of the sightings scattered throughout sundry lists, most often unpublished, and to work out the coordinates for as many useful points as possible to form the first catalogue with any serious guarantee of accuracy. It appeared necessary to set a limit to the scope of this list, and we decided to give only five hundred sightings, since the work of codification and coordinate computation is considerable. On the other hand, these five hundred cases (listed in Appendix III) are more than merely a sample; from the point of view of distribution in time, the 1954 cases make up the bulk of the catalogue, especially those sufficiently well defined to be used in the computation of the networks. But in order to preserve the general aspect of the phenomenon, we have included the sightings most commonly quoted in the specialized works on the subject and even a number of old sightings—for example, the 1908 explosion of a mysterious body in the Siberian *taiga*.

We have sought to present a fairly complete series of cases of Types I, II and III, such cases being theoretically the most representative of the phenomenon. These reports were selected from extensive material: collections of newspapers and files of letters from readers of several large dailies, made available by the news media in Paris; the personal files of early sightings compiled by Raymond Veillith, the publisher of the lively periodical *Lumieres dans la nuit,* Charles Garreau, a professional newspaper man with a local daily sold in the east of France, and Roger Vervisch; the early compilations of similar data by the independent investigative group Ouranos, under the direction of Marc Thirouin; Guy Quincy's special catalogue on landings, a systematic and clear presentation of the observations; the files of Michel, a staggering volume of documents; and, of course, the fine presentation of the material by Michel in his two books. In addition, we have also made use of the material published by Mebane (6), Keyhoe (23, 24, 25), and E. J. Ruppelt (2), as well as the publications issued by APRO for the happenings in the United States. Finally, we included documentary material secured in the course of our own investigations, particularly testimony from officials that was never released to the press.

The sightings in the catalogue are listed chronologically, numbered sequentially and coded as described in (203). This data is punched on IBM cards, following a standard format, for subsequent computer manipulations. This catalogue was completed in 1962. Since then, much progress has been made, both in the selection of representative UFO events and in the design of computer codes for research in this area. In 1963–64 a much larger catalogue was developed, comprising more than three thousand sightings; most of the studies discussed later in this book were based on the newer list. However, it is our purpose here merely to illustrate how the need for standardized information has arisen in the course of the discussion of Michel's hypotheses, to which we now return.

THE NETWORKS EXIST

Now that we are in possession of an accurate list of coordinates for the sightings of the period studied by Michel, we can undertake a systematic verification of his statements. Many people have tried, long before us, to achieve this verification by joining the points with straight lines drawn across detailed maps. This approach can give only uncertain, confused and unreliable results. The computation of the great circles, on the contrary, gives exact tables that allow the position of the lines to be plotted on the maps precisely. The average distance from the places of the sightings to the mean Bayonne-Vichy line, for example, was found to be less than one kilometer, a result that encouraged us to compute all the other straight lines. Quite a few of them, it turned out, were verified with similar precision. When we plotted the large networks on local maps, the phenomenon announced by Michel was absolutely confirmed: the lines intersected with a high degree of precision on the center of the "star-shaped" networks.

The precision of these intersections was the important finding. In the case of the October 2 network, we found that the smallest circle we could draw touching all the alignments was indeed centered on Poncey and had a radius of 600 meters, while the circle containing all the points of intersection of the lines had a radius of 4 kilometers. But in the case of Montlevicq, we obtained a distinctly poorer result (1.4 and 5.0 kilometers, respectively) and for the third network (October 11) it did not seem to us that the star intersection was verified.

At this point we had verified the claims of Michel: the straight lines—which had been laughed out of court by so many scientists*——came out of our computer with splendid precision, and in the two really important cases, the star-shaped networks also seemed to be verified. Yet all our efforts to discover more about the underlying order, the internal structure Michel's theory predicted, failed to produce any result, although practically every sighting in the catalogue had been weighted and compared by the computer to every possible line in the networks. To find the answer to this mystery, we first had to take another hard look at the whole idea of "orthoteny"—and the part chance might have played in the design of the networks.

ORTHOTENY CHALLENGED

Although there was room for improvement in determining the exact locations of the sightings, the material available to us showed that the calculations of the great circles were well founded, at least for France. The sightings reported as being along the arcs of great circles were indeed aligned, and the alignments claimed to form networks did indeed intersect with acceptable precision, at least far as the two main networks (October 2 and 7) are concerned. Michel's observations are consequently correct.

But there is more. As soon as Michel learned the results of our calculations for the Bayonne-Vichy (BAVIC) circle, at the end of August, 1961, he noticed a fact that seemed indeed very remarkable: the line crossed Spain, Brazil and Argentina, three countries where important "waves" had taken place. It passed over New Zealand, intersecting the mountainous area near Wellington, where reports had been made in unusual number; and it divided New Guinea in half, crossing the area of the remarkable phenomena of 1959. It seemed, therefore, that not only was BAVIC an unusually well-defined alignment, on the basis of the

---

* A French cosmologist told Michel: "Your straight lines cannot not exist, because flying saucers cannot exist"!

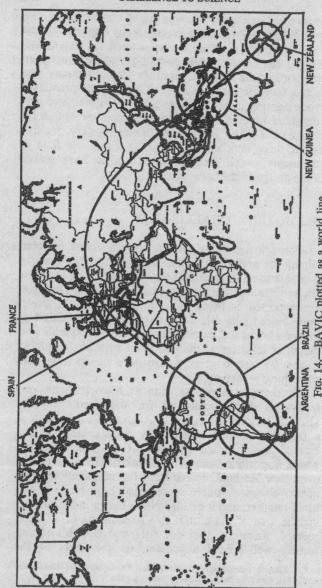

FIG. 14.—BAVIC plotted as a world line.

French sightings, it also provided a link of exceptional value between the most significant periods of UFO history (excluding the American waves). This connection is illustrated in Figure 14, where we have plotted BAVIC as a world line. It was the basis of a generalized theory presented by Michel as "global orthoteny": the hypothesis that there existed an underlying order in the manifestations of the UFO phenomenon on a planetary scale. Knowledge of this order could give us considerable insight into the nature of the phenomenon itself. An understanding of these laws would perhaps help determine if the cause of the sightings was natural or artificial, and what its origin was.

The idea of a structure of alignments, however, in extricating us from one perplexity, had only plunged us into another. It might seem that we have here a key of some importance, but is this really true? What existence can we attach to these great circles? To what physical fact can we link the alignment? Does the phenomenon appear selectively on great circles? Does not all this add further complications to a situation already plagued with uncertainties?

Must we conclude that the majority of the alignments (particularly the three-point ones) are due to mere chance, but that certain well-defined great circles, such as BAVIC, are indeed significant? If so, the accumulation of larger and larger masses of information ought to show up the structure of alignments more precisely. But the research done on this point has not been encouraging. In France, the lines cross countless sighting points for which insufficient research has been done; areas with numerous observations deserve close scrutiny before coordinates are adopted. In South America and New Guinea, where our correspondents plotted the projection of BAVIC from copies of the computer tables, none of the structures they found seemed to hold a preferred orientation along the BAVIC great circle. Similar tests of other great circles crossing Italy were also negative. When we tried to show the existence of an internal structure, while remaining willing to accept as significant an alignment on which new points appeared at any interval in time, we found our efforts hampered by the density of the lines.

The time has therefore come for us to reconsider the problem entirely and to ask ourselves whether the part played by chance in the formation of the networks has not perhaps been radically underestimated, not only by the supporters of "orthoteny," but even by its opponents, whose formulas fail to account for the phenomenon of Michel's star-shaped networks. The problem posed here is quite typical of a whole series of questions that can be tackled in a systematic manner only by the use of impersonal methods; what we need is an automatic, "push-button" technique with no human bias, capable of describing the situation completely without introducing at the very start the oversimplifications manual calculation imposes. The method suited to the study of a problem of this kind is simulation.

WE SIMULATE A WAVE

In order to simulate the alignment networks, we generated points at random on a spherical surface representing France, i.e., an imaginary surface of comparable dimensions and geometry, and endeavored to show all the alignments, or, to be more precise, all the great circles on which at least three of these points fall. This required an entirely automatic method to eliminate the factor of the psychology of the experimenter in perceiving the organization of the lines.

This psychological element has been considerably underestimated in the statistical tests suggested by Mebane, Davis and Menzel for checking the validity of the alignments. It even enters into the very definition of the notion of "straight line," as can be seen in Figure 15, in which we have three sighting points, A, B, and C. If the lack of precision on each point is, say, one-half mile, each "sighting" must in reality be represented as a disk one-half mile in radius. Thus one finds cases

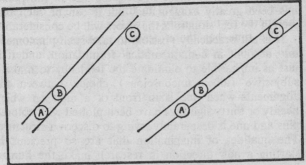

FIG. 15.—A common difficulty in the study of the alignments: A is aligned with B and C, but C is not aligned with A and B.

where the alignment BC can pass through A while the alignment AB does not pass through C.

In Figure 16, A and B are so close to one another that a whole series of points C can form the alignment, in the sense that the center of the disk B will be in the

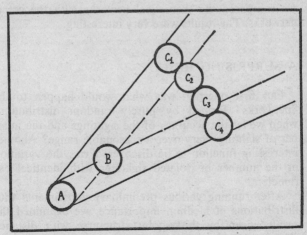

FIG. 16.—In the situation shown above, all the points called C may be considered as "aligned" with points A and B.

"corridor" AC. In these figures, the size of the points has been greatly exaggerated, but it can be seen that even in the real situations the errors will be considerable.

It is not practically possible to take such phenomena into account in a mathematical formulation, and it is just as impossible to eliminate the tendency to make a subjective (albeit unconscious) choice between the alignments when one is in front of a map on which twenty or thirty sightings have been plotted with colored pins and one is desperately trying to discern a structure. The qualities of imagination that are so precious in starting a new direction in research make the human brain an untrustworthy instrument in checking hypotheses. Here the computer is a useful tool.

Given any distribution of points on a surface, the appearance of alignments between these points is a problem of criteria. Since the number of points included in the distribution, their size and the shape of the surface can all vary, discussion must be related to a concrete case. We decided to "simulate" a wave comparable to that of 1954 in France, following a technique that is developed in detail in Appendix II. In this way we compared the theoretical neworks with the actual networks. The results were very interesting.

A SURPRISING RESULT

Our first question was what would happen to the "networks" formed by purely random distributions when we let the accuracy of the sightings and the number of sightings vary over a reasonable range? Another interesting function to be discovered was the variation in the number of isolated sightings with identical parameters.

After running various preliminary experiments with distributions of medium importance, we examined the results given by thirty-point structures with distance criteria of 1.0 and 2.5 km. Taking out one, two, three points from the network, we deduced the distribution

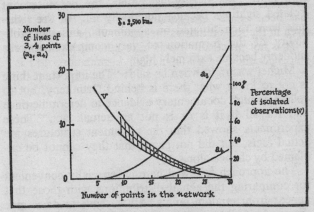

FIG. 17.—The statistical law governing the generation of the networks. Note how rapidly the percentage of isolated observations approaches zero when the number of points increases.

at different stages, i.e., with thirty points, twenty-nine, twenty-eight, etc. The curves obtained (average of the experiments done) are shown in Figure 17.

Figures 18 *a* and *b* show random networks produced by the computer. These structures were in no respect inferior to the most complex networks advanced as proofs of the straight-line theory. For any distribution

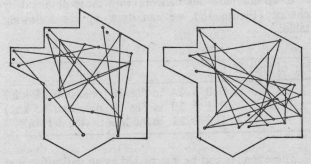

FIG. 18.—(left) Random network, accuracy 1.0 km.
(right) Random network, accuracy 2.5 km.

with more than twenty-five points, the percentage of isolated sightings became practically nil. All the sightings were then situated on alignments, and the probability of the formation of very complex networks suddenly became extremely high.

Michel was right when he said: "The important thing is not to know what there is behind Orthoteny, but to collect enough documentary evidence to determine once and for all if it is or is not an actual fact." These experiments showed that the alignment structures are actual facts, but did not prove that they cannot be explained by chance alone.

The approach followed here is especially convenient for comparing the actual distributions with those that appear from random points. All we have to do is give the machine the coordinates of actual sightings, instead of random numbers, and let it grind through the tedious task of computing and selecting all the possible alignments. Figure 19 shows the Montlevicq network (the structure discovered by Michel for the French observations of October 7, 1954) as it was "rediscovered" by the electronic machine in about four minutes. There are only one or two very minor differences between this network and that published by Michel, a fact that constitutes another tribute to the extreme care and precision with which the French researcher conducted his analysis.

If we compare this network with those obtained by chance (Figure 18) we can draw up the following table:

No. of lines of	6	5	4	3	points
	0	0	4	24	in Fig. 18 (precision 1.0 km.)
	0	1	5	20	in Fig. 18 (precision 2.5 km.)
	1	0	0	21	in the Montlevicq network

These figures can be interpreted as an indication that the actual accuracy in the real sightings is of the order

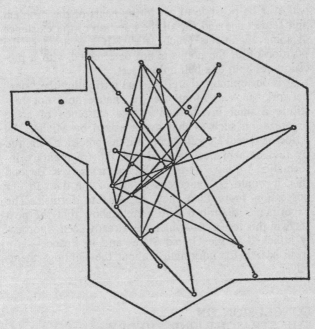

Fig. 19.—Motlevic network.

of 2.5 km.; thus there is no reason to differentiate between the alignment structures obtained on the basis of real sightings and those appearing as the result of mere chance. The phenomenon of the intersection in the form of stars completely loses its exceptional character for distributions with a large number of points.

In the actual network (Figure 19), there is an alignment of six points, two of the points being in reality very close to each other. Such an alignment would deserve to be the subject of a special study. Unfortunately, we find here the same obstacle mentioned in the course of the preliminary calculations: because scant official consideration was given to the sightings, often the only data at our disposal are the descriptions given by the newspapers. It seems doubtful to us whether it will ever be possible to get to the heart of the problem and settle once and for all the question of the existence of some alignments (such as BAVIC) so long as the position of *all* the points is not determined with a precision of about one-half mile or less.

It is our opinion, therefore, that attributing the "star" networks such as Montlevicq to chance does not constitute a final invalidation of the existence of some organization such as that hypothesized by Michel. All it does is reveal a conflict between the precision required by the mathematical method and the fragmentary information we have on the sightings themselves. Beyond this, it would be dangerous to ask of the data in our possession more than they are able to furnish. The experiments described here merely show that the next stage in this research—which has already been vigorously attacked in the United States and in France—is a fresh search for information about the sightings themselves.

CONCLUSION ON THE STRAIGHT-LINE THEORY

The results we have just presented will probably be considered by some to be a total refutation of the theory of alignments. We shall not be so categorical, because our data have not yet been independently checked by other groups of scientists, and because we have been drastically limited in the amount of computer time that we could devote to this project outside official support. Besides, no general conclusion as to the nonexistence of certain alignments can be drawn from the present work. The analyses carried out merely establish that, among the proposed alignments, the great majority, if not all, must be attributed to pure chance. In the two star-shaped networks we have verified, we see nothing but the superposition of a random effect and the dispersion usually associated with Type II sightings, which has been well established by Michel.

The fact remains that we are once again facing the original problem: the study of the individual sightings as reports. The first general clue that seemed to have presented itself has evaporated before our eyes; although work will continue on certain details of Michel's discoveries that may be the occasion for new evidence, the elucidation of the UFO problem "orthoteny" seemed to announce has not come about. Then why devote so much time to the straight-line theory?

The point is that while the straight-line theory, as far as we can say, is not the key to the mystery, *a body of knowledge has been accumulated and a large edifice of techniques has been built, and this development reaches far beyond the negative conclusion on the straight-line hypothesis.*

The significance of Michel's theory remains great, because it has taken the problem out of the dilemma where believers and non-believers had buried it for fifteen years. It has shaken the many scientists who previously could not see in the reports anything for science to analyze. Orthoteny is not the final solution, but it is a splendid avenue of approach to the scientific, objective study of the reports. For the first time, a calm, dispassionate debate has gathered the opponents and supporters of different interpretations of the reports—from Menzel to Michel—in a controversy of the highest caliber. For the first time, hypotheses have been presented, analyzed, tested, and rejected by students of the phenomenon. The subject of UFO's has thus been taken out of the list of "odd phenomena" and "strange events" —such as tales of witchcraft and stories of haunted houses—and placed under the light of scientific analysis.

Thanks to Michel's fertile mind, the study of UFO's today is no longer an area of wild rumors, uncontrollable theories and unjustified hypotheses. It was in view of the study of the straight-line phenomenon that the first classification of UFO sightings and the first codification systems were introduced, five years ago. It was to check the alignments that the first catalogue was designed and about twelve different computer programs written for a variety of machines.

Slowly, as the descriptions written by the witnesses were stripped of the sensational aura added by the newspapers, reduced to bare facts, converted into numbers and codes, localized on maps, and processed, these reports lost their unbelievable character. They ceased to be occasions of amazement or ridicule; no longer were they merely subjects for the belief of some and the disbelief of others; they became elements of information, pieces of scientific data.

The problem with which we find ourselves confronted is no longer the global verification of a large body of networks but the detailed study of local reports and of the remarkable laws followed by the phenomenon in its development in time and in its physical manifestations. These other aspects remain to be elucidated, and they will involve more intricate discussions; but the study of the straight-line mystery has given us the tools to attack this new challenge with some degree of confidence.

5

THE SIGNAL AND THE NOISE

SCOPE OF THE PROBLEM

IN CHAPTERS 3 AND 4, we dealt with the situation in space of the UFO's sighted since 1946 without considering the particularities presented by each account, thus limiting ourselves to the search for a possible law covering the topographical distribution of the sightings. We are now going to expand this study by recalling, first of all, how the phenomenon appears to the witness.

The "flying saucer" (whether an actual material object, a known physical phenomenon misinterpreted, or even a vision) is the image of an object of variable complexity, usually deriving from the spherical form. At times ellipsoid, discoid, ovoid, spindle-shaped, cylindrical, or cone-shaped, this image is that of a self-contained object whose visible aerofoil surface seems to play only a secondary role in the motion (as opposed to the wings of an airplane).

The essential characteristic of the movement is often elusiveness (especially in Type IV cases). When associated with a spherical or "mandala" (tear-drop)

97

shape, this elusiveness appears to impart a confused and distressing sensation, like a waking dream or delirium, not only to the witness but, to a lesser degree, to the investigator who questions him and the person who reads his testimony. Reactions to observations of "flying saucers" consequently appear complex and unsuited for direct rational analysis. It is interesting to note that it was a psychoanalyst, Jung, who took the first step in the study of the phenomenon (110). Although his conclusions throw little light on the physical nature and the material existence of the "saucers," they do permit a better understanding of the psychological atmosphere created by the reports and of the state of mind in which scientific circles have established their opinion.

This opinion is actually fashioned from remarks of a general and vague nature about either the possibilities of misinterpretation of man-made objects or the various physical causes likely to produce the images. The majority of scientists, who know nothing about the phenomenon—and see nothing in it but accounts by deluded witnesses of sightings of meteors, balloons and aircraft, together with the photographic hoaxes perpetrated by a few—have chosen to deny the existence of the "saucer-object" and maintain that all the sightings can be attributed to hallucinations, mirages, errors, or pranks. We shall discuss this attitude later in connection with specific examples.

HOW WAVES DEVELOP

When we move from a consideration of individual accounts to the study of the evolution of the problem as a whole since 1946, an important characteristic of the UFO phenomenon comes to light: the sightings are not randomly distributed in time. Long periods may elapse without a new case unless the newspapers of several countries are examined very closely. Then once again the problem reappears on the front pages of the papers and assumes a sensational character, which deters people of common sense from studying it. At other times, when the press has grown tired of a subject it has over-exploited, only by patiently building up card indexes from private reports is a sudden change in the density of sightings over a given period established, several years after the event.

This characteristic is important, for, just as in the case of the theories bearing on the shape or the kinematic behavior of the "objects," any attempt to explain the phenomenon will have to account for these variations in the number of reports, which are termed "waves."

None of the waves has been limited to a particular region of the globe. However, each has had its peak in a precise region. The wave of 1946 had a maximum in Scandinavia; those of 1947, 1950 and 1952 were observed principally in the United States, but also gave rise to a substantial number of cases in France, where the autumn of 1954 was particularly rich in precise reports. In 1956, the whole globe experienced a resurgence of cases, while the United States had a sudden peak in 1957. South America, where there had been numerous sightings during previous waves, next began to take the lead over other regions of the globe. While 1962 was an active year, 1963 was one of the quietest ever recorded. Both 1964 and 1965 were active years. As this is being written (spring, 1966), the wave that reached its maximum in the summer of 1965 is still being felt around the world, and there is no sign that activity is about to subside.

The development of a wave in any given country generally occurs independent of the happenings recorded elsewhere, news of which reaches the public of the country in question only much later. The newspapers are filled with reports once the interest of public opinion has been triggered by the first important cases, but it does not appear that there is any psychological influence of one country over another in this aspect. Frequently, as a wave develops, it is accompanied by an unusual occurrence, something of a "phenomenon" itself, in the press: the subject appears later and lasts longer in the newspapers than in reality; at first the press is slow to admit it, then it seeks to prolong its existence.

In the course of our research, we found that the picture of the development of the phenomenon obtained from the examination of the reports in a single country is extremely poor. The official agencies that investigate the UFO phenomenon in the United States do not yet seem to understand this.

Naturally, both on the local and the global scene, a big story disturbs the law of variation; it encourages the witnesses of recent sightings to make their reports public, and, of course, it creates an ideal market for hoaxes of all kinds. Accordingly, certain spasmodic gaps in the sustained mean variation are to be expected. As our task here is to describe the evolution of the problem in its main lines, we will not go into these secondary effects.

CELESTIAL SIGNS

According to Jung, the idea of lenticular machines that could perform rapid, silent evolutions existed long before modern times; traces of them are found in the rumors and legends of a past so remote that Jung placed them in the general picture of the "collective unconscious" of humanity and put them on the same footing as the modern phenomena.

For instance, at a time when there was little distinction between physical events, moral truths, and spiritual experiences, and when ideas were not, as they are today, separated into categories (scientific, ethical, theological, philosophical, etc.), Hildegard of Bingen wrote in her book of visions, the *Scivias,* about 1145:

I saw a great star most splendid and beautiful, and with it an exceeding multitude of falling sparks which with the star followed southward. And they examined Him upon His throne almost as something hostile, and turning from Him they sought rather the north. And suddenly they were all annihilated, being turned into black coals . . . and cast into the abyss that I could see them no more.

This vision, illustrated by the beautiful figure of stars falling into the waves, is interpreted by Hildegard as signifying the Fall of the Angels.

In his remarkable book *From Magic to Science* (Dover, 1957), one of the most penetrating works on the rise and development of the scientific spirit, Charles Singer, commenting on the *Scivias,* notes:

The concentric circles appear in numerous visions. . . . It is in this concentric form that Hildegard most frequently pictures the Almighty, and the idea again appears in the eleventh miniature, which she describes as "a most shining light and within it the appearance of a human form of a sapphire color which glittered with a gentle but sparkling glow." Appearances of this type are recorded again and again.

Elsewhere in the same book Singer remarks:

All or nearly all the visions present certain characters in common. In all a prominent feature is a point or a group of points of light, which shimmer and move, usually in a wavelike manner, and are most often interpreted as stars or flaming eyes. In quite a number of cases one light, larger than the rest, exhibits a series of concentric circular figures of wavering form. . . . Often the lights give the impression of *working,* boiling, or fermenting, described by so many visionaries, from Ezekiel onwards.

The reference to Ezekiel is a singularly appropriate one: the descriptions of the twelfth-century visionary are thus seen to converge with those of prophets before Christ. We touch here a fundamental branch of human inspiration, which culminated with Dante and to which other great thinkers such as Paracelsus (who lived from 1491 to 1541 and was not ignorant of Hildegard's works) contributed. These visions were often of great power and beauty, as shown in another description by Hildegard; this one accompanies a curious engraving (used by Jung in his book on "flying saucers") of the soul, depicted as a "fiery sphere," coming down to possess the body of an infant:

> And I saw that many circling eddies possessed the sphere and brought it earthward, but with ever renewed force it returned upward and with wailing asked,
> —I, wanderer that I am, where am I?
> —In Death's shadow.
> —And where go I?
> —In the way of sinners.
> —And what is my hope?
> —That of all wanderers.

It is difficult to lump together ancient and modern eyewitness accounts before detailed evidence is forthcoming, however, for the frequency of the observations before the nineteenth century does not indicate any clear succession of waves. We can only note that certain years or epochs have been richer in sightings than others; the period 1916–44 was one of the poorest, a little-known fact that throws the present-day sightings into even greater relief.

We shall return to the subject of the cases dating from before 1946 later, for, if they do pertain to the same fundamental problem, they present several serious questions, regardless of the type of interpretation given them. Their geographical distribution covers all seven continents.

The sightings of 1946 and 1947 exhibited strong geographical correlations, being centered in Scandinavia (primarily in Sweden, Denmark and over the Baltic Sea) and in the United States, respectively. Among the 1947 sightings that have reached us there are three from France, however: Col de Serres in April, Montusson in July, and Les Moutiers in August. There was a clearly defined peak in July, and the number of cases rose far above the average during June and July, 1947.

The interest of the American press was triggered by the account given on June 24, 1947, by a businessman, Kenneth Arnold. The first investigation by the U.S. Air Force was then initiated. A statement attributing the Arnold event to hallucination terminated the investigation on July 4, the very day the wave seems to have reached its peak. At the same time, astronomer G. Kuiper declared that the phenomena described corresponded to no known type of meteor and were patently a case of man-made objects.

The problem of the investigation of the UFO phenomenon was clearly propounded from that moment. The common reaction of scientific circles and of the general public, still very much impressed with the secrecy that had surrounded Project Manhattan—the preparation of the atomic bomb—was to credit the army with the manufacture of the "machines," while the long string of eyewitness accounts from military pilots led the air force to rule out—at least in private conversations—the idea of hallucinations, prototypes being tested by some American research body, or spy aircraft from another country. But it was hard to prove that the phenomena were of natural origin.

A new official explanation (or, we should say, interpretation), calculated to reassure the public (which was not entirely satisfied with the "hallucination" theory), had to be supplied. A commission was set up by an order of December 30, 1947, signed by Secretary of Defense James Forrestal. Under the authority of the Air Material Command at Wright Field Air Force Base, the commission had among its members Dr. J. Allen Hynek, then an astrophysicist with Ohio State University in Dayton.

Despite its official definition as a research body, this commission was never in a position to define precisely its own line of action. Despite the efforts of its scientific members, the commission assumed the character of an investigation center, designed to provide the air force with explanations of individual reports, rather than a research center. At the same time the very existence of this official commission prevented other scientific investigators from contemplating independent studies, more dynamically oriented toward research.

The struggle between the air force and the scientists continued behind the scenes from 1948 to 1966; it can be traced from the published statements of both sides. It has either been misinterpreted by the popular UFO writers or escaped their view completely. Hynek has been the most vocal of the scientists closely connected with Project Blue Book in his attempts to broaden the official investigative policy. An expert on artificial satellites (he organized the present worldwide tracking system for the U.S. in 1957) and an internationally known authority on stellar evolution, he accepted the responsibility to investigate UFO reports, in the face of strong criticism from his scientific colleagues and constant distasteful attacks in the pamphlets of the believers. During his nineteen years with Project Blue Book, he investigated well over one hundred cases in the field, sometimes spending several days in remote places where puzzling observations had been made. His name is mentioned in every major report in the air force records: He was with Ruppelt in Bismarck in 1953, in Levelland in 1957, the Socorro (which he visited three times) and Monticello in 1964, to mention only a few cases.

He also had innumerable phone conversations with witnesses of sightings the air force decided not to investigate in the field. This position within the "inner sanctum" afforded total awareness—he has demonstrated that he knew the files of Blue Book better than anyone in the air force and was more familiar with the French sightings in 1954 and the UFO situation abroad than anybody among the American "amateur" groups—but no real power to improve the existing policies. Since 1952 he has taken every opportunity to call the attention of the scientific community to the significance of the problem and has made every effort to convince the air force that the activity of Blue Book has to be redesigned; but his recommendations were always ignored.

It was only in 1965, when he placed the matter before the Secretary of the Air Force, that he got the Scientific Advisory Board to reconsider the offcial handling of the problem. The conclusions of the board vindicated entirely Hynek's continuous efforts and his oft-repeated statement that the UFO problem was primarily a scientific one. As this is being written, the air force has just decided to turn the task of investigating the most significant cases over to teams of university scientists. Nineteen years after the creation of the original commission, a new phase has thus been opened in the study of the sightings in the United States.

On January 7, 1948, Captain Thomas Mantell of the Kentucky National Guard died while attempting to intercept an unidentified object, in dramatic circumstances that were widely publicized. Otherwise the number of cases remained stationary and then, in 1949, diminished. On December 27, 1949, the commission was disbanded. In a statement of April 27, 1949, it had discretely *admitted the real existence of the unidentified objects and the possibility of their extraterrestrial origin.* The statements made by the air force, however, were based on an entirely different attitude, and spun a web of nonsense and naive, even childish interpretations around the problem.

After the commission was disbanded, the investigations were taken over entirely by the air force. In 1950 the frequency of the reported cases rose once more. This wave was marked by both the first eyewitness accounts given by eminent scientists and the first move on the part of authorities in the scientific world to take up a position against the material and physical reality of the phenomenon. Already, on August 20, 1949, Dr. Clyde Tombaugh had described a sighting that has remained a classic. On May 22, Dr. Seymour Hess witnessed at Flagstaff, Arizona, a UFO phenomenon which he described in minute detail. This sighting was discussed by Dr. G. de Vaucouleurs in his correspondence with Dr. Hess. This growing interest of scientists in the UFO phenomenon helped to give a purely academic character to the partial researches undertaken at that time. The opinion even seems to have prevailed that events themselves would settle the matter shortly, with the investigations finally bringing to light the physical phenomenon behind the sightings or "extraterrestrial visitors" making definite contact with the authorities.

The number of cases dropped to a minimum in 1951. The following year it went up again, and this time the character the phenomenon assumed seemed to indicate that the second of these eventualities was about to materialize: on July 20 and 26, 1952, a succession of objects flew over the White House and the Capitol. Detected simultaneously on radar by several posts, observed from the ground, and pursued by aircraft, some of the objects performed a "dance" above the Capitol. Speeds as high as three kilometers per second were recorded.

Subsequently, countless numbers of reports were received from radar stations, often supported by the evidence of pilots. The Air Technical Intelligence Center collected all the files and started to study them; unfortunately, the military personnel at ATIC are rotated every two years, and this hampers a long-term, scholarly approach to the files. The men in charge of the project barely have time to become acquainted with the various types of reports before they are reassigned by the Pentagon.

Conscious of the lack of continuity in the air force's investigations, Donald Keyhoe, a retired Marine major, privately began his own inquiries, which he published in a series of books. Also in 1952 the oldest civilian group, APRO, was founded in Arizona by Mr. and

Mrs. James Lorenzen. For a list of the major civilian UFO groups in the United States, *see* Appendix V.

The 1952 wave is interesting because it shows the phenomenon in its definite aspect: entire series of sightings sweeping a given country. It is impossible to explain them all as hoaxes or jokes. During this period the bases for scientific discussion were laid down, and the tendencies associated with various types of explanations were established. The phenomenon had finally assumed a worldwide aspect.

The most striking sightings of this wave, those at Oloron and Gaillac and the reported landing at Marignane (described in Chapter 1), took place in Europe, where the Spanish and North African cases of 1950 were practically unknown. Nevertheless, discussion of the problem remained strictly academic. The "objects" were treated as aerial phenomena, and the absence of any material fragments was discouraging to the engineer and the physicist alike. If the manifestations were caused by machines, many argued, wouldn't these machines be subject to wear and breakdown?

In 1953 the number of cases dropped off, but 1954 was a period of fundamental importance. The whole globe experienced an enormous increase in sightings. As many cases were gathered in Europe for the months of September and October, 1954, as had been for the whole world since 1946. France in particular presented an extraordinary density of cases.

The "flying saucer" began to lose its academic character and entered the experience of daily life. It completely monopolized the press and general conversation. The eyewitnesses were scientists, doctors, actors, engineers, peasants, pilots, politicians, writers. The reports were coherent; totally independent groups of witnesses described identical appearances and behaviors.

Photographs were taken showing disks, "cigars," bell-shaped objects—but few details. Landings reported by apparently sincere witnesses numbered over two hundred. Local panics occurred. Reporters scoured the countryside by night, hoping for a sensational picture.

"Little men" four feet high, with globulous eyes and shaggy eyebrows and wearing "diving suits," were reported alighting from the machines. Beings similar to humans were seen in their company, always taking great care to stay near the craft. These beings were described as lavish in their demonstrations of friendship toward the witnesses, but any curiosity in their direction met with inhibiting "rays."

A pensioner at Bethune who manufactured his own "flying saucers" nearly set fire to some crops. Several tramps were taken for "Martians" and shot at. Traces were found at spots where landings were said to have occurred. At Quarouble, depressions caused by a weight estimated by the French Air Force Intelligence at thirty tons were found in railroad ties after a sighting there. Unverifiable rumors flew about.

"Saucers" were seen in all parts of the world. Once the initial astonishment subsided, they were accepted with good humor. A drawing by a Paris cartoonist entitled "The Village Idiot" shows a shy individual surrounded by laughing farmers; the caption reads, "He's the one who hasn't seen a flying saucer yet!"

The number of sightings diminished in 1955, although more slowly than in the periods following previous waves. In 1956 there was again an increase in activity, which passed unnoticed at the time because the press, still saturated with the sensationalism of the preceding wave, gave it no publicity. In 1957 a series of phenomena with all the fantastic features of the 1954 wave burst upon the American scene, where the reports of the 1954 French wave had been brushed off as "obviously unbelievable." This wave coincided with the launching of the earth's second satellite, Sputnik II, but the reports mentioned globes and luminous disks, settled on the ground or flying over cities, that stopped the engines of cars, and apparently were not connected with misinterpretations of the satellite.

The phenomenon continued into 1958 and the following years. It presented well-established features and thus aroused little interest. In reports from all over the world, successions of peaks and troughs are found, but no wave in the proper sense. The Scandinavian and South American sightings were little known. Most of the significant reports came from New Guinea, New Zealand, and countries of the Communist bloc.

Between 1958 and 1963, the "flying saucers" became a queer memory in the mind of the public. Scientists, particularly astronomers, carefully avoided the subject. The phenomenon was shrouded in total discredit, and any discussion about it only produced boredom. Even to mention the subject was a *faux pas*. Observatories made a point to deny loudly every sighting reported to them. Scientific conservatism made disbelief in the sincerity of the witnesses the fashion. In military circles the same kind of autocensorship prevailed. To report a UFO sighting was to endanger one's promotion. Certain pilots were said to be "seeing things." Some airline companies demanded that crew members who reported UFO's undergo psychiatric examinations and grounded them until these tests were completed. Publishers discouraged books on the subject. Science fiction dropped the subject. Even the spiritualists and the occulists fell into line beside the most hardened skeptics: entities from other planets, they argued, travel in their "ethereal bodies" and have no need for spaceships! The vote against the "saucers" was unanimous: of more than 110 unexplained sightings made around the world in 1962, only 2 were mentioned by French radio. The best solution seemed to be: if you don't talk about it, maybe it will go away.

The views propounded by a few individuals who had decided to devote their time and labor to the study of the mystery passed undiscussed. Michel's book, which we reviewed above, was greeted, not even with opposition, but with silence. No voice was raised to contradict him. Engineers, teachers, psychologists, medical people discussed his book in private, but said nothing publicly.

Yet independent and isolated views were uttered here and there: Jung adopted a strange position in his baffling, indeed almost prophetic, book, *Flying Saucers: A*

Modern Myth of Things Seen in the Sky. Meanwhile, the crooks who had been making a living by exploiting popular credulity looked around for other sources of revenue. Telepathic contact with Venus was no longer profitable. The journals published by the "enlightened" began to come out on ordinary paper, then on stencilled sheets.

Because professional scientists were reluctant to study the phenomenon, which had become so unfashionable, none of the few serious investigative groups set up in the United States was in a position to initiate a true inquiry into the problem. The role of NICAP and APRO was limited to the gathering of documented reports preserved in the hope that some day a full-scale investigation would be conducted. Although they have made some unavoidable errors, and their policies have not always shown a great deal of practicality, both groups have gained many friends in the scientific community by the sincerity of their efforts. Only because of them have some of the most significant American sightings been preserved. Unfortunately, these laudable efforts have too often been overshadowed by the "way-out" claims of a minority of irresponsible "enthusiasts."

Internationally, one periodical has emerged as the crossroad of research on aerial phenomena: the *Flying Saucer Review,* founded in 1955, which has been published every two months ever since. Its policy has varied over the years from the days when it was almost entirely devoted to discussions of the claims of "contactees" to the more recent period, when the scientific dispute over "orthoteny" several times brought to its table of contents the name of Menzel himself. Since the end of 1964, under the skillful and competent editorship of Charles Bowen, the *Review* has clearly emerged from its past. It now has readers and contributors in all countries of the world (more than five hundred copies reach the United States) and is read even in the Communist countries.

Despite the almost total silence of the press and official circles, the period from 1958 to 1963 was very fruitful in more than one respect. Because the activity of the phenomenon diminished greatly, the sensationalism attached to the subject subsided and there was no longer any violent passion to cloud the issue; hence it became possible to study it with fresh eyes, in an objective manner. The evident failure of the traditional explanations opened a field of inquiry to young scientists, some of whom viewed the problem as a worthy challenge. Finally, the imminence of the first human expeditions toward the planets made it incumbent upon engineers and space specialists to begin a serious study of the possibility of encountering other civilizations. Indeed, this possibility is present in any study of the UFO phenomenon, as the official commissions explicitly affirmed on several occasions. As for the *theoretical* possibility of existence of other civilizations in our own and other galaxies, that has already been established by astronomy.

In 1964, when sightings were again made in large numbers in the Western world, both the observations and the official interpretations were greeted by a totally new attitude on the part of the public. People were no longer so skeptical of the witnesses as they were of the official explanations for the sightings. Although tangible evidence was still lacking, the public seemed to place the burden of the proof on those who claimed the sightings could be explained as natural or conventional effects. A Gallup poll in 1966 disclosed that five million Americans had observed something they believed to be an unidentified flying object and that ten times as many —fifty million—thought there was a real phenomenon involved in the reported manifestations. When the percentages are broken down according to educational levels, the proportion of persons inclined to attribute the sightings to imagination and fraud is highest among the least educated strata of the population.

The renewal of interest in the "celestial signs" culminated in hearings by the Committee on the Armed Services of the U.S. Congress, held on April 5, 1966. The discussion centered on the need for a new scientific investigation of the reports—the recommendation made several times to the air force by its panels of scientific advisers. Such an investigative scientific body, if it is ever formed, will find that the nature and quality of the reports have changed significantly during the history of the phenomenon.

In the early period (1946–54) the nature of the sightings reported to the air force was such that classical physical explanations (mirages, balloons, etc.) could indeed be sought. In the second period, after 1954, the accounts became at the same time so coherent and so incredible that they could no longer be dismissed as familiar phenomena. While a luminous body briefly seen speeding through the night sky by an airline pilot can lead to a number of hypotheses from the physicist's point of view, the "Martian" that was shot at by a terrified family in Kentucky,* or the one that walked past a petrified steelworker in northern France, cannot. Such cases call for a full-scale study by psychologists to determine whether or not the witness really believes that he saw the thing he reported.

The explanations offered can be divided into two categories: physical explanations and psychological explanations. Each category is applicable to a certain period in the history of the phenomenon and must be discussed in relation to its own criteria.

THE EXPLAINERS

In the majority of cases the authors of the physical theories are astronomers, although the question usually falls into the domain of the atmospheric physicist. While astronomy possesses elements of general information regarding the region where the manifestations most often occur, it does not, as was noted by the astronomers on the official U.S. commission, possess observational or

---

* For a detailed account of the Kentucky incident, *see* Jacques Vallee, *Anatomy of a Phenomenon* (Chicago: Henry Regnery Co., 1965).

investigative instruments capable of studying the phenomenon in that region.

The very fact that physical explanations have been sought exclusively in the realm of traditional optical phenomena shows that the investigators have from the outset oriented themselves toward a certain type of interpretation, neglecting all other possibilities. The psychological interpretation has never been explored scientifically. No group of witnesses has been systematically studied to compare their psychological profile with average profiles in the entire population. All the efforts have been directed toward squaring the observed physical manifestations with the known effects suggested *a priori* from the field of optics or meteorology; no objective analysis of the sightings to deduce general concepts from them has ever been made.

It seems to us that this method has had a direct bearing on the cases chosen to serve as a basis for these theories: the testimonies used all relate to that portion of the reports whose physical features fall within the narrow domain where the greatest probability of confusion is found. In other words, when scientists have selected cases for detailed analysis, or when the military have presented samples from their files, or when congressmen have been shown reports, the sightings used have always been chosen from a set of borderline observations to which conventional explanations can be applied without great difficulty. There is great reticence in admitting that other cases, those that remain unidentified, might also be representative of the phenomenon. Thus, if we examine the evidence selected for presentation to the public or the scientific community as "typical" of the phenomenon, we note that it is impossible to find any indication of the existence of the well-defined types that emerge at once when the whole body of the reports is studied without prior discrimination or selection (proven errors and hoaxes, of course, being rejected).

In particular, it is impossible to find among these selected cases any traces of sightings of Types I and II,

and only rarely one of Type III. This is striking in many
works, for instance, in Ruppelt's book (2). The public
has been affected much more, of course, by manifestations occurring near the ground, close to houses and
roads, than by encounters in the air, even when they
involved military pilots. Even if the arguments propounded were indeed a perfect explanation for this
limited sample of sightings, they would still account for
only a tiny proportion of the eyewitness accounts—
and the least interesting portion, at that, since they are
the least precise in such details as the coordinates of the
sighting and the physical description of the "object."

The physical interpretations are inspired by the idea
that the observed effects are linked, not to an actual
object, but to an optical illusion or electromagnetic conditions in the atmosphere. Menzel, in particular, has
directed his attention toward this area. While these interpretations may apply to a large number of Type IV
cases, especially those in the air-visual category, attempts to establish a correlation between the occurrence
of the phenomenon and some special range of meteorological conditions have ended in failure in most cases,
just as attempts to establish a correlation with the geographical or climatic location of the witnesses have
failed.

In August, 1965, for instance, the wave of reports
from Texas, Oklahoma, and other central states was
"explained" as an effect of the general hot temperature
in the area, while reports that were almost exact dupli-
cates poured in from Europe, Australia (which was in
mid-winter), the high plateaus of Peru, and even Ant-
arctica.

A second category of physical interpretations accepts
the physical reality of the cause of the phenomenon.
Within this category two opposing theories can be distinguished. One denies that the physical cause has anything to do with a material object, and invokes physical
entities such as ball lightning, pockets of ionized air,
etc. The other introduces into the picture a material
object, meaning either a device of terrestrial origin (bal-

loon, artificial satellite, aircraft), a natural body orig-
inating in space (meteor, astronomical object), an ani-
mal (migratory birds), or an extraterrestrial machine
controlled by artificial intelligence or alien creatures
capable of thought.

In the following table, these various interpretations
are displayed graphically for greater clarity; to each of
them is attached the name of a scientist or author who
has been especially instrumental in developing this particular interpretation, even if he has considered others.

PHYSICAL INTERPRETATIONS	no physical reality		mirages optical illusions	Menzel
	physical reality	no material object involved	ball lightning	Haffner
		material object involved	conventional (aircraft, balloon)	Gauzit
			unknown craft	Keyhoe
PSYCHOLOGICAL INTERPRETATIONS	psychopathological		hallucinations, hysteria	Michel Heuyer
	sociological		hoaxes, rumors	Sanger

It is clear that interpretations other than the "physi-
cal-material" and "physical-non-material" ones, though
certainly applicable in numerous individual cases, fail
to account for the phenomenon *as a whole*. The most
interesting views are, on the one hand, the view that
holds the observed effects to be manifestations of ball
lightning,* plasma effects in the atmosphere, or similar

---

* Ball lightning is a rare phenomenon described as a "glowing
globe floating through the air." Such objects have been reported
diving down chimneys, boiling water in barrels and melting airplane wings. They are observed during thunderstorms and their
persistence and apparent stability intrigue physicists, who have
proposed various theoretical models. A recent theory, reported in
the *Science News Letter* of September 26, 1964, and in the *Physical Review* 135:390, 1964, by two physicists at Yeshiva University, New York, proposes that ball lightning is the result of "a
concentration around a conductor of the high electrical fields
found during a thunderstorm" and that it has no relation to the
control of thermonuclear energy, as some scientists have proposed.

phenomena that have only recently become of interest to physics (*see* 314, 318), and, on the other hand, the view that attributes the phenomenon to a material physical object obeying either an intelligent will or natural laws still largely unknown to us. In this context can be mentioned the interpretation of the Tunguska explosion of 1908 as a collision with a body of antimatter, a suggestion made by physicist Clyde Cowan and Nobel prize winner and chemist Willard Libby of the University of California at Los Angeles.

The explosion in Siberia on June 30, 1908, uprooted trees thirty miles from the epicenter and melted silver samovars forty miles away. A scene of incredible devastation confronted scientific expeditions sent to investigate. For many months afterward, the sky assumed an unusual luminosity all over Europe, and in the Caucasus the light was bright enough at midnight to read by.

Soviet author A. Kazantsev has proposed the view that antimatter might be the key to a mode of space propulsion discovered by other civilizations and that the explosion of such a "spaceship" is a more probable explanation for the *taiga* catastrophe than a collision with a meteorite of antimatter. According to the calculations of a Soviet physicist, Zolotov, the explosion appeared to be contained within an outer shell, and the energy involved was enormous. The shock wave was recorded in England, and the background radioactivity of the atmosphere rose sharply, as Libby and Cowan discovered by analyzing the rings of old trees in Arizona. In the rings of a Douglas fir tree near Tucson, for example, the rings representing 1908 showed an "unmistakably increased deposit of radioactivity." The power of the Siberian explosion is shown in Figure 20.*

Apart from these two groups of interpretations, there exists what Hynek has called a "poverty of hypotheses." We can eliminate at the outset the interpretation as balloons, which cannot explain the speeds recorded, the

---

* *See* the Russian magazine *Technika Molodezhu* ("Young Technique"), No. 2, 1966, for a complete discussion of the various hypotheses.

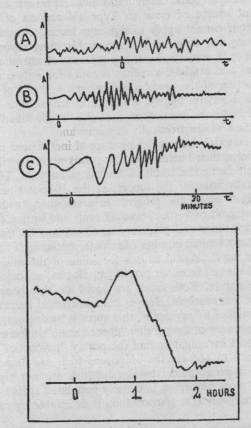

Fig. 20.—(bottom) Variations of magnetic field recorded at Irkutsk Observatory during the 1908 explosion; (top) shock waves produced by (a) a chemical explosion; (b) a thermonuclear blast of a few megatons four thousand miles from its epicenter; (c) the Tunguska explosion at approximately the same distance.

secondary luminous effects, or the changes in direction and altitude, numerous examples of which will be given later in this book. Meteors, which represent an important source of error in Type IV reports of brief duration, cannot apply to sightings lasting one minute or more and thus fail to account for most reports of Types I, II, and III. Misinterpretations of astronomical objects and artificial satellites account for only a small proportion of the unexplained reports and are of little use in a general theory. All these interpretations combined leave the phenomenon of the "unidentified" reports as a whole practically untouched.

If material devices do produce the observed manifestations, their kinetic behavior rules out the possibility of their being the result of human technology. This is especially true for the reports of the 1946–60 period. In recent years, the progress in aeronautics, with the development of vertical-take-off craft and intricate systems for lunar and planetary landings, may be responsible for a limited number of misinterpretations.

The psychological causes for some of the misinterpretations can be either psychopathological or sociological in nature. Both types are based on the theory of rumor. For example, Heuyer has constructed a theoretical model of a "psychosis" that spreads by degrees, with the assistance of the parallel "phenomenon" in the press. But most investigators find the purely "psychotic" theory hard to accept: the objections to it are based on either a geographical basis (sightings are not significantly more numerous in densely populated areas) or a physical basis (the phenomenon is detectable by radar, etc.).

Supporters of the second theory attribute the phenomenon purely and simply to fabrication, hoax, and the disturbed imagination of the modern public. Sanger has summed up this argument thus: "Until proof to the contrary is forthcoming, the expert in aviation and space flight must recognize that what we have here is a weapon—most probably an immaterial one—in the war of nerves."

Of all the theories put forward, this one strikes us as the weakest, although—like the hypothesis that attributes the manifestations to "machines"—it could in principle relate to all of the sightings. Actually, as we have seen, the occupations and psychological characteristics of the witnesses are as varied as possible, whereas hoaxes are usually linked with precise psychological features and age groups. Moreover, in many sightings the witnesses or groups of witnesses are entirely independent of each other.

There are various means for testing the evidence for or against each of these theories, but first the conditions with which each interpretation must comply in order to be accepted—those features of the UFO phenomenon for which it must account or which it must at least not contradict—must be established.

These fundamental features are: the considerable growth in the number of reports since 1946; the distribution of these sightings in series, with peaks and troughs; the absence of any correlation with solar activity, atmospheric radioactivity, or the appearance of meteors; the presence of independent features not observable in usual physical effects; and the consistency of the secondary details, which makes it possible to classify the sightings in accordance with perfectly defined criteria and thus to extract the "signal" from the "noise."

6

A STUDY IN RECOGNITION

SURVEY OF PREVIOUS EXPERIMENTS

IN THE PRECEDING CHAPTER, we made the claim that, in a study of the reports of unusual aerial phenomena, the separation of the "signal" from the "noise" was not so difficult a job as the official statements imply. We now intend to prove that claim.

We have seen that the sightings, although reported and commented on in various ways, can be reduced to a limited number of definite types, each specifically different from the others and possessing features encountered repeatedly throughout the whole field under consideration. The number of observations, however, is an obstacle to researchers who, like the groups of amateurs and the personnel of Project Blue Book, lack training in mass data storage and processing techniques and have no funds for computer time.*

No large body of information can be processed or

---

* A fact many critics of the air force's handling of the cases are unaware of is that the files of Project Blue Book have never been systematically reduced to punched cards and, therefore, the air force is not in a position to conduct statistical studies beyond a very elementary level.

handled without reference indexes based on coding procedures. The definition of an optimum code for a given problem is a matter for professional attention, and attempts to analyze large collections of reports without such a system can only result in confusion.

Some air force consultants, aware of this problem, have made use of partial codification systems. One such example is the coding that led to the results of *Special Report No. 14;* the system, however, was not retained by the air force in its later handling of reports. Other air force consultants have devised codification systems for their own use. In all these studies, the reports were given a code, but not a classification.

The first system applied to the UFO phenomenon *as such* was the classification/codification method we published in 1963. It was derived from our experience with European sightings and had been used in several digital computer applications since 1961. The preliminary catalogue of five hundred observations given in Appendix III used this code. Researchers in the United States are now working along the same line. Techniques derived from methods of literature searching and automatic indexing are under development (Olsen), while other systems for the automatic preselection of significant cases have been suggested (Powers) but not tested.

Such systems are particularly essential during waves, when reports arrive by the dozens every day and it is critical to decide immediately which sightings deserve further study. In the fall of 1957, so many reports reached the Air Technical Information Center that the lines of communication between main air force bases were badly jammed for several weeks. The stream of reports carried good and bad data alike, at such a rate that no real analysis work was possible for several months with the methods then (and still) in use at Dayton. An efficient system of the type suggested here would have eliminated non-significant reports, reduced considerably the transmission time through the lines, and given investigators a clear picture of each significant case, with general indications of reliability and the direction in which a plausible study of the case could have been researched.

The second job very easily performed with a good system of classification is the compilation of general catalogues containing the history of the phenomenon in one compact, directly accessible package. Here a good codification system is more helpful than a literature-searching technique, which is cumbersome and may lead to multiple problems of relevancy. Our group has used several versions of catalogues of this type, the latest version containing more than three thousand sightings. A critical part of the preparation of such a catalogue is the selection of cases for inclusion in the list.

RECORDING AND COMPILING

Any catalogue of broad scope is the result of the combination of various sources, each of which tends to cover a particular period better. These different indications tend sometimes to confirm, sometimes to contradict, one another, and it is then necessary to make a choice. Our interest has centered on the year 1954 because of the homogeneity, geographical correlation, and large amount of documentation the reports of that year exhibit. We were able to conduct a meticulous check of all the sources by going back to the original eyewitness accounts, using newspapers, letters, private files and our own personal papers.

Several groups have published general lists covering wide intervals. In Europe the largest available catalogue is that compiled by Guy Quincy (privately distributed). In the United States the most extensive files are, of course, those of the air force, supplemented by those of NICAP and APRO. In 1965 NICAP published most of its files in a well-documented report entitled *UFO Evidence*. Generally speaking, each sighting in our catalogue has been checked against at least two independent sources.

All sightings reported from notoriously fanciful sources, as well as obviously ludicrous accounts, were entered in a special list for the purpose of checking their possible recurrence. We also removed from the main sample all cases where a simple explanation was found, either by an official investigation or as a result of our own analysis, and all cases where the "phenomenon" sighted was proven to be conventional in origin. Next, the essential periods in the history of the phenomenon were gone over in detail, and finally the whole catalogue was checked, sighting by sighting.

This analysis was performed in accordance with the following rules:

1. All sightings reported by witnesses spread over an area wider than four or five miles in radius were subjected to a special study to determine the possibility of their being meteors. The method followed for the elimination of these cases is illustrated below.

2. For the period after 1957, every sighting of a continuously moving point source (with due allowance for psychological and visual aberrations) made between dusk and dawn was examined to see if an artificial satellite visible to the naked eye had been misinterpreted. An example of such a misinterpretation is given below.

3. Special care was exercised in the critical study of the "recurrent" sightings, for such sightings may indicate a local peculiarity leading to an interesting line of research, as in the Exeter case.

4. Particularly remarkable accounts, such as reports of landings, were reviewed in great detail.

METEORS AND SHOOTING STARS

Studies of the time distribution of the most significant sightings showed no correlation whatsoever with the periods of activity of the principal groups of meteors.

The interpretation of a sighting as a meteor was therefore an isolated, well-defined fact, and the demonstration of the natural character of the object presented no difficulty.

When the dispersal of the witnesses throughout a vast region called for a special analysis of the case, the second feature investigated was the duration of the sightings. If it was less than one minute, the case was considered with great caution, even if it presented apparently significant secondary characteristics. If the duration was several minutes, but there was no evidence that the timing was accurate, the case was still regarded with suspicion. But if the object was proved to have been in view more than one minute, it was definitely not a meteor.

When both the dispersal of the witnesses and the duration of the sighting had been considered, the statements given by the various groups of witnesses were examined and plotted on a map, and a chronological law for the events was sought. In general, times were distributed at random around a mean value, as in the example below. It was then a simple task to conclude the demonstration. The following case is an example of such an analysis.

On November 22, 1952, eight sightings were reported in the western part of France between 7:00 and 7:30 A.M. The duration of each sighting was very short. The accounts can be summarized as follows:

(1) *Between Secondigny and Bressuire, Deux-Sevres.* —Time unknown; large blue "cigar-shaped object" hidden by clouds.

(2) *Cormenon, Loir-et-Cher.*—Time unknown; dazzling sphere and noise of explosion; stream of multicolored stars.

(3) *Malicorne, Sarthe.*—7:00 A.M.; abnormal blinding flash.

(4) *Lhomme and Picoiseau, Sarthe.*—7:00 A.M.; multicolored cigar, red and yellow predominating; length seventeen to twenty times greater than width; climbed at 80° angle; emitted white smoke.

(5) *Between Cholet and Saint-Aubin, Deux-Sevres.*—7:00 A.M.; luminous cigar of great size; descended point-first and changed color; climbed again, slowly, with luminous trail, and then disappeared in mid-air.

(6) *Asse-le-Boisne, Sarthe.*—7:15 A.M.; very luminous cylindrical object; blue in front, red at rear.

(7) *Mamers, Sarthe.*—7:20 A.M.; powerful light, as if from a rocket.

(8) *Malicorne, Sarthe.*—7:30 A.M.; very brilliant circle, with a "wave of shooting stars."

The object of these sightings appears to have been very large and very fast. It is consequently improbable, in the absence of any serious means of timing, that the various times given by the witnesses could have any significance, any more than the shapes suggested (cylinder, circle, cigar) do. It would seem, rather, that the object in question was seen by all these people simultaneously, and that differences in their watches—or in their calculation of the time—were responsible for the time range indicated. Note too that no estimates of duration were given.

The witnesses were dispersed over a rectangular zone one hundred kilometers wide and twice as long. At Cormenon the sound of an explosion was heard accompanying a "dazzling sphere" and multicolored sparks or stars. At Mamers a "powerful light" was seen. At Malicorne it was a "blinding flash." These data clearly indicate a meteor whose trajectory must have been very flat, indeed even horizontal, until the explosion. Observers 4 and 5 speak of a rising object, a common illusion when a meteor crosses the sky very rapidly with such a trajectory.

The series of sightings made in western France on the morning of November 22, 1952, is therefore interpreted as the movement of a meteor, traveling east-northeast with a flat trajectory, which broke up in the area of Dreux.

ARTIFICIAL SATELLITES

Since 1957, artificial satellites of the earth have introduced a new source of error and important additional "noise" into our study. Many persons who lack information on the satellites have misinterpreted them as "mysterious objects."

Here again, the psychologist finds matter for reflection. The passage of a satellite, which seems detached from all earthly connections, is a sight stamped with great purity. The mind finds in it a satisfaction that can easily be magnified when the witness is prepared to believe in the fantastic nature of what he has seen; misinterpretation then takes the form of flight from the things of everyday life. Once the first seconds of the sighting suggest this other-wordly provenance, the witness is no longer able to perceive the evidence: he "dreams" through the remainder of the experience.

Some persons feel that the UFO phenomenon is entirely a product of such a psychological state. At any rate, this tendency is found in extreme aberrations, such as the accounts given by "contactees" who report that the "saucers" are piloted by perfect beings of great physical beauty. The need for escape is joined with a search for purity. In this respect, it is indeed interesting to see so many misinterpretations of artificial satellites after all these years.

However, the movements of every object launched into space from the earth are precisely known, and the positions of the artificial satellites can be checked immediately by consulting a table. In a few cases, where the date or the time of the sighting has been reported erroneously, more elaborate methods are called for. The following account is such a case.

The photograph in Plate VI was taken by a Mr. Samper at Azazga, Algeria. The data given by the witness were: date, August 6, 1961; course of object, southwest to northeast; elevation, small; magnitude of object, less than that of Jupiter. The photograph was said to have been taken between 8:05 and 8:10 P.M., U.T.

The witness sent his negative to Michel, who in turn sent it to us. As the trajectory and magnitude of the object were very similar to those of Echo I as seen from Algeria, we asked Pierre Neirinck, a keen observer of artificial satellites, to examine the negative more closely. The identification of the object was effected in the following manner:

The extreme magnitude attained on the photograph is + 6.5 in the area of the object (And) and + 7.5 in the upper center (Lac). The apparent magnitude of the object is + 4.3 at the beginning and + 5.4 at the end. Declination of comparison: + 47° Reduction to declination 20°: 4.0 at the beginning. Magnitude of Echo I at that declination (mean value of near transits at average altitude): + 3.0. True magnitude of the object assuming an altitude of 1500 kilometers: + 1.5 at the beginning.

Length of arc recorded: 14°6. Angular velocity from the data supplied by witness (five minute duration): 0°049 per second, a velocity very inferior to that of Echo I, even for an angular elevation of 15°. Verification of stated exposure-time by means of the traces left by the stars on the photographic film: measured star 15 And (declination + 40°) chosen for its polar distance and average brightness. Its trace, as that of the traces of its near neighbors, is 0°49, plus or minus 0°03. The direction of the vibrations of the camera seems without incidence on the length of the trace. Therefore the exposure lasted 0°49/0°191 or in other words 154 seconds = 2.56 minutes, hence the true speed of the object was 14°6/154 = 0°095 per second. This speed agrees perfectly with the speed of Echo I for the portion of trajectory that has been recorded.

If it is Echo I that is involved, we must conclude that an error has occurred as regards the time or the date. Three cases are possible: error of one or two days: possible transits are August 5, 1961 (Apex 20.05.21), or August 8 (Apex 20.10.9). Error of one hour: possible transit August 6, Apex 21.25.26.

The question can be settled by a study of the coordinates of the first point of the recorded trajectory. These coordinates are: 23 h 01, + 47° and the corresponding local coordinates:

reported data:

August 6 at 20.05 U.T. Azimuth 52° Elevation 27°0

third case:

August 6 at 21.05 U.T. Azimuth 55° Elevation 36°5

first case:

August 5 at 20.05 U.T. Azimuth 52° Elevation 26°4

second case:

August 8 at 20.05 U.T. Azimuth 53° Elevation 28°3

The third case gives a point too distant for the azimuth and elevation indicated (for an altitude of 1500 kilometers) and 21.29 hours U.T. No correspondence in this case. The second case gives a point at 20.12 hours, but 300 kilometers further on. The first case situates the point corresponding to the given azimuth and elevation at 20.01.4 and at a geocentric distance, with respect to the observer, exactly equal to the observed elevation: 18° or 2000 kilometers. The straight-line distance is 2670 kilometers. The apparent magnitude of Echo I (+ 3 for near transits, on photographs) is at that distance + 4 on photographs. The angular velocity checks also. Therefore the photograph corresponds to the following data:

Artificial satellite Echo I. Date: August 5, 1961. Duration of exposure: from 20.01.4 to 20.04.0 U.T. Place: Azazga, Algeria.

The sun having set locally at 18:52 U.T., the picture must be quite well exposed, despite the brief exposure time.

THE PLANET VENUS

No single object has been misinterpreted as a "flying saucer" more often than the planet Venus. The study of these mistakes proves quite instructive, for it shows beyond all possible dispute the limitations of sensory perception and the weakness of the accounts relating shapes and motions of point sources or objects with small apparent diameters.

The identification of a report as a misinterpretation of Venus or another bright planet or star, when the analyst has worked from an adequate description and precise positional data, is irrefutable. The appearance of the object, its apparent diameter, its color, its progressive reddening when it reaches the horizon, its apparent changes of shape and color when seen through a mediocre optical instrument (binoculars, small-aperture telescope), the duration of sighting and the slow westward course all furnish positive criteria. In numerous cases we have seen in the air force files, the witnesses have given measurements of position, in local coordinates, and even photographs, all of which can be checked precisely by reference to astronomical tables for the given day and hour. We are going to review certain descriptions found in sightings of Venus that report "flying saucers." These mistakes were common in the United States during the 1957 wave. Thanks to a simple analysis, such undesirable reports can be eliminated. All the sightings are from November, 1957 (files of Project Blue Book). All times are reduced to GMT.

1. Detroit, Michigan, November 1, 11:35. Round object, size of a pea, green and white. Observed stationary for one hour. Flickering.

2. Long Beach, New York, November 3, 9:30. Round object, size of a dime when at maximum brightness, of a pin-head at minimum. Emitting "beams of light."

3. Milwaukie, Oregon, November 5, 2:00. Large

oval object, brilliant orange, mixed with white. Faded away at the horizon. Seen for one hour.

4. Port Arthur, Ontario, Canada, November 5, 11:15. Oval-shaped object, size between that of a pea and that of a pin-head. Size estimated twenty times as large as Polaris. Shining white, changing to orange and then again to white. Seemed surrounded by a shining mist. According to some observers in the group, the inside of the lighted area presented a "scaly" appearance. A black speck was moving slowly on the object, in a counterclockwise rotation, from which the witnesses were able to deduce that the object completed one revolution per minute; the mist surrounding the object was three times its diameter. The color changed to red when it reached the horizon. The object followed a westerly course throughout the observation, which was made with binoculars and lasted one hour and thirty-five minutes.

5. Aiken, South Carolina, November 5, 11:30. Cigar-shaped object. Size of a pea at arm's length. Shining white with a fluorescent appearance. Shining white points inside the object. Long tail with three blue trails —taken to be "blue flames"—almost as large as the object. No sound. Stationary most of the time, with sudden sideways motions. Seemed to move away from the observer, and then faded away gradually, becoming red and then amber. Observed with binoculars for about one hour.

6. Texas and New Mexico, November 6, 3:00. Object the size of a basketball. Silvery, then red, seeming to be spinning, descended toward the southwest and faded out. Seen for twenty minutes with binoculars.

7. Buffalo, New York, November 6, 10:30. Pear-shaped object, size of a B-52, metallic, hovering in the southwest and then fading out. Seen with binoculars for approximately twenty minutes.

8. Hopkins and Saint Paul, Minnesota, November 11, 00:30. Object with changing color, red to orange, sometimes turning to bright white, size of a baseball. Observed with binoculars and telescope for thirty min-

utes. Moved three times in three minutes. It would move, stop, move again, and so on. General course, southwest.

9. Saint Charles, Missouri, November 12, 00:10. Round object with a triangular section on top. Size of a big star. Observed toward the south for one hour. The round part was white and the triangular part was red. The latter was spinning "like the streamers on a pole at the fair." No sound. The object made vertical and lateral motions.

10. Harrisburg, Pennsylvania, November 15, 11:20. Egg-shaped object seen for one-half hour with binoculars. White at first, then disappeared, leaving red dots in the sky. It was spinning and seemed to give off points of light.

11. Dayton, Ohio, November 20, 10:15. Object that looked solid, stationary for twenty minutes. Pure white color. Seemed to have four points. Size of a car headlight. Seen toward the southwest.

12. Santa Rosa, Texas, November 25, 8:45. Object seen for more than three hours, moving west. Round, size of a baseball. Color: brown in the binoculars, white with the naked eye!

The study of the many reports in this category is interesting, for it leads to certain observations regarding the reliability of the witnesses, or at least the majority of them. All these people were mistaken and were poor observers—to look at Venus through binoculars for three hours and not recognize it is not exactly a bright performance—and all were led astray by their imagination. In their reports to the air force, they affirmed that they had seen a "flying saucer." But what did they describe? A perfectly natural phenomenon, with due allowance for atmospheric distortion, poor optical instruments and human imagination. They described exactly *what they saw*. Did they claim they were "paralyzed"? No. Did they see "portholes" or was the engine of their car or their television affected by the object? No. Their errors are entirely within natural limits, and they illustrate equally well both the fallibility of the human senses and imagination and *the perfect sincerity and honesty of the witnesses*. They gave descriptions so clear and honest that the air force was able to identify the origin of the sighting from their own descriptions, even when the imagination had played a considerable role, as in case No. 9. We believe that this observation is an important one, because it demonstrates that the witnesses, sometimes referred to as an untrained, unskilled bunch of over-imaginative people, are in reality perfectly responsible and reliable citizens who, by sending their reports to the military authorities, have even demonstrated a level of civic awareness well above average.

To use the erroneous sightings—numerous as they may be—to support the claim that the UFO phenomenon does not exist is simply dishonest, for objective and calm analysis of the facts shows that the "rumor," the "noise," can be eliminated precisely *because* of the reliability of the witnesses. The criteria for this elimination are so simple and clear that this work could be performed automatically by a computer, just as the bulk of the work of coding the sightings could be. We only stress these false sightings to show that we are perfectly aware of them, that they obey clear laws, and that the honest and properly trained investigator can eliminate them with great ease. The reports that remain on his table when this elimination has been performed have an altogether different character.

7

A WORLD OF REPORTS

EVENTS IN PERSPECTIVE

Sightings very similar to those reported since 1946, and accompanied by the same sort of repercussion in public opinion, occurred in the past. Their inclusion in a study of the phenomenon depends on the point of view—physical or psychological—adopted in dealing with the problem.

For Jung, the assimilation of the ancient sightings of circular objects into the modern eyewitness accounts required no particular justification, since the psychologist is concerned with the "flying saucer" as an archetype. Indeed, as Jung said,

> If the round shining objects that appear in the sky be regarded as visions, we can hardly avoid interpreting them as archetypal images (110).

Those who approach the problem from another direction, and notably those who seek physical interpretations, cannot resist justifying this assimilation on a more concrete basis. Popular tradition, they say, furnishes us with many legends, and that same tradition is at the origin of the strange inventions of today; therefore those earlier pieces of evidence, particularly those that describe bodies circulating at a great distance from the earth, are to be mistrusted.

Here, however, the astronomical archives provide interesting reference material. They contain numerous examples of opaque "celestial bodies" glimpsed by professional astronomers. In the eighteenth and nineteenth centuries such bodies were frequently seen against the disk of the sun or the moon. Some of these sightings were so well established that the French astronomer Leverrier used them to compute the orbit of Vulcan, the hypothetical planet that was then thought to revolve between the sun and the orbit of Mercury but was never discovered (112). In 1947 L. Rudaux wrote:

Observers of the solar disk have sometimes seen enigmatic celestial bodies, in the form of small black spots, passing in front of it; they behave in exactly the same way as the planets Mercury and Venus—all due allowance being made—when these two planets interpose themselves, at fixed and specific times, exactly between the sun and the earth; the description of these bodies as enigmatic means that we do not know what they are and what place they occupy among the other bodies (113).

Charles Fort has applied himself, in several enjoyable books, to the compilation of long lists of such observations. While we have retained them within our general scheme of analysis, we feel that, in the absence of any modern evidence for their existence, the nature of these "bodies" lies for the moment outside the scope of any serious discussion. We will consider only those sightings whose latitude and longitude can be at least roughly defined, that is, eyewitness accounts describing the sighting of a body in the atmosphere.

The number of such sightings in the past in which the question of identification with the UFO phenomenon arises is nevertheless quite considerable. We will mention particularly the cases of "exceptional meteors" reported in several scientific publications, to which Camille Flammarion gave the name "bradytes." As we have seen (in Chapter 1, "The Case of the Crooked Bolides"), the observers usually report a circular or star-like body that moved through the sky too slowly to be a falling meteor. Furthermore, some of these reports mention right-angle changes of direction, changes of acceleration and even the descent of one or a number of objects to the vicinity of the ground—the very characteristics of present-day sightings.

Although cases reported by popular tradition must be approached with considerable caution, they should not always be rejected. From the psychological viewpoint, they are more interesting in many respects than sightings made by professional scientists, inasmuch as they partake more directly in the characteristics of rumor. On the other hand, their resemblance to the sightings of the present day, and the similarity in the effects produced on public opinion, indicate that the UFO phenomenon is not solely a feature of the "Space Age" and that the objective cause of its manifestations —whatever that cause may be—is not of recent appearance.

It is important to bear in mind that these visions were not attributed to beings from another planet but were generally received as signs from Heaven; the objective phenomena were at times so mixed with the visionary rumor that it is extremely difficult to establish the limits of the phenomenon. Some recent sightings in South America and other areas where relatively primitive modes of civilization prevail are still interpreted in the same context, as religious omens. People in Cuernavaca, Mexico, believed that the Second Coming of Christ was taking place when a large disk of fantastic brilliance came close to the ground on September 23, 1965, and the electric power mysteriously broke down. Indeed, the psychiatrist and the sociologist will be tempted to include in a study of UFO's certain reports of "miracles" and other unusual happenings that are unquestionably linked, just as the "flying saucer" sightings are, to an emotional matrix. We feel that physicists should not let themselves be drawn into discussion of these cases beyond a general review of the theories about them; they should center their study on reports that can be pinpointed in longitude and latitude and are free of any typically religious or legendary context. With these reservations, sightings handed down to our epoch from previous times should be included in an objective analysis of the UFO phenomenon.

THE AMERICAN PERIOD

Observations by pilots

Reports of objects resembling "flying saucers" made during the latter part of World War II are vague and difficult to analyze. Both sides in the conflict were quite excited about these observations of what they thought were secret devices developed by the other side. They came up with a delightful name for these early "saucers": "high altitude, high velocity balloons"! Another name was popular among the pilots, who called the mysterious bodies "foo-fighters."

The majority of the accounts that have been preserved from this period were made by the crews of Allied bomber squadrons. The fact that the so-called balloons were capable of flying in formation against the wind and of passing the best aircraft at any speed worried many people, but the reports created no stir in public opinion; graver happenings were occurring daily. The accounts were studied exclusively by the Intelligence services of the various powers, who were all anxious to get to the bottom of the mystery.

The impossibility of identifying the "objects" as propelled machines of any imaginable sort soon became

evident. When the investigations conducted at the close
of the war established that no flying machines of terrestrial origin were involved, the subject was forgotten,
to be taken up again only when the waves developed
from 1947 onward.

Most sightings of "foo-fighters" occurred after 1944
(although they may have been seen in Sweden as early
as 1939), particularly in Northern Europe, Japan, and
the Mediterranean Basin from Portugal to Turkey. At
times they involved isolated "bodies," at other times
"formations." In one case, for instance, a B-24 bomber
was said to have been followed by thirteen disks.

From this period on, precise features began to appear: the phenomenon consisted of the observation of
a definite object, of a globular or discoidal shape.
When several of these "objects" appeared together,
their evolutions were linked to each other. The altitude
at which the phenomenon occurred was the same as
the aircraft's, but the speed and maneuverability of the
unknown "objects" were superior to those of the aircraft, whose evolutions they appeared to be following
without engaging in movements that could be interpreted as offensive.

Later this type of phenomenon was reported in combination with other features. Reports mentioned objects
of different shapes performing evolutions in concert
and motionless disks at medium altitude; but before
1947 the "foo-fighters" were always fleeting and at
high altitude. After that date the sightings became frequent along airline routes. The "objects" described were
no longer always described as disks.

A classical account in this respect is that of Chiles
and Whitted, two Eastern Airlines pilots who, aboard
a DC-3 at 2:45 A.M. on July 25, 1948, saw what they
described as a cigar of metallic appearance, some thirty
meters long, twice the thickness of a Dakota and without wings, giving out an intense blue light, which
"quivered" up and down the fuselage like the light
along a neon tube. This "cigar," the pilots said, had

two rows of portholes "shining with supernatural brilliance," as though magnesium were being burnt in the interior of the craft. In front, Chiles said, the machine had a point like a radar antenna. Behind it, there trailed a jet of flame some ten to fifteen meters long, reddish-orange in the middle and lighter at the edges. When it seemed only a few score meters from the airplane, the flame behind the object became a powerful beam and, rocking the D-C 3 with its blast, the machine zoomed like a rocket into the sky and vanished in a few seconds.

Observations of "balls of light"

On several occasions, and under the same conditions as those just described, military pilots have reported sightings of "aerial bodies" with quite different characteristics. While objects such as the "cigar" observed by Chiles and Whitted were commonly interpreted as "machines," those we are going to review were characterized by their small diameter, their agility and the duration of the sightings. A classic report is the one given by Lieutenant G. F. Gorman, a member of the North Dakota National Guard.

The witness was preparing to land his Mustang F-51 on the airfield at Fargo, North Dakota, on October 1, 1948, when he distinctly saw a light trailing his plane. It was "a ball of intensely white light, completely spherical, with a sort of halo around the edges." Its diameter did not appear to exceed thirty centimeters (about one foot) and it had a sort of pulsation: "When I approached," said Gorman, "it suddenly became fixed, just before making a tight turn and moving away."

For thirty minutes Gorman tried to catch the "ball," while his efforts were observed by two people aboard another aircraft and by two witnesses in the control tower.

At the end of the period of observation, the ball of light rose steadily, leading the aircraft up to the limit of its climbing capacity, and then, after a vertical leap, vanished "at a stupendous speed." Various explanations have been suggested, and some of them are plausible. The witness himself declared that he was convinced that he had been struggling against "something controlled by an intelligence." He told the investigators that he was convinced that the object was governed by the laws of inertia because its accelerations, although sharp, were not immediate, and although it was capable of making extremely tight turns at great speed, it followed a curved trajectory.

There have been several sightings of this type, for example the one made by Lieutenant H. G. Combs at Andrews Field near Washington, D. C., on November 18, 1948.

Early sightings of objects near the ground

These features are observed from 1946 on; some of the "ghost-rockets" of the Scandinavian wave were said to have "landed," then taken off again, but these incidents were treated as quite unbelievable and passed unnoticed amid the numerous reports made by military or civilian pilots.

In April, 1947, in France, on the Col-de-Serres (valley of the river Clarry, Cantal) a Mr. Orliange claimed to have seen "a disk with a cupola," thirty meters in diameter, which flew at a low altitude. On August 13, 1947, a disk was seen at Twin Falls, Idaho, again at a low altitude. As it passed above a forest, the trees were said to have been seen bending over, as if under a fierce wind.

So far as we know, these are the earliest examples of "flying saucers" with a definite structure (cupola) and producing physical effects (bending trees) on the surface of the earth, in the postwar period. The sightings are not so well documented as one would hope, but like that of Chiles and Whitted (with the portholes, the turbulence affecting the aircraft, and the thirty-meter diameter) they are coherent and should be considered.

The fundamental features of the concept of the "flying saucer" as an object seem to have become already established at this time (1947). Two kinds of objects, one of them of small dimensions and comparable to a sphere of pure light, the other described as cigars or disks and commonly interpreted as machines, are encountered.

The movement of these bodies is neither the falling motion of a meteor nor the slow drifting of a balloon. The vision is not fleeting; it does not end with the sudden vanishing or the explosion or "disintegration" of the object. It persists for at least several minutes, develops in a continuous and coherent fashion (movements interpreted as "maneuvers") and ends with these bodies making off at great speed when pursued. No indication is found of propulsion resembling the techniques used by us. The objects are silent.

THE EUROPEAN PERIOD

From 1947 to 1952 most of the observations were made in the United States. In 1952 sightings that revealed certain well-defined patterns of great general interest were made in Europe.

Early cases of Type II

A detailed review of the sightings at Oloron and Gaillac will complete the roster of characteristic features of the phenomenon. These accounts represent one of the pinnacles in the history of the phenomenon, and they introduce a type of sighting that could turn out to be of great importance in deciding once and for all between the two groups of interpretations—physical or psychological.

The chief witness of the Oloron sighting (seen by hundreds of people) was Yves Prigent, of Oloron College, who gave the following account to the press:

To the north, against the background of the blue sky, a fleecy cloud of curious shape was floating along. Above it, a long, narrow cylinder, apparently tilted at a 45° angle, was slowly heading southwest. I estimated its altitude at two or three kilometers. The object was whitish in color, not luminous, and very distinct in outline. A sort of wreath of white smoke was escaping from its upper end. Some distance ahead of this cylindrical object, about thirty other objects were traveling on the same course. To the naked eye they looked like shapeless balls resembling puffs of smoke, but with the binoculars one could distinguish a red central ball and all around it a sort of yellowish ring inclined at a considerable angle from it. This inclination hid the lower part of the central sphere almost completely, but left the upper part visible. These objects were traveling in pairs, following a broken trajectory characterized, in short, by a swift zigzag. When two of them moved close to each other, a whitish trail appeared between them, like an electric arc. All these strange objects left behind them an abundant trail, which disintegrated as it fell slowly toward the ground. For several hours, there were lumps of it hanging on the trees, the telephone lines, and the roofs of the houses.

This sighting took place on October 17, 1952. Ten days later "a long cigar inclined at a 45° angle, with a plume of smoke on it, traveling slowly toward the southwest, surrounded by twenty objects that sparkled in the sunlight and flew in pairs in a rapid zigzag," was observed at Gaillac.

These descriptions seem to fit in with three groups of sightings: first, the cases from historical times, such as those reported by Jung, with descriptions of large groups of spherical objects accompanying "cylinders" and "tubes" in vertical or inclined positions; second, the sightings of cigars of great size, reported at very high altitudes, in the American files (of these objects,

Keyhoe writes that experienced observers estimate their length between two hundred and three hundred meters, with certain reports mentioning even greater lengths); and, finally, the French sightings from the fall of 1954, which furnish even more detailed descriptions of these large, cigar-shaped objects. We will return to their features in a study of the physical aspect of the reports in Chapter 9.

Stationary objects

The density of the population of Western Europe, where the UFO phenomenon was particularly widespread during the fall of 1954, made it possible to obtain good descriptions of the behavior of the objects, including numerous cases of stationary sightings. In certain circumstances the witnesses even reported motionless objects at low altitudes.

An example of a sighting possessing this feature is the case that occurred at Feyzin, France, at 11:20 P.M. on September 15, 1954. The witness was Roland M., aged 19. He gave the following account to the press:

> I was riding on my motorcycle between La Begude and Corbas, on local road V 02. I was about two hundred meters from the fort of Feyzin when suddenly a white light, coming down from the sky, swept the road and crossed it. I stopped and looked at the light, which had halted. I then discovered that it came from the upper part of a dark mass that was hovering about ten meters above the ground and fifty meters away from me. The black mass appeared elliptical. I watched for a while, and then I heard a faint sound, like a damp fuse; sparks shot out beneath the craft, which rose up with lightning speed.

At about 8:30 P.M. on September 18, 1954, two sightings displaying the same features took place in an entirely different part of the world: the Ivory Coast in Africa.

At Danae a luminous red object, circular or elliptical in shape, was seen by a large number of people. Arriving overhead at a brisk speed, it came to a halt in mid-air and remained motionless for five minutes, shining brightly all the while; then it vanished at high speed. At Soubre (250 kilometers northwest of Abidjan) a similar sighting took place. An "object" arrived at high speed, halted for several minutes over the town, and then disappeared in a cloudless sky, its size and brightness rapidly diminishing. The Chief Administrator of Soubre was among the witnesses (26).

It is interesting to regroup these sightings, for, while generally well-defined coordinates are given for them because the witnesses had time to note the position of the phenomenon, they admit to only a small number of interpretations. The meteor theory in particular is ruled out. But the characteristics of the objects are no different from those we have already encountered. The witnesses report the sighting of "discoidal bodies," the dimensions and behavior of which remain identical with those objects described in continuous movement through the atmosphere.

General survey of the "landings" of 1954

Although the observation of the phenomenon at low altitudes was common before 1954, cases in which witnesses described an object in contact with the ground were exceptional until the fall of 1954. In the absence of any extensive documentation, the absolutely fantastic cases reported prior to this period must be excluded from a completely objective analysis designed to clarify the physical nature of the phenomenon. Strictly speaking, one cannot refuse to include them in a statistical study that might lead to interesting sociological observations. One such case is the Sutton, West Virginia, incident of September 12, 1952, where an object on the ground and its "occupant," referred to as a "monster," were described.

The situation was totally different after September, 1954. The number of well-described cases confirmed by official investigations, involving obviously sincere witnesses many of whom possessed technical education, rules out the possibility of many conventional interpretations. We will take as an example the remarkable case at Foussignargues on September 27, 1954.

At 2:30 A.M. a Mrs. Julien and her son Andre, of Besseges, got off a bus at Foussignargues. The bus departed in the direction of Gagnieres, and as they walked toward their house they perceived in the sky a luminous reddish object, surrounded by a lighter halo, coming down in an easterly direction; the object disappeared behind a hill. As was learned later, the people in the bus saw a similar thing from a bridge situated a few hundred meters to the northeast.

Ten minutes later, a Mrs. Roche saw from her balcony at Revety, in the hills overlooking the same road, a red light emanating from a round, luminous object that was apparently on the ground at a distance of a hundred meters lower down:

> The object put me in mind of a sort of luminous tomato. Five or six vertical stems, of considerable thickness, emerged from the center of it, on the top.

The phenomenon was also observed by Mr. Roche for twenty minutes. But as nothing further occurred, they went indoors again. As no official investigative body existed in France, there was no authority for them to call. However, Mr. Roche, disturbed over the sighting, could not sleep and went outside again at 3:30 A.M.; the object was still in the same place, giving off the same red light. His fear prevailing over his curiosity, the witness did not approach the object and went back inside the house. At dawn the object—

whatever it was—had left (French papers for October 2, and [6]).

For the same reason that the cases of the stationary objects are noteworthy, these accounts involving UFO's on the ground deserve attention. Well pinpointed as to their coordinates, they afford a sure basis for topographical studies and a search for possible patterns, as we shall see in a more detailed discussion of the "landings" in Chapter 9. Such reports are of considerable importance to the psychologist, since they have formed the basis for the rumor; public opinion is much more concerned about close approaches than air-visual observations, which are always amenable to more or less sophisticated physical explanations.

The typical features of the reports describing objects on or very near the ground can be summed up as follows:

1. The object described displays symmetrical revolution around a vertical axis. It has moderate dimensions (a few meters).

2. The outline of the object is clear and well defined. Whether dark or luminous, it is not described as being "essentially luminous," in the sense that the light radiated from it appears to be localized in one section of the object or "irradiated" by its whole surface, which is described as material.

3. The appearance and disappearance of the object in general do not occur suddenly. Its behavior (unlike that of an optical phenomenon) is continuous and consistent: the object is seen arriving, landing, remaining on the ground for a more or less extended period, and then departing again, very often with a vertical trajectory that takes it out of sight at the zenith within a few seconds.

4. The object is not visible solely in one position or from a favorable angle. It is seen by persons in different positions around it and hides from their view the objects or parts of the landscape that are situated behind it, precisely as a material body would do. Its angular dimensions can thus be gauged from those of the area

it intercepts, e.g., the Marignane landing. According to all the sightings the objects have thickness.

5. The sighting of the object is often reported by different groups of independent witnesses, i.e., groups of persons unseen by and unknown to each other.

THE WHOLE WORLD

As a result of the censorship exercised in Europe and the lack of interest on the part of the press after 1954, many people until recently believed that sightings were no longer being made and that the phenomenon had disappeared of itself.

In reality, not only has the phenomenon returned to a high level of activity after 1964, the wave phenomenon was observed without interruption during the "silent decade" of 1954–64. The characteristics of these manifestations did not differ from those we have just described. Indeed, the most remarkable aspect of the phenomenon is its stability and consistency. The new factor in the situation is the simultaneous eruption of observations in all countries of the world. In this respect, the fall of 1957 was very noteworthy, as we shall see in the course of a detailed study. In the United States, there was a sudden renewal of sightings in the first days of November, 1957—the start of a spectacular series comparable to the French occurrences of 1954. Eyewitness accounts describing large objects in the vicinity of the ground, associated with detailed secondary effects, became common.

After 1960, the emotion, excitement, and even passion with which the observations had been received changed to a sort of ill-defined malaise among the public. Nearly everyone had either "seen something" or knew someone who had. This represented a formidable accumulation of repressed personal experiences. This awareness of the phenomenon found no expression: only the local newspapers ventured to publish reports, and always with a commentary designed to make it appear that the sightings should not be taken seriously. A typical news report skillfully apologized for quoting a UFO sighting by displaying a sense of humor. For example: "The moon was full Sunday night, when two persons from our town saw a weird object. . . ." Or: "Summer, the silly season, is with us again, and we should not be surprised that flying saucers invade our skies once more. . . ."

Awareness of the UFO phenomenon seems consequently to have passed through different phases, with a certain number of characteristic features and typical kinds of behavior. Particularly sensational at certain periods, and associated with a remarkable "phenomenon" in the press and interesting psychosociological reactions, it seems to have attained a condition of stability as early as 1950. In the last two years, concern has taken the place of humor in the newspapers' treatment of the phenomenon. As an increasing number of reliable citizens have reported their sightings in great detail and perfect seriousness, scientists have become increasingly willing to recognize that a full-scale study of the facts will be unavoidable in the face of public concern. The most obvious pattern on which such a study will be focused is the wave phenomenon.

WAVES BEFORE 1954

As we have seen, the waves of 1947, 1950, and 1952 mainly concerned the United States. But the first wave of the postwar period took place in Scandinavia in 1946. Pending publication of the researches currently being conducted by Donald Hanlon on the 1896–97 wave, and by the staff of NICAP (under the direction of Richard Hall) on the nineteenth and early twentieth century sightings, we have very little to add to our observation in *Anatomy of a Phenomenon* that waves of unidentified aerial phenomena, involving reports quite similar to the modern ones, did occur. Careful historical investigation, we feel, would establish beyond doubt that such events have been recorded by reliable observers and that waves did take place, notably in Great Britain and the United States, during the period 1883–1909.

After 1952, it was not until the peak of 1957 (notable for the famous Levelland çase) that the same intensity of emotion was associated with the UFO phenomenon in America. Practically every book on the subject has included an analysis of the waves of 1947 and 1950, recalling in detail the circumstances of Arnold's sighting and those that followed. The little-known point about the 1950 reports is that a series of sightings was recorded in Spain and North Africa (27, 13) shortly after the peak of the American wave. The 1947 wave covered the months of May through August, with the peak in early July. The 1950 wave covered the months of February to May, inclusive, with its peak at the end of March.

The 1952 wave is the first for which we possess a really large number of detailed sightings from the whole world. It lasted from mid-April to mid-December, with its peak in mid-July, and consisted of European and American reports in approximately equal proportions, plus numerous sightings from Africa. The most notable cases of the European wave were in September and October. They include, of course, the Oloron and Gaillac reports. By way of illustration, we shall recall some little-known cases.

C. Vaillant, a correspondent for the newspaper *La Bourgogne Republicaine,* claimed that on July 17, 1952, at 1:00 P.M., at Belan-sur-Ource, he was astonished by a sudden whirlwind of dust. He saw in the sky a luminous object that appeared to be stationary. A second object, disk-shaped, detached itself from the first one and moved toward the west, while the first one moved off in the opposite direction. Then suddenly both objects rose straight up and vanished; thereupon the wind stopped.

On August 3, 1952, at 11 P.M., at Arbret (between Doullens and Arras), two policemen, Blondel and Darras, of Baumetz-les-Loges, saw a "ball of fire," which traveled from Doullens toward Arras, then stopped above the Arbret railroad station and climbed away vertically.

On August 13, 1952, at Fourchambault, a very brightly shining disk "with a large hemispherical turret or cupola on top" was seen circling above the town. Twelve persons in Fourchambault and Givrey, including a Mrs. Jaillette, who watched the motions of the object with binoculars, reported this sighting.

All the above sightings are from France. On September 15, 1952, at about 8:00 P.M. at Thies, Senegal (West Africa), J. Grivel saw something he described in the following account:

A large, reddish, luminous point appeared between Mu and 32 of Scorpio, moved slowly and noiselessly toward the east, passed near Khi of Scorpio and moved toward Sagittarius. Suddenly, between the stars Delta and Gamma of Sagittarius, it stopped. Later it resumed its movement toward the north, then toward the west, and finally disappeared near Phi of Ophiucus. There were no aircraft in the sky. No sound was heard. (Extract from *L'Astronomie,* Bulletin of the French Astronomical Society.)

On September 19, 1952, close to the village of Beine, near Chablis:

Mr. R. Sommer, pilot and aircraft manufacturer, writes to us as follows: "I was returning home by car, the night was dark, without moon or stars. After having passed through the village of Beine and driven on for about five minutes beyond it, we were greatly surprised to see that a dazzling unknown object had appeared in the sky, to the left of our road. The object was shaped like an olive and golden in color. Its major axis was vertical. The spectacle was magical and fairy-like. This manifestation lasted for about five minutes. The minor axis of the object was slightly smaller than the apparent diameter of the moon. A few minutes later, I visited the neighboring villages. I examined the churches, wondering whether this apparition might have been due to illuminations or reflections.* But everything was absolutely quiet and there was no prominent light to be seen. The road was deserted." (Extract from *L'Astronomie*.)

Three days later, in Bayonne, the night shift at the Mouguerre Chemical Plant observed, for twenty minutes, an object moving up and down whose luminosity varied with the motion and whose color changed from red to blue.

The American sightings of the 1952 wave have been the subject of now classic arguments. Menzel and Keyhoe, whose studies are complementary to a large extent, have analyzed the cases in detail.

THE GLOBAL WAVE OF 1954

The French wave started in mid-August and extended through the end of November. This period contains no less than fourteen cases of Type II. A detailed description of the French reports has been given by Michel in (5, 6). Their extraordinary character prompted many scientists to attribute them entirely to the "silly season." Although these sightings not only exist on record but are easily verifiable from the local newspapers, which very often give the names and addresses of the witnesses, their number and nature are still underestimated. In fact, a study of the French press enabled us to gather twice the number of cases in the original sample from which Michel had worked.

The first noteworthy events of the wave took place

---

* Many churches in France are illuminated at night. The sighting in Beine is a good example of a case of Type II-A reported by a witness of unquestionable technical education and, furthermore, published by the scientific press.

long before the period now generally considered to
have marked its beginning. The records of the U.S.
Air Force show that Germany was the first West
European country where the level of sightings rose
sharply. In mid-August the east of France recorded a
marked increase: there had already been four sightings
on August 11 at Serezin, Remiremont, Contrexeville
and Gerardmer. The next day, at Precy-sur-Thil, a
shiny object that moved in sudden jerks and left a
trail was observed. During the night of August 18–19
a "cloud-cigar" was seen in Dole; it moved slowly across
the sky, illuminating the whole town. The next day,
the reports of landings started. These Type I reports
have been very much contested, especially the description of the "occupants" of a UFO given by a Norwe-
gian witness on August 20. The same day another landing was reported, in Varennes, France. On August 23
a well-documented account of a landing near Thonon
(on the shore of Lake Geneva) and the celebrated
case of the Vernon "cigar"—watched for forty-five
minutes by policemen, a businessman, and an army
rocket engineer, from separate locations in the town
—were reported. As early as August 23—more than
one month before the flood of reports in the press—all
the basic features that were encountered in nearly *one
thousand unexplained sightings over the following three
months* were already clearly defined.

Only a person unversed in "Ufology" would claim
that these features were new. It was the number of
reports, the quality of the descriptions, and the reliability of the observers that made the 1954 wave the
subject of so much controversy and a standard for the
various theories of the UFO phenomenon. It is not
possible to go over all the cases here, as a look at the
graph of the daily number of unexplained reports
(Figure 21) will show. This number was well above
twenty for several weeks, and only a large and very
well organized official team of investigators, trained in
police methods and equipped with rapid means of trans-
portation and communications, could have coped with

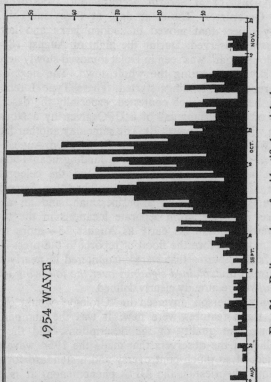

FIG. 21—Daily number of unidentified aerial phenomena reported during the 1954 wave.

such a flood. No such organization existed at that time
—or now. It would have been impossible for the armed
forces to justify the appropriation of large funds to a
commission with orders to track down "saucer" reports
while the highest scientific authorities—who had made
a hasty judgment on the basis of a few exaggerated
reports in the sensational papers—were making public
statements attributing the observations to meteors and
balloons. The situation has not significantly changed in
this respect since then. But we feel that a detailed study
of the mechanism of the 1954 wave would give us insight into the nature of the phenomenon and might suggest means of coping with a similar "invasion" in the
future, as there are no signs that the phenomenon is
about to subside.

The events of September, 1954, covered all of Western Europe, from Scandinavia to Portugal, and extended into Africa. American reports were by no means
lacking during that period, but they showed no remarkable variation. At 8 A.M. on September 5, ten
persons, including three policemen, in Graz, Austria,
saw an object shaped clearly like a disk cross the sky
on an east-west trajectory. One and one-half hours
later, a second disk was seen moving in the same direction. In the afternoon of the same day in Tangiers, a
disk-shaped object the size of an airplane was observed
for ten minutes (official French military documents).
Between September 13 and 20: *Wave over Holland*.
Unknown flying objects were reported at Zuidlaarder-
veen and near Groningen, and all over the Netherlands.
On September 17, at 6:28 P.M. *thousands of witnesses*
in Rome, among them military pilots and high-ranking
Italian Army officers, saw over the city an object
shaped like a half-cigar, at an altitude of less than one
mile. This object was simultaneously tracked on radar
by the airport personnel while the crowd watched it
perform incredible evolutions: it reached speeds of 260
to 280 kilometers per hour almost instantaneously, only
to stop suddenly again, drop down, then turn, rise,
and so on. An antenna of some sort visible in the center

of the machine left a short luminous trail when it moved. This demonstration lasted more than an hour, leaving the authorities completely astonished. Then the object rose and moved toward the northwest. The official investigation of the case was not publicized, but the incident was commented on by all the European newspapers during the following days. Observations of a similar object made elsewhere in Italy that day may refer to a later portion of the same object's trajectory.

About September 20 a series of sightings took place in the area of the Azores, with observations at Santa Maria Airport and reports by airline pilots flying over the Atlantic Ocean. At the same time there was a resurgence in sightings over the Ivory Coast of Africa. During the night of September 27, the pilot of an airliner en route from New York to Lisbon reported an extraordinary source of light, which was not a ship and yet seemed to be on the surface of the ocean, at latitude 38° 12′ N. and longitude 37° 36′ W.

On October 1 a Type I sighting that was certainly not influenced by the French wave, which was far from its peak at that time, was recorded at Dhubri, India. A "luminous plate, with a long trail behind it," landed in a field and then took off again.

On October 2 there were sightings in Canada, Tunisia (Megrine-Coteaux), and Scotland (Perth)—and the Poncey "network" in France. The following day every part of the world was represented: Switzerland (the Jungfrau), Austria (Ried), Italy (Mantau, Boscochiano), India (Bombay), Belgium (Huy), England (Northolt), and Lebanon (Beirut)!

On October 12, the French wave passed its critical peak, but the "phenomenon" was breaking loose in the press. "Flying saucers" were the sole subject of conversation, interest, and passion throughout the country. Taken by surprise, scientists, draped with dignity, refused to study reports presented with all the "frills and trimmings" of the sensational. But many of the newspaper accounts were in reality well researched and well documented, in spite of the fantastic headlines. A scientific investigation would certainly have helped to soothe the fever that swept the country. But nothing was done as the wave went on, in France and in all of Europe. The center of activity shifted: after mid-October there was a wave in Yugoslavia (with reports from Sarajevo, Ljubljana, Belgrade, and Zagreb) and a large Italian wave developed. The latter has not been very well publicized, but from what we have been able to learn it was quite as remarkable as the wave that took place in France. There were sightings at Salerno, Vietri-sul-Mare, Rovigo, Po di Gnocca, Trento, Genoa, etc. Reports of all types, including landings and low-altitude maneuvers, have been gathered.

On October 21 sightings were made in Norway, Germany, and Italy. A German sighting was published by *L'Astronomie:*

> At 6:45 P.M. on October 21, 1954, Herr Janus-zewski of Reutingen (south Germany) observed two white oval objects moving at dizzying speed toward the northwest. They vanished suddenly. Our colleague estimates their altitude at six to eight kilometers.

During the last days of October there were sightings in Italy, Angola, Algeria, Morocco, and Madagascar. A UFO was photographed in Communist Hungary by a schoolmaster (*see* newspaper *Esti Bud* and *Agence France Presse,* dispatch of October 27). Further observations of "flying saucers" were made in the French Cameroons, Spain, and Belgium.

We come now to November. So far as the French reports are concerned, the wave was nearing its end, but sightings from other parts of the world continued to pile up. The wave in South America was just beginning. There were several observations in India, Africa, Australia, and Spain. On November 12, the Director of the meteorological observatory in Terceira, Azores, related a sighting. On November 21, nineteen disk-shaped objects were seen by the passengers of a Brazilian airliner over the Paraiba River. On November 27, the sightings came from Brazil, Portugal, and the Soviet Union.

By this extensive accumulation of material, we intend only to show the necessity for a serious investigation on a worldwide scale. It is interesting that if the U.S. Air Force had set up a scientific research group in 1954, this group would have remained totally unaware of the wave and its remarkable features, because it affected North America only in a very minor way. Hence we feel that *the task of analyzing this planetary phenomenon should be given to an international scientific body,* with authority to pursue investigations locally through national research groups.

Certainly many of the reports to which we have just referred would—by the criteria of the air force—be classed under the label "insufficient information." But if the work of a few people, consisting simply in the careful reading of the newspapers, gathered so much material, what would professional investigators, well briefed as to the facts of the problem and supplied with some funds, have been able to do?

Moreover, the idea that the events of 1954 essentially centered on France, are confined to the facts related in Michel's book, and should be interpreted within the framework of a mere sociological phenomenon affecting one small country with very dense population is simply incorrect. On the contrary, the list of reports we have given suggests that a little research would discover a similar density of sightings in any European country, and it would be very apparent that the whole earth was affected simultaneously by the same phenomenon. Although mass psychology has frequently been invoked in the interpretations placed upon eyewitness accounts, this science, to the best of our knowledge, does not possess in its records a single example of the propagation of a hallucinatory rumor in a practically instantaneous manner over the whole of the planet, and a rumor based on descriptions showing constant features at that!

Engraving published in the *San Francisco Call* in November, 1896. Donald Hanlon, who has catalogued more than 150 sightings for the 1896-97 wave, reports that the object was seen throughout the United States and became popularly known as "The Airship." It was highly maneuverable and was equipped with powerful lights; it landed several times and was definitely not the work of local craftsmen.

Drawing published by the British paper *Peterborough Citizen and Advertiser*, March 24, 1909. It shows the "aerial ship" observed by a constable, P.C. Kettle, "an absolutely trustworthy witness." Kettle's attention was drawn to the object by the noise it produced, "similar to that of a car." The object seemed to be equipped with a powerful searchlight. Compare with Plate 1.

These three photographs were taken near Namur, Belgium, on June 5, 1955. They are believed to be authentic because on exposure No. 2 the object is seen behind a condensation trail, which could not have formed at an altitude lower than 1,500 meters, according to the professional meteorologists by whom the photographs were analyzed. On that basis, the minimum diameter of the object must have been twelve meters. Also, a professional astronomer examined the negatives and reached the conclusion that they had not been faked.

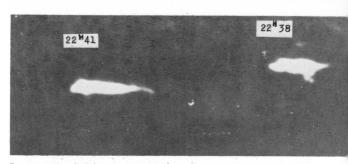

Images recorded by the trajectory analyzers at Forcalquier Observatory in France during the night of May 3/4, 1957 (see Chapter One). The top photograph was taken by the fixed camera, the bottom by the rotating camera, showing less detail. Note the change in the relative position of the two images, proving this is not a case of emulsion defect.

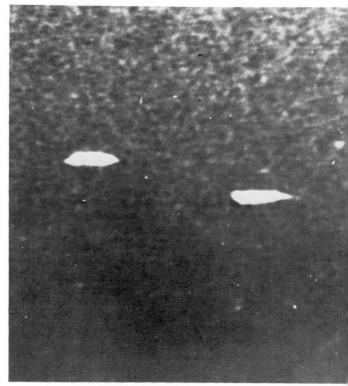

The scene of the Loch Raven Dam observation, in October, 1958. This air force photograph was taken from the point where the witnesses' car stopped as they were approaching a brightly lit object hovering over the bridge (see Chapter Ten).

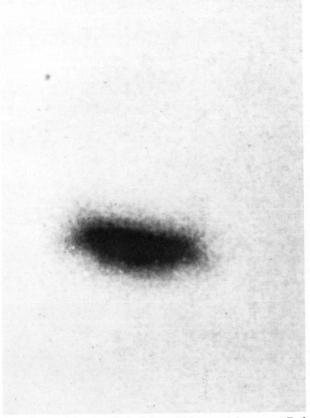

This photograph of a dark flying object was taken over Red China in 1961.

◀

An example of a frequent misinterpretation: this "unidentified object" photographed in Northern Africa in August, 1961, by a puzzled witness is actually the artificial satellite Echo 1 (see Chapter Six). Such errors are common but easily recognized.

The imprint found at the site of the Socorro, New Mexico, landing in April, 1964, by the air force investigating team (see Chapter Two).

An abnormal echo or a flight of wild birds may, in many cases, explain this or that piece of evidence. But what known effect gives rise to reports of circular objects made at the same moment and in the same terms (sometimes word for word) by hundreds of Hindus armed with sticks and thousands of Italians equipped with radars? And when a peasant from the Millevache Plateau in France—a man who is certainly no science-fiction fanatic—comes to us with the same description, this goes beyond the bounds of hallucination or psychosis as described in the textbooks.

THE WAVE OF 1957

After the wave of 1954, to which so much emotion is still attached, the most important global wave was that of 1957. Its particular character derived from the fact that it reached its greatest intensity in the United States, where means of communications are most developed and where public opinion is most sensitive to any emotional stimulus.

The wave began in South America. There were many reports from Brazil, and toward the end of the summer the observations in North America started to pile up. Then came the Sputniks. The most widely publicized observation, that of Levelland, Texas, coincided with the launching of the second satellite.* All eyes turned toward the sky. Suddenly "flying saucers" shared the headlines with the satellites. This brief flareup of interest on the part of the newspapers made the wave appear to have a peak of short duration, and it was widely interpreted by the "enthusiasts" as an indication of the saucers' interest in earth's achievements in

---

* The Levelland case and the related observations have been studied in detail in *Anatomy of a Phenomenon*. The first artificial satellite (Sputnik I) was launched on October 4, 1957. Sputnik II was probably launched during the night of November 3/4, possibly on November 4 at 04:40 U.T. Therefore the remark by Mebane in (6) is not applicable.

space. In reality, the wave had been going on for a long time.

A number of unfavorable circumstances enter into the picture in the study of these reports: first, the emotional tension of the American people after two successful satellite launchings by the Soviet Union; second, the richness of this period (particularly after November 10) in brilliant meteors; and finally, the exceptional brightness of the planet Venus throughout the whole period. The distance of Venus from the earth, however, was far from its minimum, which came in February of the following year.

In spite of these unfavorable circumstances, the job of tracking down errors of this sort is not so difficult as is sometimes implied; the fact that a large number of the reports indicate a truly puzzling phenomenon cannot be denied. It is interesting to note that at the time of the series of sightings in Texas on November 2, a pilot of the Union of South Africa was pursuing two "disks" maneuvering separately over Johannesburg and that another UFO was seen at Cracow, Poland, at 7:30 P.M. on November 4. For November 5, the list of observations outside the United States includes Santo Domingo, Italy, and Belgium. The Belgian sighting took place at Wegnez, and phenomena very similar to those recorded in Theriot, Louisiana, on the same day were described there. The two accounts are almost identical, word for word. On November 6 we have reports from Seoul, Korea; Kagoshima, Japan; and Itaipu, Brazil, where a military fort experienced a general power failure as a "large disk" flew overhead at a low altitude. On November 7 the reports came from Chile, Australia, and France. The French sighting was at 6:45 P.M. over the atomic plant at Marcoule.

The next day, November 8, was a day for landings in the United States. But it was also marked by the Toulouse case (see Chapter 1, "The Case of the Spinning Disk"). On November 16 a UFO was photographed in Madrid, and a week later a veritable wave started in Europe. The South American reports con-

tinued to be frequent, although insufficiently documented, throughout this period.

CONCLUSION

It is not enough to recognize the existence of a wave
phenomenon and to study the process of the development of the waves, as we have done with the most
"typical" periods, 1952, 1954, and 1957. Such a study
is only the first step in a global investigation of UFO
activity, i.e., of the patterns that govern the recurrence
of the waves on a planetary scale. The methods for such
an investigation will be discussed in the next chapter.

Unfortunately, as we have seen, the observations of
unusual aerial phenomena have not been gathered by
official centers in a truly scientific spirit, and we must
rely on carefully selected samples drawn from either
the files of amateurs or the collections of the U.S. Air
Force. Both sources are far from satisfactory to the
scientist, for the consistency in the documentation of
the cases is poor—the former's because of lack of funds
and the latter's because of lack of scientific curiosity.
In all the studies conducted so far, scientific research
has been absent. Individual sightings have been carefully scrutinized, but patterns of possible general interest
have been ignored. Scientists have been asked to examine special cases, but no consultant has been called
upon to make a long-term appraisal of the *total nature
of the phenomenon*. Just as an astronomer who devotes
his entire attention to only one star will remain unaware
of the laws of stellar evolution, the responsible agencies in the United States, which possess only fragmentary information on the very large field they pre-
tend to explore, miss the phenomenon's most general
laws. Their research ends when a case is called "unidentified." They review the file from time to time to
see if a conventional explanation has come up, and
sometimes they succeed in finding one. They assume
that, given infinite time and no new observations, the

proportion of "unidentifieds" will statistically approach zero asymptotically. This official philosophy is a total fallacy for two reasons: first, the number of "unidentifieds" added each year is not negligible; second, the passage from a statistical law ("the UFO phenomenon represents a very small percentage of the reports") to a physical statement ("the UFO phenomenon does not exist") is not justifiable.

This is not the way science works. Although our data are more fragmentary than we would desire as a base of solid investigation, they warrant a review of the methods available for an analysis in depth of the UFO mystery.

8

CYCLES OF ACTIVITY

IS THERE A HIDDEN LAW?

WHAT ARE THE METHODS that would permit a systematic study of the recurrence of UFO phenomena, if such research ever came to be officially recommended?

The remote similarity between the unfolding of the waves of observations and the idea of an "invasion" or "exploration" of the earth by creatures from another planet was first pointed out in 1947. It was in pursuit of this childish idea—entirely borrowed from science fiction—that the early researchers acted when they ventured to seek a periodicity in the phenomenon, or a coincidence between its peaks and the oppositions of Mars or even of Venus. All these studies were done by means of graphs and seemed to show a certain correlation with the distance of Mars.

According to our previous experiments, recorded in (107), it would seem that the coincidence with the Martian cycle is very well verified for the period covering the four peaks of 1950–1952–1954–1956 (*see* Figure 22), but loses its validity beyond this period. This would explain why more roughly made studies

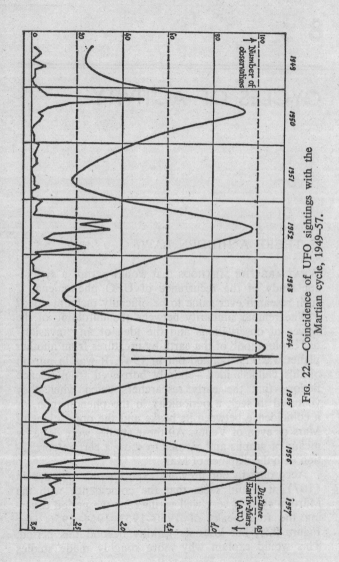

FIG. 22.—Coincidence of UFO sightings with the Martian cycle, 1949–57.

over a wider period have sometimes seemed to result in a reasonable correlation.

The critical factor here—and all studies made so far are inadequate on this point—is the number of basic data. The total number of sightings actually made since 1946 is impossible to calculate. Five million American citizens are estimated to have made what they believe to be a UFO sighting. More than ten thousand, a very small proportion, have reported their sightings to the air force. Of these, only 5 per cent or 10 per cent remain unidentified. This is too small a sample, both in terms of statistical validity and of geographic origin, for an accurate frequency study. Because of the shifts in the center of activity of each wave, which we have carefully studied in the previous chapters, any investigation conducted in a single country will completely miss the general law. If we take the observations coming from all parts of the world, as our team has done, the sample is both more representative and much larger. The number of significant sightings reaches five or six thousand, or about ten times the number of significant American cases. Within the framework of an official study, this number could probably double. Our own estimate of the correlation with Mars in 1962 was based on one thousand sightings. The estimates made before us by Michel, Guieu, Buelta, and others were based on a few hundred sightings. The investigation reported here used our revised catalogue of three thousand sightings.

The periodicity of the phenomenon is not the only interesting objective of such a study. Its by-products enable the research to be oriented toward certain types of physical explanations. It would be interesting, for instance, to find a general eleven-year cycle in correlation with solar activity, or a function following the sequence of thermonuclear explosions and the corresponding increases of atmospheric radioactivity. On the other hand, what is really needed is a total analysis, in which the cyclic effects are clearly separated from the trend of the rumor over the years. Some theoretical refinements have been proposed in an interesting discussion of the phenomenon by Buelta. They involve the use of parameters designed to compensate for variations of population density, geographic area, climatic conditions, etc. We feel that, in the present state of the data, these weighting factors would tend to mask the objective phenomena and complicate the interpretation of the results, and we have therefore confined ourselves to the raw data and their direct derivatives.

CYCLIC VARIATIONS

In studies of this type a frequency distribution is usually broken into fundamental functions termed "components." They are classified under four main groups: (1) long-term variation or "trend"; (2) cyclic variations; (3) seasonal variations; and (4) irregular, accidental variations.

The analysis of the series consists in the description (usually in mathematical terms) of these components, starting from the hypothesis that the observed function of time can be written as the product of four functions, which are respectively responsible for the fundamental variations. The techniques used in this analysis can be found in many books and lie outside the scope of this work. We eliminated the seasonal component since our data were planet-wide, and we tried to arrive at an empirical, intuitive representation of these data. We took one-fourth of a month as our elementary time unit and examined the variation defined by a total of 2,708 sightings distributed into 768 periods from 1947 to 1962. Over 300 of these cases were Type I (landings), 44 Type II, and 270 Type III. The curves of yearly frequencies for Types I and III are shown on Figure 23, where they can be compared with Type V, a test category where we grouped the observations of "lights seen at night" and unexplained but poorly defined objects. The greater selectivity of Types I and III is clearly apparent.

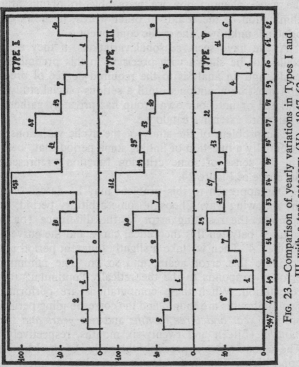

Fig. 23.—Comparison of yearly variations in Types I and III with a test category (V), 1947–62.

Here the existence of a strong "trend" helps to mask any cyclic effects that may be present. This general trend was computed by a "moving average" technique we introduced in other scientific applications (256); it also helped to eliminate a major part of the irregularities. The resulting function is shown in Figure 24, which displays the best mathematical representation of the wave phenomenon we were able to obtain after elimination of the trend. In other words, it shows our principal unknown, the cyclic component.

As we have seen, seasonal variations, if they exist, could not be shown with precision in this preliminary study, and an analysis to the required degree of precision must be abandoned until a serious official study is initiated or until our own group has privately gathered a far more extensive catalogue.

The problem of the study of the cyclic variations is essentially a question of finding some period that "best" (in the sense of some criterion function) represents the curve of Figure 24.

Our approach to this problem may be described in the following way. Choosing some arbitrary period, we compute the resulting error by the difference (or its square) between this theoretical curve and the curve of Figure 24. Then we take a slightly different period and compute this error again, and so on. The minimum error corresponds to the theoretically "optimum" representation. When these computations are performed two minimums are found, and the corresponding periods are *one year and three months* and *two years and two months* (fifteen and twenty-six months, respectively). The second value is precisely the period of the Martian oppositions. The first value is very close to the half-period. When the error is evaluated by least squares, the first minimum vanishes.

The fact that a period very close to that of the Martian cycle has been found is clearly important. It could be regarded as a confirmation of the correlations found earlier (107). But we are still far from a result that could be taken as a clear proof of the correlation,

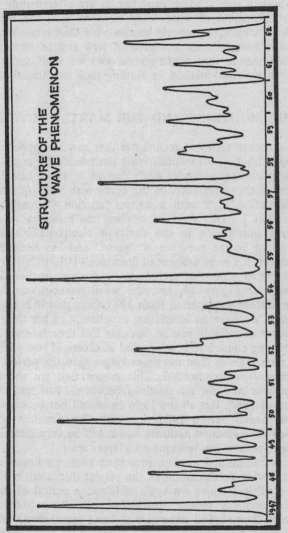

Fig. 24.—Structure of the wave phenomenon, 1947–62.

and we are certainly not prepared to claim that we have proved it exists; these experiments are offered only as an illustration of what *could be done with the UFO files* if they were properly handled. We shall retain these indications only as a source of new insight into the phenomenon that confronts us, and we shall apply a more rigorous method in seeking their confirmation.

THE SIGHTINGS AND THE MARTIAN CYCLE

Another series of techniques that can be applied to the extraction of an underlying periodicity (if any) in the phenomenon under study derives from the calculation of the correlation of the curve with itself ("auto-correlation") or with a known function ("cross-correlation"). This field of applied mathematics is of great importance in the study of electronic systems working in the presence of "noise" and has been the subject of a large amount of literature (101, 102, 103). We have used this technique to analyze further the curve of Figure 24, i.e., the wave phenomenon for the sixteen-year period from 1947 through 1962. Here again, we have an interesting experiment rather than a source of reliable results, because this time interval is not long enough to test a period in excess of two years; a time span at least ten times longer than the period is generally recommended. This means that we should consider at least all sightings between 1946 and the end of 1966. But all the 1966 cases will not be known and coded before 1967 or 1968. The problem will then have reached maturity and it will be very interesting to resume this research on a larger scale.

In the limited attempt presented here, we found an interesting confirmation of the results discussed in the preceding section; we again obtained a period of one year and one month, the half-period of the Martian cycle. The second experiment (cross-correlation) was conducted using a list of the distances of Mars, using four values per month. Again, a good correlation was obtained; in view of the preceding results, this cannot, of course, come as a surprise. As a test we ran the same calculation with the distance of Venus, and we found only a poor correlation.

These results are very difficult to interpret, and for that reason we have constantly emphasized the need for a larger sample. When these new data are obtained, it will be possible to make a serious appraisal of the hypotheses advanced concerning a larger periodicity. Dr. Olavo Fontes, in particular, has theorized a fundamental five-year cycle, illustrated by the three waves of 1947–1952–1957, which would allow a simple representation of the large variations of the frequency of reports (108). But no means of checking this theory exists at the present time. The distribution can obviously be accounted for by many diverse combinations of two periodic phenomena. It would be more interesting to take up this question again if certain waves were qualitatively different from certain others or if the lag between the peaks of activity and the Mars oppositions were consistent with the passage of the Martian seasons, as some astronomers have suggested. These studies have not yet been undertaken. In any case, they could not have any validity if they depended only upon the limited lists of sightings available today to the various private groups or even, for that matter, to the U.S. Air Force itself. These samples are much too limited and too affected by selection effects, not to mention their strong geographical bias. These is consequently, in our opinion, an urgent need for centralization and development of a fast codification method.

A DIFFICULT PROBLEM

Any attempt to associate a terrestrial physical effect with an astronomical phenomenon is exceedingly dangerous and the conclusions drawn from such experiments should be scrutinized with skepticism. Present-day analytical methods can investigate such relationships safely only as long as we do not try to extract from the results more than the data themselves are worth.

At the present time we know of numerous terrestrial phenomena linked to astronomical cycles, particularly to those related to our sun. But a relationship with the distance of a planet can only be interpreted at two levels: first, at the psychological level—the proximity of the planet and hence its brightness and apparent diameter in the sky being at the origin of certain illusions (cf. our review of misinterpretations of Venus in Chapter 6, where the raw data show a component in correlation with Venus because of these errors); second, in the sense of actual interplanetary travel. We have here an additional means of deciding between the principal theories with which we are faced.

In any research involving the use of statistical methods, the transition from mathematical correlation to physical correlation is hazardous. In this chapter, we have treated the variation of the number of reports as a "signal," without any hypothesis as to its origin or nature. But many factors may have intervened to mask or falsify certain features of this variation.

The first such factor is the geographical one. Most of our data were of American (North and South) and European or North African origin. Does this mean that the entire continent of Asia or the enormous area of Africa south of the Sahara Desert has been touched only exceptionally by the phenomenon? Numerous indications favor the opposite view, especially in the Communist world, where waves have indeed occurred; their approximate dates are known, but details are not yet available.

A second important factor is population density. It would seem that a very dense region, such as France, would yield a large number of cases and an African country produce few.

On the other hand, are we not running the risk of exaggerating the importance of these factors? We know that waves have occurred in regions of the world far removed from the Western centers of communications, in sparsely populated regions, even in desert areas; the accounts are even more numerous in those areas. We shall see a striking proof of this fact in the study of the French landings.

The absence of any strong correlation, in a given country, between the density of unidentified sightings and the density of population is interesting. Men who live out in the country look up at the sky more, and they know it much better. It is true that they are often more credulous, but they are also closer to nature and more observant. If the actual number of sightings made during the peaks is related to these factors, their situation in time seems fairly independent of secondary conditions. For this reason we have paid particular attention to the need to define each wave carefully.

The maximums in the distribution are generated, not by reports from any one country, but by a large number of observations coming suddenly from all over the world. For example, we discovered a large-scale increase of activity in 1956, although at the time no wave was reported from any definite country. Only by collecting the sightings were we able to discover this phenomenon several years later.

To summarize, the frequency variation of UFO sightings can be regarded as the superposition of a constant "background" generation of reports and of sudden increases of large amplitude in well-defined time intervals, which we term waves. This variation involves a strong cyclic component, which the current military investigations ignore entirely. The correlation of this cyclic component with the Martian cycle is interesting, but it is far from being absolutely demonstrated.

If a correlation, not only of a numerical but also of a physical nature, does exist between Mars and the distribution of UFO reports, how could it be interpreted? Would we be able to decide definitely between the two main theories that confront us? Unfortunately, we do not think so. In fact, those who do not believe in the material reality of the saucers will see in this result *the confirmation that the phenomenon is to be attributed to mass psychology:* visions of a hallucinatory nature, of a mild form, are stimulated by the close approach of Mars, they will say; misinterpretations of the image of the planet by pilots or by people on the ground add to the confusion. The same interpretation works for any series of sightings, if Venus and Jupiter are brought into the picture. Indeed, in a psychological theory, there is no reason for these two planets to play a less important role than Mars.

Those who believe in the reality of the "flying saucers" will not consider the conclusion reached here as proof either. The proof, or at least convincing evidence, of their theory is found by them in the very character of accounts in which the sighting conditions and the sincerity of the witnesses seem to them to be sufficient guarantees. They will interpret a correlation with Mars as lending support to the idea that the "saucers" are interplanetary craft that use either a satellite of Mars or the planet itself as a base in their exploration of our solar system. In the present state of our ignorance of the nature of the Martian satellites, it is not impossible to think that they are large interstellar vehicles, placed into orbit more than a century ago (they were first observed in 1877) by an advanced scientific community coming from elsewhere in the universe. This interpretation would at least be more plausible than the idea that intelligent life has developed on Mars and has constructed these satellites.

It is important not to lose sight of the fact that any phenomenon whatever that appears in a more or less strange context can be linked with some astronomical body. One can always manage to find some heavenly object whose opposition, or conjunction, or quadrature, or maximum brightness falls reasonably close to the time of the reported event. The periodic phenomena are even more dangerous for, among the infinitely varied play of the periods ruling astronomical cycles, one can always find a value "not too far away" from that of the pseudo-period in question. Then, if we admit that two periodic motions are involved, or superimposed, we can account, with good precision, for practically anything we like, with the aid of planetary cycles.

It is for this reason that we have refrained from carrying the calculations beyond a very elementary level. A more sophisticated construction based on the sixteen years of sightings that have been coded would be nothing more than an intellectual exercise. It is also for this reason that we decline to pronounce an opinion on the proposed five-year cycle. That the phenomenon under study manifests itself in the form of waves is beyond doubt. That it exists outside these waves is equally certain, since significant sightings have been found throughout the period under study, even between waves. The correlation of the times of the peaks with the oppositions of Mars is sometimes curious. The coincidence of the period with the Martian cycle is also interesting. But to attribute the phenomenon purely and simply to the "Martians" on the basis of the data available today is as absurd as the view that would explain away all the sightings as the "unusual twinklings" of planets!

9

THE SEARCH FOR PATTERNS

A QUESTION OF METHOD

ONCE THE ERRORS, misinterpretations, and obvious hoaxes are eliminated, the remaining sightings—those that fit our definitions of the UFO phenomenon—can be studied.

Whether this list contains anything other than misinterpretations and errors remains of course an open question. If the phenomenon exists outside and beyond the conventional explanations, it must be possible to extract it from this sample by a suitable treatment using simple considerations of physics.

We feel that many previous investigations have failed at this point because they either attempted to establish an overall descriptive study, too general in scope, or focused entirely on "the best reports," reverting to the cases one by one in order to subject them to the classical explanations. Yet the remaining reports still exhibit considerable diversity and must be studied in groups of fair homogeneity; some residue of facts will remain unexplained in any case, even if only because of the fragmentary nature of the information at our disposal.

Previous studies, therefore, whether conducted by the air force or by the "Ufologists," have merely shifted the problem around while dissipating the capital of information.

This approach is not very scientific, yet it has often been used to "explain" a large percentage of the American reports. Nature offers infinite combinations of phenomena. If one sets out with the idea that all the sightings *must* possess a conventional explanation, one is led to introduce natural phenomena fanning out into an infinitely complex structure, where every sighting will have to submit to a lodging at one level or another. But does this analysis offer really serious guarantees? Are the final "explanations" plausible? Is not the study soon engulfed in the unverifiable, in a domain where the hypotheses become totally arbitrary?

The techniques used to investigate phenomena affected by observational distortion, which are well known and are used every day in conventional problems, are relevant here. But scientists have been discouraged from applying them to the UFO phenomenon because of the mystery and the ridicule that surrounded it. We feel that this ridicule should be totally disregarded. If the phenomenon has been surrounded with an aura of mystery and exploited by false prophets and charlatans, that is only one more reason it should be brought under the light of analysis—to prevent the spreading of new, and possibly harmful, forms of sociological disturbance. Even if physics derives nothing from the study of the phenomenon, and even if it turns out that the witnesses have described only products of their own imaginations, a serious investigation will have great interest for the psychologist.

Scientific honesty calls for an extensive research excluding no possible hypothesis. Such a research would start with the definition of classification criteria and the gathering of a sample of significant sightings and would proceed to a qualitative study of this material. Such a description would be directed first to the times and durations of the sightings and would seek to pinpoint the phenomena of the most clearly defined types; in this respect, without entering into the detail of all the investigations under development now, we will use the "landings" as an example of an area of great potential interest. Of course, we will introduce no external consideration in this analysis and will concern ourselves only with the physical characteristics that emerge from the eyewitness accounts.

TIME AND DURATION OF THE SIGHTINGS

If you ask an amateur group or the U.S. Air Force at what time of day most people report flying saucers and for how long they are seen, they will answer about the same thing: people see flying saucers mostly at night and some sightings last longer than others. The least one can say about such a statement is that it lacks accuracy and that after so many years of investigation we should be able to define the phenomenon a little better.

The fact is that the question, obvious as it is, cannot be answered properly without breaking down the figures according to the various types of UFO events; this approach was not used, either officially or otherwise, until the French cases of 1954 were systematically studied, as we have seen. The analysis has now been extended to all the sightings available, including the American cases, and the following information has been accumulated:

1. The frequency of Type III reports shows a marked increase between 8 P.M. and 9 P.M. As the night continues, the number of sightings drops rapidly. The number of Type III observations made in the early morning hours and during the day is not negligible, but the large majority are made between 6 P.M. and 12 P.M.

2. Type I sightings (landings) occur only rarely in the daytime, between 6 A.M. and 6 P.M. There is a sudden rise in the frequency of sightings at sunset, and

the maximum is reached almost immediately, while the maximum for Type III observations is reached about three hours after sunset. On the other hand, the number of Type I reports decreases gradually during the night, in direct proportion with the number of potential observers (as people return home from work and go to sleep). The frequency of Type III sightings decreases more rapidly (*see* Figure 25).

3. The frequency of the "landings" has a second maximum at dawn (as people who go to work early wake up and leave their homes) but returns to zero

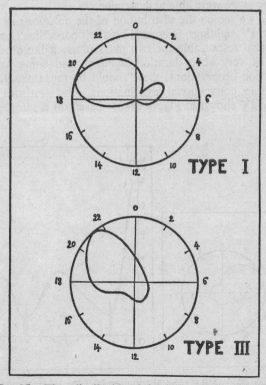

Fig. 25.—Time distribution of sightings of Types I and III.

about 6 A.M. This is especially interesting in contrast with the distribution of Type III sightings.

4. Type IV sightings occur most often during the day, although the maximum is toward sunset.

5. The Type II phenomena, which represent a small number of reports, are studied in detail in the next chapter and have no bearing here because of their higher "noise" level arising from misinterpretations of balloons, aircraft, and astronomical phenomena. The distributions of cases of Types I and III are based on samples of several hundred data each.

6. The distributions are the same in every country, as far as we were able to determine.

As we see on the distribution of the *durations* of the Type IV sightings (Figure 26), the "borderline" cases are also responsible for two maximums: a large number of very short-duration sightings and some long-duration observations; these should be reexamined for possible conventional explanations. The statistics of Type IV shown in Figure 26 are based on a sample of

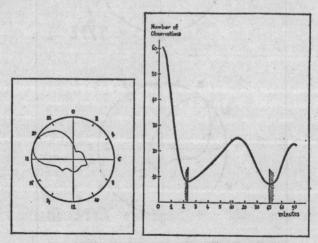

FIG. 26.—(left) Time distribution of Type IV sightings; (right) duration of Type IV sightings.

six hundred cases. Sixty per cent of them were observed between 5 P.M. and 11 P.M. A considerable proportion show a duration of several minutes, some even from ten minutes to half an hour. Obviously we cannot say much about the short-duration cases, except that further investigation should be made to see whether they could be cases of extreme meteors. On the other hand, some of the cases of very long duration, such as the Washington incident of 1952, are very difficult to discuss. Our data were not sufficient to warrant a comparative study of the same distributions for the various waves. If there is any variation, it is certainly not obvious. At any rate, this study did reveal that the manifestations of the UFO phenomenon were of considerable duration, often in excess of five minutes and commonly of fifteen or twenty minutes. This is ample time for the witnesses to make a good observation, once the surprise of the first moments has been overcome.

THE "MARTIAN" IN THE TWILIGHT

Fatigue may account for errors of judgment and misinterpretations in reports of Type I sightings made during their peak period, from dusk to dawn. Reports in which "beings" are described as emerging from the craft and remaining outside for some time present greater complications.

The official investigators frequently reject these accounts without examining them at all. Ruppelt himself said: "Next to the 'Insufficient Data' file was a file marked 'C.P.' This meant crackpot. Into this file went all reports from people who had . . . inspected flying saucers that had landed in the United States . . ." (2). This is a truly enormous admission. If this "C.P." file had not been invented in order to eliminate *a priori* peculiar reports, those reports could have been studied by the psychologists; if they were simply fantasies, the question of the landings would have been resolved by now.

This is an important question, because the mythomaniacal tendency is not so widespread as some would have us believe; it consists of a well-known pattern of psychological characteristics easily detected by the specialist. We cannot dispose of the sightings made by pilots, customs officers, and railroad engineers, people who are not prone to go berserk, by saying that they have "merely" had hallucinations or invented a science-fiction story. The security of our society requires more consideration of the question than that.

Since we do not refuse to study the UFO as an aerial object, we cannot logically refuse to study it when it is reported to have landed. Furthermore, if we do not rule out the possibility of these objects' being controlled devices, there is no reason for not granting them —within this hypothesis—the capability to approach the surface of the earth, to settle on it, and for their "occupants" to come out of their machines. But in this domain the physicist should advance no hypothesis before the psychologist has analyzed the reports and given his conclusions, and before some preliminary classification has been made on the body of reports.

The psychologist finds in these descriptions an admirable subject of study. Not only do the witnesses declare that they have seen the "beings," their sincerity is, in many of the cases, quite obvious. In a minority of the cases, which have come to be known as the "contactee" stories, we find the too-familiar pattern of the witnesses who have been "taken for a ride" aboard a "flying saucer" and have been told of the purpose of the UFO's. Generally in reports of this type the "occupants" are described as benevolent beings (our "space brothers") come to save us from atomic destruction. Such accounts should be definitely separated from reports made by psychologically stable and genuinely puzzled citizens. What the witnesses of this latter group describe is very different from the "space brother" image.

The typical "visitor" of these reports is a man of small stature, dressed in shiny clothing or in an ordinary one-piece suit. The suit may hide his head; if the face is visible, it is generally described as larger than the human head, with large, protruding eyes. Some of the reports insist that the dwarfs have hair on their faces, and sometimes all over their bodies, either their own or dark fur clothing.

In all these reports, the most interesting person—until some evidence is obtained that the "visitors" do exist—is the eyewitness himself. An evaluation of those cases where the witness has given clear signs of sincerity, indeed frequently of extreme terror, and the creation of an official investigation commission empowered to pursue such investigations would be the logical tools with which to work here.

THE PATTERN BEHIND THE LANDINGS

How would such a commission go about studying the landings? A complete analysis of the Type I sightings would be directed to the following four groups of questions:

1. Who makes reports of landing? What are the ages and professions of the witnesses?

2. Under what conditions are the observations made? How far from the witnesses do the "objects" land? At what time of the day and in what terrain do the landings take place? How long do the "objects" remain on the ground? How do they disappear?

3. Do the witnesses describe the "occupants" of the "craft"? If so, in what terms? Are their descriptions consistent?

4. What are the main characteristics of the "craft" as deduced from the reports?

Contrary to what has sometimes been said by the American enthusiasts, who like to think they see in the development of UFO activity the unfolding of a "master plan," with the landings a characteristic of the recent period, such incidents have been present in all phases of the phenomenon. Charles Fort mentions a few. An American researcher, Orvil Hartle, has published several accounts of early twentieth-century landings of a remarkable character. Similar cases were noted during the 1946 Scandinavian wave and the first clear descriptions of "little men" were made in 1947. Hanlon, in his excellent analysis of the 1897 wave in the United States, came across a surprising number of Type I reports that had escaped the attention of all other researchers, yet were readily available in the daily newspaper collections. Some of the incidents he discovered describe the "occupants" of the craft as beings of small stature.

Reports of landings were not rare during the "American Period" of 1947–52, but, as we have seen, Ruppelt's team conscientiously eliminated them. It was only when careful and organized civilian researchers such as Leonard Stringfield and Carol Lorenzen started to investigate the American landing cases and to publish their findings that the proper light was cast on the subject.

In the meantime, however, something of the greatest significance had happened in Europe. The 1954 wave, which reached its peak there, produced thousands of reports, and among them a large number of Type I cases. All reports circulated freely. Valuable details, first-hand documents, and personal interviews were promptly centralized by able researchers. Italy, Spain, Northern Africa, and Germany also produced a wealth of data.

The problem of the landings has since gained widespread interest, but the 1954 reports are the nucleus of any general study. In this preliminary investigation we have chosen to limit our analysis to two hundred of the most significant cases of that year, excluding of course all recognized hoaxes, misidentifications of common objects, "contactee" claims, etc. These two hundred cases represent about one-fourth of our present file on landings.*

The first impression on viewing these cases is one of shock and disbelief; it does not seem possible to introduce any semblance of order in events so far out of the ordinary. Two comments, however, will open an avenue of discussion.

1. The main series of the 1954 landings started with a clear, sudden burst of activity in September and tended to subside early in November. The center of this activity shifted geographically during the second part of October, with the most remarkable reports from Italy and South America rather than France. This is the *first hint* that this activity, strange as it may appear, may be linked to some physical or psychological reality that can be studied with profit. At the same time, the fact that the majority of the reports came from France indicates the possibility that sightings were made with equal density in other countries but did not receive equal attention.

2. The obvious explanation that comes to mind is that the cause of the landing reports, the "stimulus," is indeed real: it is psychological in nature; in other words, all the witnesses were the victims of their imagination. This theory was formally presented by Heuyer in a celebrated communication to the French Academy of Medicine; it has been tacitly accepted by the scientific community as a whole and forms the basis of the official attitude on the subject: people are the victims of a "flying saucer psychosis"; the stories they read in the newspapers have a strong effect on their imagination; under this influence, feeble-minded individuals start generating rumors that spread from building to building and from block to block; such rumors, of course, are typical of the tensions of modern society, and they culminate in the vision of the "flying saucers" and their operators on the ground.

---

* *See* the special issue on "landings" of the *Flying Saucer Review* (October, 1966) for a complete description of these two hundred cases.

That this theory concerning the Type I reports has gained acceptance even in the ranks of the "Ufologists" is evidenced by the failure of most American groups to take seriously the researches made by Michel and by other foreign researchers ten years ago, and by the fact that comments on this category of events are conspicuous by their absence in the UFO literature in the English language. It is quite remarkable to see how Keyhoe and some of his followers have consistently avoided the issue while Menzel and most scientific skeptics constantly point to the reports of landings as the critical area of any serious discussion of the UFO phenomenon.

We intend to prove that the Heuyer theory is false by showing that there *is* order in the reports of landings and that what seems to be an unorganized mass of rumors is in reality correlated very strongly with phenomena of a physical, rather than psychological, nature. We shall first show negative correlations with all the factors upon which the psychological theory could be based. Then we shall reconsider the laws of the phenomenon, observing their coherence, their consistency with the hypothesis that the great majority of the reported incidents are real. This conclusion will open the way to some interesting speculations that, in turn, should help to eliminate some of the obscurities that have surrounded the UFO mystery for nearly twenty years.

The first negative law: population density

The "flying saucer psychosis," as described by Heuyer, would obey very strict rules. Psychoses are *not* erratic, random phenomena; they arise and become observable only in those areas where conditions are favorable to their development. In the fall of 1954, the conditions for such a craze would have been found in Paris, where rumors circulate very fast and are easily amplified, where political and social conditions were in a poor state (the "Baranes scandal" was raging), and where there was a public for science-fiction ideas. To a lesser degree, the crowded areas of Marseilles, Bordeaux, and Lille and the heavily industrialized regins of the east would have been vast reservoirs of potential "Heuyeritis" victims.

We have plotted on Figure 27 all the unexplained French landings of 1954. Not only is there no heavy concentration around Paris, the *six departments* of Seine, Seine-et-Oise, Seine-et-Marne, Marne, Meuse, Loiret and Loir-et-Cher, which should have provided the greatest contribution of psychotic elements, since

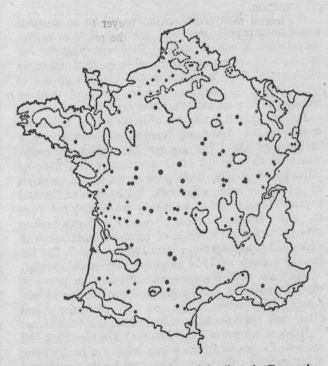

FIG. 27.—Unexplained reports of landings in France in 1954; dotted lines indicate areas with a population density above sixty per square kilometer.

they include nearly one-third of the total French population, *did not contribute a single report!* The other densely populated regions (with the single exception of the Lille area) were similarly "avoided" by the phenomenon, in direct contradiction with Heuyer's theory. This allows us to state our first law:

The geographic repartition of the landing sites in 1954 is inversely correlated with population density.

The second negative law: witness reliability

A typical "Heuyeritis" victim would be an unstable single or unhappily married clerk with little or no responsibility, a college student filled with youthful enthusiasm, or some spiritualist soul in quest of unearthly experiences. Such a person would perhaps go out at night *hoping* to see the "saucers"; wishful thinking would thus be responsible for many reports.

Indeed, this is what we observe among the noisy crowd of the American "contactees" and among a majority of the UFO groups that spring up everywhere as soon as the UFO question regains national publicity. Typically, these persons go to the outskirts of the city or town, after dark, led by strange "mental impulses" and they find what they are looking for: contact with beings from other planets. They hurry back to town to organize a series of lectures, complete with slides and tape recordings from Jupiter Area 7. Did the landing reports of 1954 originate from such sources?

They did not. We have here the data to prove it; the reports in the local press gave the number of witnesses, their names, addresses, and professions, and often their ages. Statistics compiled on this basis show:

1. Most witnesses (71 per cent) are identified and are well known where they live. Most are family men; observations by the whole family, or by the family and its neighbors, are not rare.

2. The report from the main witness, who describes

an object on the ground, is confirmed by independent witnesses, i.e., persons who did not see the first witness and did not know of his observation, in eighteen cases. In four cases, objects that remained on the ground were seen by different persons at intervals of from ten to twenty minutes. In most cases, the police were immediately called and took statements from the witnesses within an hour of the sighting.

3. In practically all cases, the site of the observation was quite familiar to the witness. In twenty-two cases the machine landed literally in his backyard or in the immediate vicinity of his house or property (field, pasture). In no fewer than seventy-five cases it landed directly on the road or in the immediate vicinity of the road the witness used to go to and from work. In fifteen cases it landed where the witnesses (firemen, nightwatchmen, military personnel) were working.

4. In forty-three cases the witnesses were at work when they saw the object for the first time. In nine cases they were on their way to work. In twenty-one cases they were returning from work. In twelve cases the witnesses were guards, firemen, or policemen *on duty*.

5. Reports are made equally often by persons of both sexes. There is no abnormal frequency of certain age groups. Reports made by children do not differ significantly from reports made by men or women, except in wording, as could be expected.

6. In twenty-one cases the main witness showed signs of extreme terror and in four cases he fainted either during the experience or immediately afterward. In six cases he had to receive medical attention. The reaction of animals is also one of panic in many cases.

7. Out of a minimum of 624 persons connected with the two hundred landings, *only 98 (15 per cent)* were alone when they observed the object. In terms of sightings, less than half of the observations (exactly 49 per cent) had only one witness; this is not surprising when we take into account the time of the observations and their locations in rural areas. In thirteen

cases there were more than 10 witnesses. In one case a crowd of 150 people reported seeing the craft and its operators.

These statistics are an eloquent support for the reality of the reported phenomena. They can be summarized as our second law:

In the 1954 landings, the population of witnesses was typically rural, with a natural proportion of men, women and children. Most witnesses held steady jobs, often positions of social responsibility, and observed an unusual phenomenon while engaged in their usual occupation and in their usual environment.

This law is further illustrated by the diagram of Figure 28, where we have plotted the number of witnesses versus the *distance* of the object, i.e., the minimum distance between the main witness and the reported object. Both of these figures are known in sixty-six cases. The filled circles on Figure 28 represent observations with reported physiological effects. It is interesting to observe that the dots are scattered through the diagram with no special pattern; very close sightings (where the witnesses said they were close enough to have touched the object) are not necessarily "one-witness" cases. The distribution reinforces our conclusion that the "stimulus" is not psychological.

The positive laws

We have now established that Heuyer has not satisfactorily explained the observations. But neither have we.

The statement that the phenomena were caused by "some sort of spaceship" or by "extraterrestrial intelligence" is too easy a way out. If by spaceship is meant a machine, unless it is the product of an intelligence totally foreign to mankind it must have been engineered according to precise principles of design. If

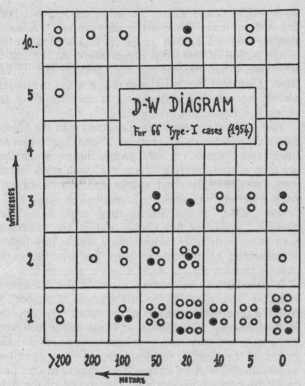

Fig. 28.—Number of witnesses versus the distance of the object in sixty-six Type I cases of 1954.

this is so, it must be possible to test the objectivity of the phenomenon by reference to the reports themselves; in other words, there must exist, in spite of differences in wording, certain invariants in the characteristics of the craft that could not have been invented by the witness and that can be retrieved analytically.

As noted in an American compilation *(The UFO Evidence),* all the reported objects present a symmetry of revolution and sometimes produce strong electromagnetic effects; but this is certainly not enough. Even in the 1954 cases, where the witnesses had not been exposed to many descriptions of "saucers," Arnold's sighting was well known, and there had been some talk of the notion of flying disks from Mars. At the end of the wave, it had become the most popular idea in Europe. Therefore, neither the shape, nor the maneuverability, nor physical disturbance in the vicinity of the object is a dependable invariant.

The luminous phenomena connected with the objects are of more interest. The reported "craft" are observed under two "phases": a *dark phase*, during which they are seen as dull, metallic "machines" with solid bodies, sometimes emitting short sparks and sometimes supported by legs and showing luminous openings; and a *bright phase*, during which they look like "fiery spheres," globes of fire whose centers are sometimes seen as transparent envelopes inside which dark figures are observed. Many witnesses were first attracted to the objects because they thought a house was on fire.

It is extremely interesting to study the *transitions* from the dark phase to the bright phase in connection with the reported maneuvers of the "craft" and hypotheses concerning its technology. These are indeed very consistent, and they lead to several strange results: the inside of the "craft," for instance, is often described as illuminated with an intense light, similar to that produced by burning magnesium. The source of the light is so powerful that it lights up the countryside over an area of several kilometers sometimes. Not only is there nothing in our technology that can duplicate this performance in a small volume and in perfect silence, the conditions inside such a "machine" would be quite intolerable to a human being.

The strongest invariant is the diameter of the "machine" itself. These estimates should be reliable because the objects are seen on or very close to the ground, against a familiar background of buildings and trees. It is also much easier to estimate distance from an object near the ground than from one in the sky. Do reports that give both an estimate of the "craft's" di-

ameter and also its distance from the witnesses give us
a coherent picture ?

They do, and it is a most remarkable one. On Figure
29 we have plotted these reports along with the average
of each class. We find that the estimated diameter of
the "craft" is a constant for all witnesses whose closest
approach was between five meters and one hundred
meters. Witnesses who came very close to the "craft"

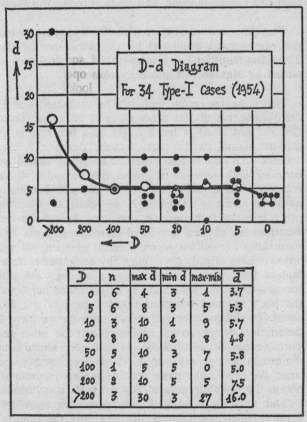

D	n	max d	min d	max-min	d̄
0	6	4	3	1	3.7
5	6	8	3	5	5.3
10	3	10	1	9	5.7
20	8	10	2	8	4.8
50	5	10	3	7	5.8
100	1	5	5	0	5.0
200	2	10	5	5	7.5
>200	3	30	3	27	16.0

FIG. 29.—Estimates of the diameter of the "machine"
versus distance of the witnesses, with the average for
each class.

give a slightly smaller estimate; those who were far from it give a much larger one. The latter phenomenon is familiar to psychologists and to astronomers: it is called the "moon illusion," because the rising moon gives a much exaggerated apparent diameter. But if the objects in question were not real, physical objects, our diagram would not show this "moon illusion"! If the witnesses were liars, or the victims of a delusion, no such effect would appear. This leads us to our third law:

The data are consistent with the hypothesis that the phenomena reported by the witnesses of the 1954 landings had a symmetry of revolution and an actual diameter of about five meters.

This is an important finding. The estimated size of the objects that display other types of behavior (those that did not land) is much larger than five meters. Is this intentional on the part of their "designer"? Why are not such objects also observed in flight? Should we consider with renewed attention the accounts where the "craft" were said to "vanish" in mid-air? Too many questions remain unanswered; we need to discover other laws, or technological principles, before we can ascertain the physical nature of these phenomena. *But these laws are within reach.* Certain elements of the answers have already been found, by computer correlation of the reported characteristics; but they are still too new and too fragmentary to be published here, and the body of good observations of Type I is still too small. In eighty cases (of 1954) only do we have a description of the arrival of the object; the other reports on our list involve objects that were already on the ground and generally took off when witnesses came near. We need many more detailed reports in order to obtain the scientific data to support such conclusions.

This scientific investigation appears even more imperative when we discover that not only the objects' dimensions but other parameters of the phenomenon follow well-defined rules. We have already seen, early in this chapter, the *law of the times,* where we observed that only a few of the landings took place during the day. It would be interesting to make the same study on a larger sample of data, to determine whether or not the boundaries of this activity period follow the sunset and sunrise.

Another pattern evident from Figure 27 is the distribution of the landing sites. There is, as we have seen, a large avoidance area, which includes six departments in a diagonal band from Belgium to the Atlantic. North of that zone, there is an area of fairly uniform density along the English Channel from Le Havre to Boulogne, extending about 200 kilometers into the interior. There is also a very loose distribution of sightings in the south. The great majority of the landing sites are situated within a diagonal band about 250 kilometers wide; no less than eighty landings, 51 per cent of the 1954 French landings, took place in that band during the last three months of that year. This observation cannot be correlated with any obvious regional characteristic: the band in question stretches from busy Alsace-Lorraine, where most of the sightings were in dense woods, to the quiet valley of the Loire River. It includes wild, sometimes desolate areas of Vendee and the central plateaus; oddly enough, the density of landings is higher in those hard-to-reach spots, where people have little or no interest in current events and where life is traditionally slow. Certainly, nothing could be more out of place than a science-fiction drama in a spot as removed from modern civilization as the Millevaches plateau. This is the area of France where some of the toughest groups of the Resistance were entrenched during World War II; one of the officials who investigated the landings in that area commented that the UFO's seemed to follow a pattern of activity quite similar to that of the *Maquisards,* staying in the densest woods and the wildest areas.

The clusters

Another finding noticeable on the map is that the landings tend to occur in "clusters": two, three, or four observations are made by different people at different times within a small, well-defined area a few kilometers wide. Since this map has been plotted, Fuller's analysis of the Exeter observations in New Hampshire has shown that a similar pattern existed in the United States.

We will report here on two clusters of special interest: the Mezieres cluster and the Saint Quirin cluster.* Of the three observations near Mezieres, none has ever been reported in a national newspaper or a specialized publication. Two come from obscure local papers; the third one is a police report. They were unknown to Michel and Carrouges when they wrote their books. They have received no publicity. The sightings took place on October 4, 16, and 27—roughly twelve days apart. The first case was reported by a child, who said he saw an object "shaped like a tent" and an unknown individual near it. In the second case, a woman fainted as she saw an object land within thirty meters of her. In the third case, policemen in the immediate vicinity of the two other sightings saw a flying object that took off at dawn.

The same pattern is observed in the dense woods of Alsace, near Saint Quirin, Schirmeck, and Moussey: six days after the observation by a Mr. Schoubrenner (who was driving in the area when he saw a luminous object on the highway, felt a sensation of heat, and was overcome by a sort of paralysis when his car stalled about twenty yards away from the object) a tractor was stopped in the same manner as an object flew over it at low altitude. The next day a boy and a

* A special investigation of this point is in progress within the framework of a complete study of the distribution of the landing sites over the French territory.

school director saw a "craft" on the ground; it left marks forming a triangle.

This pattern of "multiple samplings" is observed in many other cases—in the northern regions, in Brittany, and near Toulouse and Perpignan, but mainly inside the diagonal band indicated earlier.

The "operators"

Out of the 200 landings considered here, 156 took place in France; 133 of them involved objects that actually stopped in flight. Of these, 118 landed (while others remained at very low altitude, sometimes flying slowly on) and were observed in that situation for durations ranging from seconds to hours. Of these 118 cases, 42 involved descriptions of the "pilots" of the "craft," the "operators."

In 5 cases, they were described inside the craft; this leaves 37 cases where operators were seen outside the object, of which 23 give detailed descriptions. On a worldwide scale, we find 18 similarly detailed reports of "entities."

The descriptions always involve creatures near-human in appearance; sometimes they are absolutely human. In ten cases the "operators" were of average or above-average height, with Caucasian features; in one report a human "operator" was seen in the company of two "humanoids." The "humans" are always "European," with a few variations; they wear coveralls, never respiratory devices or diving suits.

To many these descriptions constitute a setback to the theory of the extraterrestrial origin of UFO's as it is usually stated. Fictional beings from other planets are seldom of human form; when H. G. Wells or Brian Adliss creates a "Martian," it is not humanoid. The human body, biology teaches, is typical of this planet; the earth's gravity, the pressure and chemical composition of its atmosphere, and its distance from the sun all go to make up the form of life found here.

Some of the humanoids as well as the human operators are described as air-breathing creatures. In at least eight instances dwarfs whose faces and bodies were covered with abundant hair have been described. Diving suits are occasionally mentioned, but they are reserved to the humanoids, whose suits are compared to armor, glowing suits, or shiny coveralls:

It was a small creature, with a normal human face, from 1 meter to 1.20 meters tall; he was wearing a transparent suit that covered him completely: he reminded me of a child wrapped in a cellophane bag.

A fascinating aspect of the study of these phenomena is that no theory of their origin and nature can be constructed without reference to theories of the origin of man and the nature of life. It would be presumptuous to claim that we have enough data to add to the body of existing knowledge on these subjects. *But the facts must be recorded*. They may be only interesting bits of folklore—or they may involve much more. At least we can say this much: the witnesses are not insane people. They are perfectly normal, simple men and women who did not *choose* to play a role in this mystery. They are not inclined to prophecy, and they return to anonymity after telling their stories. Should we take this silence as a proof of delusion, or as a sign that they have closed their minds to the experience? The study of an actual report and the circumstances that surrounded the sighting may help to explain these actions.

THE LANDING AT PREMANON

We have seen that landings seem to be reported more often in areas far from population centers, in quiet surroundings. In this respect, the landing at Premanon on September 27, 1954, is typical. Premanon is a tiny French village perched in the magnificent mountains of the Jura, very close to the Swiss border. All the witnesses were children. The incident—one of the first landings of the wave, called by Michel "perhaps the most interesting of the entire autumn"—took place on a rainy night at the farm of the Romand family, on a desolate area far from the center of the village.

At eight o'clock, twelve-year-old Raymond Romand decided to go out for a walk. Just as he closed the door, he froze on the spot: in the yard of the farm was a strange object, vaguely shining, that looked like a vertical aluminum box: "It was as tall as a door, and shiny, like a wardrobe with a mirror."

This "object"—or "entity"—approached the boy and gently touched him. The thing was cold; terrified, Raymond fell on the ground. He tried to call for help but could not. He managed to get up on his feet, but in spite of his fear decided not to go back inside the house; he was more afraid of his parents than he was of the "thing"; he would be unable to hide his excitement and would surely be accused of lying if he told of "seeing a ghost." Besides, he was now more fascinated than terrified by his adventure.

At that point, Raymond was no longer alone. His nine-year-old sister, Janine, and the two smaller children had followed Raymond outside. Janine saw the "entity" and managed to hide in the barn. Encouraged by their presence, Raymond picked up stones and started to throw them at the "ghost." One of the stones hit something metallic as the thing walked away. Leaving the yard of the farm, it went to a luminous, reddish object in a pasture downhill, and this "ball of fire" soon took off. The next day the police investigators from Saint Claude and from Les Rousses found four triangular holes in a heavily flattened area at that spot. In addition a pole fence had been grazed and the bark of a pine tree was scorched five feet above the ground. Charles Garreau reports that over the flattened area, which was twelve feet in diameter, the grass was flattened counterclockwise in the pattern of a whirlwind, and meadow flowers looked as if they had been put through a press. The edge of the circle was clearly defined, and the four holes were arranged in a square.

After the departure of the "ghost," the children soon realized that they would be much better off if they did not talk about what they had seen; they remained silent throughout the evening and the night. But the next day, Raymond told the story to another boy at school; the rumor spread and reached the young teacher, Miss Huguette Genillon, who called the police.

Captain Prustel, from Saint Claude, conducted the investigation himself. Thoroughly familiar with the region and its people, he was not surprised at the reaction of the children; he interviewed them separately and at length, and he had them reenact the whole scene.

Throughout this investigation, Mrs. Romand displayed a very strange attitude. She seemed deeply shocked by the whole affair and reluctant to let the interview take place. She refused to believe that Raymond might have seen something. A very pious, devout woman, she stated plainly that "flying saucers" and "Martians" could not exist and that she would rather believe that an evil spirit, or the Devil himself, was prompting her son to lie. God has created us, she said; beyond God and his creatures, no live being exists, and particularly no "Martians." A newspaper reporter who went to Premanon and spoke to the woman remarked that her home was probably one of the very few places in France where the subject of "flying saucers" had never been discussed at the dinner table. The children themselves never used the term "saucer" or "Martian." They said and repeated that they had seen a "ghost." The idea of a "flying saucer" was started by the adults in Premanon.

This was the beginning of an incredible period in the life of the little village. Mrs. Romand wanted to force her son to admit he had been lying, that he had seen no "Martian." To her it was a question of faith, and she also felt that the good reputation of her farm was at stake. As Raymond did not change his story, he was punished and confined to the house. He still maintained that he had seen it. The mother was further vexed because the child had not confided in her, for it was now common knowledge that the young school teacher had first heard the story. Sympathies were split between the two camps, and soon the "Martian" had become an ideological issue in this little mountain community.

We should do well to consider this reaction among the population of Premanon with care. It gives the UFO phenomenon its true dimension as a sociological fact. The cause of the sightings can be discussed according to physics, but their most important consequences are psychological and social. Whatever its physical nature, the phenomenon has made us aware of the limitations of our philosophies, of the obscurities in our beliefs, of the weakness of our knowledge. It has generated conflicts and produced changes in our awareness of the world about us that are not easy to weigh or even to perceive, although we are all affected.

The Premanon incident has not been the occasion of great debates. No grave philosopher has stopped to ponder the story. As for the professional scientists, to brush away such accounts with a smile is for them one of the tests of fashion. This silence in high places should disturb us greatly.

10

THE TECHNOLOGICAL PROBLEM

CLOUD-CIGARS

WE HAVE NOW GAINED SOME INSIGHT into the conditions of the observations, their time of occurrence and their duration; we have studied reports of landings; and we have made certain remarks concerning the witnesses. All this has led us to retain the hypothesis that the objects have material reality as a potentially significant one. Now the time has come to consider the other types of sightings and to examine their characteristics in the light of this hypothesis.

Among the four main types of reports we have defined, the landings are not the only instance of a clearcut choice between extreme theories; the nature of the phenomenon is equally well illustrated by Type II sightings, or "cloud-cigars." The treatment given these sightings in the French publications (5, 26) has, it is true, discouraged American specialists from studying them. They thought that if cases of such lengthy duration, and with such clearly defined features, were really linked with the "flying saucers," then the problem would indeed be very different. But the American files give no example at all of this type of object, suggesting that these reports must be the result of the fantastic rumor generated by the 1954 wave and must be regarded as exaggerations or delusions.

Because we were aware of these objections, and of the complete absence of Type II reports in the publications of the amateur groups on this side of the Atlantic, we reexamined their data and those of the U.S. Air Force with considerable care; this study not only led to the discovery of numerous Type II cases in the United States, it showed them to be as clearly defined as the European sightings. Why then have these reports escaped the attention of both official and private investigators? In our opinion, the problem is again one of method. A selection effect has caused these rare but highly significant facts to pass unnoticed. The official files, as we have seen, have never been studied as a whole. Project Blue Book has never thought of its files as a body of data susceptible to classification, to global analysis, but as a collection of accounts to be explained one by one. The American amateurs start from opposite principles but their method is exactly the same: they regard their files as a collection of valuable occasions of amazement. No one has considered the lists of observations as an astronomer would consider a catalogue of stars, for instance; these "Ufologists" see their data much as chemists thought of the elements before the discovery of the periodic table: as an infinite combination of facts without organization and definite classes.

In the military files, the sightings are listed by names of witnesses and degree of "explanation." In the private files, the profession of the witness, his "public relations" value, seems to come before anything else. If a plumber observes an object approaching at a low altitude from the south and a jet pilot reports a similar object landing two miles north of the plumber's position ten minutes later, the military and the amateurs file two separate reports and place them in different cabinets; then they try to find patterns.

In the air force's files, most of the Type II phenomena we found bore the note "insufficient information." This meant that they had been swamped, dispersed within a statistical category that grouped together hundreds of vague meteors, dubious balloons, abortive hoaxes, and possible birds. This sort of system is anything but a classification. In the work published by NICAP, which has made a laudable effort to organize the data, there is one clear Type II case (observation by Frank Halstead on November 1, 1955), but it is not identified as such and appears under a paragraph entitled "Observations by Astronomers" in the section "Scientists and Engineers." No reference is made to the pattern of UFO generation observed elsewhere. As for the remaining groups, they are content with ecstatic references to "mother-ships." Only a coherent system of classification can reject the rumor, put the observations in order and bring the descriptions down to categories.

When this is done, the Type II cases command attention as much as the landings do. These cases are fairly rare, but their features are so clear-cut that they embody the UFO phenomenon in the fullest sense. These characteristic features are as follows:

Duration of sighting

The object reported in a Type II case has a slow and sometimes erratic movement; its altitude is a few miles. The duration is always at least several minutes (even for the Type II-A cases) and commonly in excess of ten minutes. This rules out most common misinterpretations. Sightings lasting about ten minutes, involving an "object" in the sky at a moderate altitude either moving slowly or stationary, with occasional sudden and brief accelerations, are typical of the Type II reports.

Atmospheric turbulence

Generally the main object described by the witnesses

is associated with a sharply defined cloud formation; often the attention of the witnesses, is first attracted by a "strange, elongated cloud," a "cigar-shaped cloud formation," etc. Other reports mention that "there was only one cloud in the sky, and its peculiar shape attracted my attention," or state that "a funny cloud flying against the wind" was seen. These indications lead to the idea that thermodynamic conditions in the vicinity of UFO phenomena are affected. In one case a radar return was obtained from a UFO phenomenon of this type, indicating some activity, not necessarily a material object, inside the cloud. Sometimes the disturbance of the cloud, the "boiling motion," can be observed visually. In the Homer, New York, case, which lasted forty-five minutes, we recall that the witnesses declared that they observed this "boiling motion" with binoculars and were shocked to see "wisps of smoke actually streaming out" (*see* Chapter 2, page 43).

Shape, luminosity, color

The shape of the object is often that of a cigar, sometimes—in the clearest cases—in a vertical position. Descriptions of "cylinders," "tubes," "ovoids" or "cloud-spheres" are also recorded. These phenomena are often luminous of themselves, not from reflected light. In several instances the "vertical cylinder" was compared to a "white rod" when seen with the naked eye, a "neon tube" when seen with binoculars. The terms "pencil" or "tube" are often used in the descriptions.

Generation of secondary phenomena

Type II-B cases are those that present the process of generation. Objects smaller and more sharply defined than the main "cloud" are seen emerging from it. Their number varies from one to a dozen. They may be said to "float away" from the first object or to fall freely from the base of the "cylinder," cease their vertical fall after a few seconds, and then set off at great speed. In some cases the witness describes their return to the main object.

It is not easy to determine how much imagination enters into these descriptions. However, the difficulty we had in extracting these cases from the files leads us to think that the likelihood of finding witnesses already aware of these features before their own sightings is extremely remote. Moveover, there is an abundance of details unlikely to be found in an imaginary account: the peculiar fluorescence, very different from the usual description of the "saucers"; the slow erratic motion; the duration of the sighting; the emission of smaller objects. All these features reappear in descriptions made all over the world. The UFO periodicals do not usually mention these sightings, and when they do, they distort them so badly that it is necessary to go back to the basic documents and statements in order to recognize their true character. Accordingly, pure invention seems to be ruled out by this remarkable similarity in the accounts.

Some reports (Oloron, Gaillac, Lemps, etc.) represent the "vertical cigars" as moving along in the midst of enormous formations of flying objects. These sightings are most impressive. The quality and the number of the witnesses who have vouched for the reality of the phenomena are other important features of Type II cases and help to rule out the idea of hoax. The luminosity and size of the formations make them visible over a considerable area, and the number of witnesses is sometimes very great. In one of the French cases, the object was seen by hundreds of people in several adjacent villages and throughout the countryside. The object was said to appear much larger than an aircraft carrier, and the reports, couched in simple terms, convey a feeling of awe and formidable might such as few phenomena of the universe can afford. We are not dealing here with the fugitive and fleeting vision of a "flying saucer" but with some of the most fantastic sights man has ever beheld. As such, they certainly deserve serious study.

Examples

In Chapter 7 we reviewed several instances of Type II cases. The more recent European accounts, such as the Vernon sighting and the other cases of 1954, have been described in detail elsewhere, as have the American reports of the last few years. A previously unpublished report is that of Reseda, California, at 10:35 P.M. on March 28, 1957. It lasted about four minutes. The witness described an object shaped like a cigar, stationary, of an apparent diameter comparable to that of a DC-6 aircraft at a distance of 1,000 or 1,500 feet. The object was surrounded by a bright elliptical light about five times less brilliant than the central object. The minor axis of this ellipse was about half, and its major axis three times, the length of the object. Although the ratios of brightness were not assessed precisely by the observer, his description of the luminosity is interesting. Placed in correlation with the other features of this account, it certainly indicates a phenomenon of Type II-A.

Similar sightings had been reported much earlier in the United States, even before the 1952 wave: on April 19, 1950, "a vertical luminous tube, of the color of a red-hot iron," was described in Dallas, Texas.

A series of five eyewitness accounts from the eastern United States on August 19, 1959, affords a clear basis for comparison with the European cases.

The first of these reports came from a radar station that recorded seven unidentified echoes at 3:37 P.M. at the latitude of Washington, eighty miles off the Atlantic coastline. These echoes corresponded to objects estimated as two or three times larger than a C-124 aircraft, but such a figure cannot be a reliable one. The estimated speeds, between three thousand and eight thousand miles per hour, are more interesting. Each of these observations lasted about one minute, and on the last occasion two blips with identical characteristics appeared simultaneously on the screen. In the absence of ground or air-visual contact or a check by another radar station, this report cannot carry much weight. It is simply one more instance of an unidentified series of blips on radar, an occurrence, *contrary to what the public is told,* with which operators of military radar are quite familiar.

At 6:55 P.M., six miles west of Mitchell Air Force Base on Long Island, New York, a Mrs. N. described the passage of a vertical luminous red object, moving fast and at a high altitude, following a straight-line course toward the southeast.

The third sighting took place on the north side of Trenton, New Jersey, at 7:45 P.M. The witness was a Mr. S., who found his attention drawn by the unusual brightness of an object slightly above the horizon in the southeast. He described this object as an elongated, vertical cigar, very bright, surrounded by a bluish-green area, and orange in the center. During the first twenty-five minutes of the observation, it made eight or ten apparent right-angle turns. This point was explicitly stated by the witness in his reply to a request for information sent by the investigators. He interrupted his observation only once, after watching continuously for twenty-five minutes, in order to make a telephone call. The main object was thereafter surrounded by five shining objects. They all appeared to regroup before disappearing in the northeast.

The night was clear and cloudless. The moon was full and there was good visibility. The sighting lasted fifty minutes in all, and the object's direction of departure shows that the witness cannot have misinterpreted the moon or the common atmospheric phenomenon known as a "moondog." No unidentified radar echo was reported. All investigations regarding balloon launchings or training operations, refueling missions, etc. that might have provided a basis for the identification of the objects proved negative. The witness was a former mechanic on B-24 aircraft and had served in the second experimental electronic squadron.

The same day, at 8:30 P.M., the pilot and copilot on United Airlines Flight 333, en route to Des Moines, Iowa, saw over Elburn, Illinois, a series of three or four bright lights compared to car headlights seen from a distance of one city block. This report also mentioned that the moon was bright and many stars were visible. The objects were white with sharp outlines, about the size of a pea at arm's length. They were first seen in the west-northwest, and vanished toward the north-northwest.

Still later (*see* Figure 30), at 9:10 P.M., at Shelton,

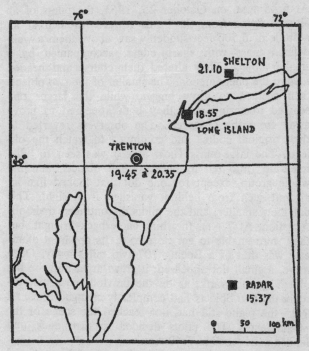

FIG. 30.—The observations of August 19, 1959, excluding the Elburn, Illinois, sighting.

Connecticut, an object that resembled a first magnitude star, but followed a spiral trajectory, was seen. The object passed overhead and disappeared in three minutes.

These occurrences may not have been connected, but Type II sightings are generally centers of activity on a regional scale, as Michel has demonstrated. Such concentrations of sightings in one specific area during a period unmarked by great activity and widespread reports in the press deserve serious study.

Some Type II phenomena are very difficult to interpret, and the search for a conventional explanation could certainly be conducted more actively than it now is. The following case pertains to this category. At 6:45 P.M. on October 25, 1963, the pilots of an aircraft flying from St. Louis toward Mitchell at an altitude of 6,500 feet suddenly saw above them a well-defined mass with sharp edges, accompanied by a smaller object. They altered their course and headed toward the phenomenon. The smaller of the two objects then seemed to grow bigger, while the larger one seemed to shrink, and they both appeared to move away from the observers. The observers reverted to their original course and continued to watch the objects. The large mass (now alone) was seen to "disintegrate" into ten to twenty small objects, and the whole group, except for one dot that looked like an aircraft seen from behind, vanished from sight. This dot grew smaller, and the pilots discontinued their observation. At 7 P.M. the thing came back in sight, but they were unable to get close to it. Its apparent diameter was that of a Boeing 707 two miles away. Once more, a small dot appeared; it grew larger and the big object again shrank, as on the previous occasion. Finally the two objects had completely changed roles. At 7:15 the plane still had not reached the scene of the phenomenon. The pilots decided to turn back and landed at Mitchell at 7:40 P.M.

Few interpretations can fit such a report. Very special atmospheric conditions could have formed an image, considerably distorted, of a refueling operation that was taking place toward the west at approximately that time; but careful investigation shows that the tankers could not have been less than 120 miles from the witnesses. On the other hand, the above description can be compared with that given by the pilots of the BOAC Centaurus over Labrador in 1954, a case that has never been solved. In both instances the search for a natural physical explanation must obviously continue.

POVERTY OF HYPOTHESES

Having reviewed the major hypotheses on the origin of the UFO's as objectively as possible, it is our opinion that: (1) all the sightings cannot be attributed to conventional causes; (2) the existence of alien intelligence must be *considered;* but (3) extreme caution must be used in developing this latter hypothesis, with due regard for the complexity of the phenomenon.

Science fiction has done much to prepare our imaginations to accept the idea of extraterrestrial visitors, and the last obstacles to the acceptance of this possibility are gradually being weakened by our own technological achievements in space. But between the recognition of our ignorance of the cause of the phenomenon and the construction of a complete theory that could be presented in a coherent fashion to the world scientific community *is a very wide gap and many years of hard work*. The extraterrestrial hypothesis, in its current presentation, meets none of the criteria for a scientific theory. Let us point to a few obscure points in this hypothesis.

In the first place, the supporters of the extraterrestrial origin of UFO's tell us that the disk-shaped objects that have been observed close to the ground are space-traveling craft. This view is supported by the appearance of the objects themselves, their seemingly perfect technology, and the speeds recorded on the radar. But we have seen that the reported dimensions of the objects are far too small to give the pilots any sort of protection against space radiation (*see* 205, 206). Michel and his co-workers have suggested that the Type-II objects may be gigantic carriers serving as local bases for the small objects. But then why are these huge space-stations not seen more often, not only by people on the ground and by pilots, but by the radar and astronomers, amateur and professional? The reported size of these objects would make them one of the most conspicuous things in the whole solar system; certainly no material construction larger than an aircraft carrier would pass unnoticed even at the distance of Jupiter.

If the objects are somehow capable of leaving our space-time continuum, they could bridge the interstellar gap with little trouble and could escape radar and visual detection as they approach and leave the terrestrial surface. But this hypothesis, which few amateur groups are willing to consider, does not really clarify the situation; it complicates the problem of determining the origin of the supposed craft and their motivation in coming here. Furthermore, it makes any attempt at detection by teams of visual observers a very unrealistic enterprise.

If the "cloud-cigars" are the key to the generation of the secondary objects, then the "luminous spheres emerging from a shining cylinder" that were reported at Augermanland in 1752 tie in with this automatically. If this is true, then what we have been seeing since 1946 is merely a recrudescence of phenomena as old as our civilization. Then why hasn't the technology of the "visitors" evolved in the course of the centuries? Should we assume that they are time-travelers? We are far from the nice, simple theory that was going to explain everything!

The hypothesis that UFO's are controlled by an alien intelligence deserves serious consideration and close study, but only within rigid scientific guidelines; a scientific investigation would seek to ascertain, on the basis of the best-defined sightings, the physical characteristics of the objects, without trying to credit the results *a priori* to a particular story.

In the remainder of this book, we will consider the UFO as a physical object, without any prejudgment as to its nature. We feel very strongly that when analysis has shown the witnesses' testimony to be sincere and detailed, the reported data as to the shapes, dimensions, and behavior of the objects cannot be overlooked.

SIZES AND SHAPES

In the unexplained sightings, the UFO's are not vaguely described as aeroforms of variable shapes and diameters. On the contrary, in the great majority of the cases the phenomenon is reported as centered on a material object of uniform characteristics. We have already stressed this point in the reports made by groups of people in different villages who simultaneously describe the same phenomena or give differing descriptions that, when replaced in their chronological order, show a logical pattern of size, shape, and maneuver. On the other hand, a certain portion of the sky, or the clouds, or the landscape, is masked by the objects: the descriptions given by the witnesses who see it from various angles generally agree, showing that the objects do in fact occupy a certain portion of space. Thus the witnesses have had no reason to believe that what they saw was anything other than a material, physical body. Our first problem is to estimate the approximate dimensions of the objects from the figures contained in the reports.

In the absence of any bearing or reference point or a recognizable structure on the object, the reported dimensions are useful mainly on a statistical basis, as we saw in our study of the reports of landings in the preceding chapter. If we plot all the reports that give size estimates on one graph (Figure 31), nearly six out of ten objects seen on the ground have a diameter between two and five meters. When the same plot is

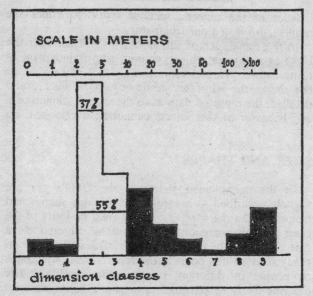

FIG. 31.—Estimated dimension of objects observed on the ground, based on ninety-one reports.

made on the basis of Type IV observations (168 reports give size estimates) the result is completely different: the objects are sometimes as large as ten, twenty, or even thirty meters (about one hundred feet), but seldom larger.

Sightings made by trained specialists and observations where reference points (clouds whose height could be calculated with some precision, etc.) were available confirm this estimate; a diameter of fifteen to thirty meters is indeed typical of the objects reported in continuous flight.

Does this mean that on the basis of these sightings we should regard the reports of landings as misleading? Certainly not, because in some of the Type I cases, e.g., the Marignane case, the witnesses have been able to check the dimensions with precision. Thus we see that *different sizes are associated with two distinct categories of behaviors: the objects responsible for the reports of Type I are of small dimensions (about fifteen feet) and those responsible for the reports of Type IV (objects seen in flight) have a diameter of sixty to one hundred feet.*

In a preliminary survey, leaving out the Type II sightings, the shapes described always derive from the disk, the cigar (ovoid form sometimes described as "torpedo-shaped"), and, more rarely, the sphere. The best-defined objects are the disks. According to their dimensions, they fall into two groups:

1. The type of disk-shaped object most commonly described in flight through the atmosphere has a diameter of twenty to thirty meters. On the photographs (such as the one taken by Paul Trent in Mac Minnville, Oregon, in 1950, or the one taken in Rouen, France, in 1954) it appears as an upside down plate with a sort of protuberance in the center of the upper part.

2. The type of disk-shaped object most commonly described at low altitude or resting on the ground is much smaller and its characteristics are very uniform. In 1954, a Mr. Farnier, a member of the French Society of Civil Engineers, gave the following excellent description to the French newspapers:

I saw a big disk, some eight to twelve meters in diameter, pass over my property at Jouy-sur-Morin, spinning as it flew and giving off a reddish-violet light together with a whistling sound somewhat reminiscent of the approach of a jet aircraft. The machine was at an altitude of about four hundred meters and hovered above me for more than twenty minutes; thus I had plenty of time to study it well. It then departed in the direction of Coulommiers.

As a former manager with the Aero-Club of France and having served in the air force, I have not been the victim of a hallucination, and this machine was not a balloon, but a thick circular wing that hovered over one spot, then moved off at very great speed, climbing steadily as it did so.

Among those objects whose shapes are said to resemble torpedoes or cigars is that described by Chiles and Whitted, the two pilots who reported an object thirty meters long and twice as wide as a Dakota.

The object called by Michel a "jellyfish" is derived from the sphere. It is a hemispherical body whose underpart is a source of light; the emission is often localized in vertical stalks or stems hanging beneath the center of the object; sometimes these stems change colors in sequence and thus give the illusion of rotating. Also of spherical derivation are the "top-shaped" objects, such as the one reported at Vins (see Chapter 1, "The Case of the Intelligent Machine"), in Georgia, and on several other occasions. The reported "separation" of a secondary object in some of the recent New Hampshire sightings is by no means an uncommon feature; the French files in particular contain quite a few instances of small (about one-foot), bright objects, described in some cases as "probes" that separate from a disk-shaped object hovering in mid-air and come down, sometimes to the point of touching the ground (in the New Hampshire cases one was reported touching a power line), before they rejoin the main object.

FLIGHT CHARACTERISTICS

The features of the reported objects that first attracted the attention of the scientists and aroused their incredulity were the kinematic characteristics. Objects reported traveling in sustained flight at medium speeds can be misinterpreted aircraft; even those reports that mention "shining disks" or "luminous spheres" can be explained as reflections of the surface of modern aircraft. Refueling missions at night can account for many reports of "nocturnal meandering lights," even those forming very complex patterns.

Unfortunately, none of these explanations holds for the flight characteristics reported in the typical UFO sightings. Present-day aircraft capabilities—and naturally even more so their performances at the time of the great waves of ten years ago—are limited to precise regions of the altitude/speed diagram (213).

Of course the points falling in the extreme regions of the diagram are somewhat unreliable, for how can such fantastically high speeds be measured? As for the steep accelerations, they can be estimated on the radar scope, but the precision becomes very poor as the velocity increases. However, there are cases of precise recordings showing truly unconventional variations of speed and altitude. Such a case is charted in Figure 32, on the basis of the observations of a French military radar tracking an unknown object in Ceuta, Morocco; a fighter aircraft was in visual contact with the object at the same time. This flight pattern is unequalled by our aircraft technology—and the observation was made at the end of 1954.

Similar indications can be sought from all reports of objects seen from the ground during the day at medium altitude. When the files of UFO sightings are sorted on punched cards to select these characteristics the number of such cases is sufficient for a serious study of flight characteristics. These reports generally refer to the large disks; the most uniform features of their behavior in flight are: (1) oblique position of the object during acceleration and deceleration; (2) ability to stop completely at any altitude with no appreciable noise; (3) change of color as a function of acceleration; (4) ability to travel extremely fast over short distances; (5) in discontinuous flight, frequent periods of "dead-leaf" maneuvers bringing the object to a lower altitude. (This type of behavior is often called "pendulum motion"; it is described by E. L. Trouvelot in a note to the French Academy of Sciences [observation made at noon on August 28, 1871, and published in the *Comptes-*

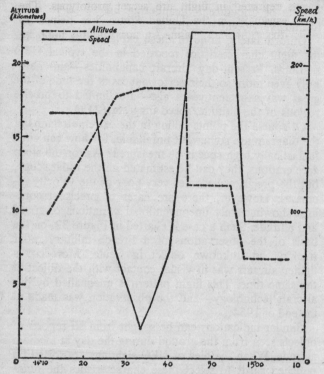

FIG. 32.—Altitude/speed record of the flight of an unidentified object tracked by radar and observed by French military pilots in Ceuta, Morocco, on December 2, 1954.

Rendus in 1885, Vol. 101, p. 154] as "a motion similar to that of a disk falling through water"); (6) in continuous flight, motion is commonly compared to that of a wave, sometimes even to a zig-zig; (7) frequent reports of objects in geometric formations and in continuous flight.

In the discussion of the flight characteristics of the UFO's, the reader should be guarded against two very common mistakes. One arises from the claim sometimes put forward by the U.S. Air Force that the disk-shaped objects reported in flight are secret prototypes. The press, especially in the United States, has helped to spread this ridiculous claim. An authoritative book by John P. Campbell, published in 1962, *Vertical Take-off and Landing Aircraft,* reveals that only two prototypes developed in this country have had any resemblance to a flat disk-shaped object. The first one, Charles H. Zimmerman's "flying pancake" (V-173), was tried and abandoned in 1942. It would hardly fit the description of a "flying saucer," for it had two large propellers and, although intended to be a VTOL (vertical take-off and landing) airplane, it lacked the power to hover. The second prototype was the Avro Avrocar VZ-9, which does look like a "flying saucer." It is supported by an annular jet, so that it rests on a cushion of air. But besides the fact that the Avrocar, powered by three Continental J-69 turbine engines, can hardly be compared for silent performance with the "soft whirring sound" described by most witnesses of UFO sightings, it has never flown out of ground effect; in other words, it has never risen more than a few feet above the ground and has never flown more than a short distance. As Campbell puts it: "The work to date has not been very successful."

The tests made on such experimental craft and on models in wind-tunnels have shown several interesting points, however. They have revealed that a disk-shaped aircraft with VTOL capability is unstable in forward flight. When it hovers, its center of gravity must remain close to the center of vertical lift, which coincides with the center of the disk. But this becomes catastrophic in forward flight: the center of lift moves ahead of the center of gravity and the craft tends to nose up or down at large angles and to go out of control. If the "flying saucers" are powered craft, their aerodynamic principle is drastically different from that of our own aircraft, and the term "flying" is quite inappropriate.

The second mistake is contained in the claim that the UFO's would produce sonic booms as they in-

crease their speed and, therefore, that the witnesses
who report an object silently leaping upward at a dizzying speed have had a hallucination or are lying. Actually, when an object goes straight up while constantly increasing its speed (initial vertical velocity being
zero) there will be a sonic boom, but persons in the
vicinity of the craft at the lowest point will not hear it.
Even assuming that the UFO is a conventional machine,
producing a cone-shaped perturbation, the disturbance
will move normally to the wall of the cone and witnesses
located inside the cone will hear nothing. Someone
miles away may hear a boom but will fail to see the
object. The same is true for trajectories other than the
strictly vertical, of course. Besides, a sonic boom is
sometimes clearly reported by the witnesses who were
in a suitable position with respect to the object; *see* the
report by Mr. S. in the Loch Raven Dam case, below.

SECONDARY EFFECTS

Six different kinds of secondary effects are referred
to in the reports. They can be classified as follows:
(1) air displacement and noise of variable intensity;
(2) perturbation of the compass; (3) production of
material imprints, traces, and burned spots; (4) burning sensations of the face, with varying degrees of concentration and gravity, felt by the witnesses at close
range; (5) disturbance of instruments in aircraft and
interference with car ignitions (hundreds of reports of
engines stalled); (6) inhibition of the voluntary motions of the witnesses.

All these effects have been noted and interpreted by
different authors. Some say that air displacement, noise,
and material traces could be caused by conventional
aircraft and that the "paralysis" of the witnesses is
only a psychological effect. Similarly, the reports of
cars stopped "mysteriously" are dismissed as caused by
the observer's panic. It is fairly clear, however, that
well-documented cases exist that show all these sec-

ondary effects. The Loch Raven Dam case, which we are going to study below in detail, is such a case.

On the other hand, the hypotheses put forward by UFO students are quite inadequate to explain these effects in terms of the UFO "technology" they assume. Michel, for instance, has summed up his discussion of the secondary effects by saying that all these effects can be explained by the production of a suitable magnetic field (5). This is obviously insufficient, particularly when the claim is extended to "the production of induced currents in the human body without touching it."

The biological effects of very powerful or very small magnetic fields are either unknown or known to be nonexistent at all degrees of intensity and at all frequencies we are able to generate (*see* 209, 210, 211, 212). The generation of purely magnetic fields is not a satisfactory hypothesis and fails to account for the reported phenomena. More directly accessible to measurement and computation are those effects that are physical, rather than biophysical, in nature, such as deviations of the compass, radio blackouts, and failure of automobile engines.

For example, Mebane reports in (6) that in a sighting made at 9:00 P.M. on November 6, 1957, near Lake Baskatong, north of Ottawa, Canada, the witnesses reported a strong interference with radio reception. A Mr. Jacobsen and three of his friends were listening to a battery-powered radio when they saw a brilliantly lighted, yellowish-white sphere with an apparent diameter inferior to that of the moon hanging motionless over a hill. The hill was about two or three miles away and the altitude of the object was estimated to be a few hundred feet. From the top and the bottom of the sphere there fanned out conical beams of light that illuminated the trees and the undersurface of the clouds. Reception on the radio was interrupted. One of the witnesses, who had with him a shortwave receiver, found that he could no longer pick up even the government time signals, but that on one shortwave frequency he was getting a very strong, rapidly modulated signal; in other words, his receiver was saturated on that particular wavelength. The signal was "something like Morse," but not Morse (which the witness, a professional engineer, said he would have recognized). Such saturation effect is familiar to those who live near a powerful transmitter. Fifteen minutes later, the object slowly moved off toward the south and entered the clouds. By 9:30 P.M. it was no longer in sight and the radios started working normally again.

A similar incident, which is documented in more detail and involves a powerful transmitter, comes from an official source in Communist Yugoslavia: on November 10, 1961, the Yugoslav news agency Tanyug published the following report, entitled "Mysterious Radioelectric Incident in Croatia":

Belgrade. A few days ago, the transmitter at the local radio station of the Croatian town of Vukovar was suddenly blacked out. In the studio the lights went out, and then flickered on and off for thirty or forty seconds. Recording instruments showed a sharp increase in voltage. At the same moment, a strange dark-gray cloud passed over the town. According to the Belgrade newspaper *Politika,* a radio technician witnessed another extraordinary phenomenon. Several sodium lamps on a shelf completely isolated from any electric apparatus or electric cable began to glow. So far, no scientific explanation has been found that would account for the connection, if there was one, between the cloud and the phenomena observed at the radio station.

One of the most significant reports with respect to secondary effects was investigated in depth by the U.S. Air Force in 1958. It deserves a description in full detail.

THE LOCH RAVEN DAM CASE

The main sighting was made by two men who declared that about 10:30 P.M. (EST) on October 26, 1958, they saw an unknown object stationary above a metal bridge near the Loch Raven Dam, north of Baltimore, Maryland. As they approached the bridge, the engine of their car stalled, and the UFO made off vertically about a minute later. The two men suffered light facial burns and were examined at St. Joseph's Hospital in Baltimore. A detailed investigation was made by the air force, which still lists the case as "unidentified." The two witnesses will be referred to here as Mr. C. and Mr. S. Here are their accounts of the experience:

REPORT BY MR. C.:

We were taking a ride out near Loch Raven Dam, Sunday, October 26. After you pass the dam itself there is a rather twisting road that goes down into a valley and obstructs your view of the lake entirely. You can't see the lake or a bridge that leads across it. Shortly after you pass the dam, you take a left turn; then the bridge looms up in front of you at 200 to 250 yards away. We took this left-hand turn and we saw, from that distance, what appeared to be a large, flat sort of egg-shaped object hanging between 100 to 150 feet off the top of the superstructure of the bridge over the lake.

We slowed and then decided to go closer and investigate the object. We crept closer to the object along the road leading toward the bridge. When we got to within 75 or 80 feet of the bridge the car went completely dead on us. It seemed as though the electrical system was affected; the dash lights went out, the head lights went out, the motor went dead. Mr. S., who was driving the car, put on his brakes and turned the ignition once or twice.

We didn't get any whirring sound. We were pretty frightened at this point.

We both got out of the car. On this road there is nowhere to hide or run, which is probably what we would have done. So we got the car between the object and ourselves. We watched it from that position for approximately thirty to forty seconds and then, I am not sure of the sequence of events here, it seemed to flash a brilliant flash of white light and we both felt heat on our faces. Concurrently, there was a loud noise that I interpreted as a dull explosion and Mr. S. heard as a thunder clap.

Then very quickly, so that you couldn't gain the proper sequence of events, the object started to rise vertically. It didn't change its position, as far as we could tell, during the rising. The only different feature it had while it was moving was that it was very bright and the edges became diffused so that we couldn't make out the shape as it rose. It took from five to ten seconds to disappear from view completely. We were very frightened.

REPORT BY MR. S:

At approximately 10:30, riding along Loch Raven Boulevard, we came around a bend. It was extremely dark, visibility was clear, there were constellations, etc., in the sky. To our recollection there was no moon. We came across an egg-shaped object hovering over Bridge Number 1. This is after you pass the dam. It was approximately, to our knowledge, 75 to 150 feet high. There is some doubt to exactly how high it was. We were rather alarmed at seeing the object and we were not qualified to tell exactly how high it was.

When we first saw the object it was approximately 300 yards away. We were going approximately twenty to thirty miles per hour as this was bad road. This was rather fast for this road and we slowed down to approximately ten to twelve miles per hour and came to within approximately seventy to eighty feet of the object. We have no way of telling the distances exactly. After we talked it over later, we figured out that it must have been approximately this distance that we were talking about. The electrical system in the car seemingly gave out, as if you had your points go up, or somebody took the battery out of the car, or some other type of disturbance of this nature. I tried to put the ignition system on but there was no whirring or anything. I put the brakes on the car and we just looked at the object through the windshield temporarily.

Then we decided to run out of the car and we decided to put the car between ourselves and the object. It was a very narrow road: on one side the lake, and on the other side a cliff. There was no place to run. We probably would have if we could've, but we were terrified at what we saw.

We thought maybe it was a navy blimp. We tried to rationalize what it was. Of course, the fact that the electrical system in our car conked out, made us a little suspicious as to what it might have been. . . .

Although we are not sure, we estimate it was approximately one hundred feet long since it occupied approximately one-third of the bridge, at the height it was at. We watched it for approximately thirty seconds and then it seemingly gave off a terrific bright light.

It had been glowing with an iridescent glow beforehand, but this light seemingly was blinding and approximately at the same time we felt a tremendous heat wave. It didn't seem like the heat of a burning object but something like an ultraviolet light or some kind of radiation. . . .

The object disappeared from view within approximately five to ten seconds after giving off a tremendous thunder clap, something approaching a plane breaking the sound barrier. After it disappeared from sight we came back into the car and turned the ignition system on and it immediately went into operation. We approached to within the bridge, backed up before crossing the bridge, and immediately, at great speed, came back to Loch Raven and Joppa Roads. . . .

At the time we were reporting the thing we noticed a burning sensation on our faces. We didn't pay too much attention at the time except to ask the police if they had noticed if our faces were red. The policemen said that they didn't but we still noticed the burning sensation. After making the report we left the police and went to St. Joseph's Hospital to try to determine if possibly they were some kind of radiation burns or any other type of thing that we might have received. The doctor looked at our faces and claimed that Mr. C.'s face was slightly red and that mine wasn't. He, of course, looked at us thoroughly, took our pressures and everything. It was only a superficial examination but he claimed we had nothing to worry about. A police sergeant at the scene, who seemingly had gone to radiation class of some kind, mentioned that if it had been a radioactive burn we wouldn't have been burned immediately and it would have taken some time to develop. This of course led us to believe that we didn't have to worry too much about the radioactivity. We left the hospital and went home that night.

The next day my face did become a little redder and it was apparently noticeable to anyone who spoke to me.

At 10:45 P.M. (EST) on October 26, 1958, a Mr. M., considered to be of above-average reliability, described a luminous white object that disappeared instantaneously after having moved in a straight line toward the northeast for one minute.

On October 26, at the time indicated by Messrs. S.

and C., several people working in a restaurant near the scene heard the noise mentioned in the account above. It is described as a "double boom," but the second sound could have been an echo of the first one. These people did not see the object.

Between 9:05 and 9:15 P.M. (EST) on October 27, 1958, Messrs L. and H. saw a luminous object motionless in mid-air above a field as they were going along Loch Raven Road, on which the bridge is situated. The object appeared and disappeared instantaneously. Two other persons, a Mr. and Mrs. H., mentioned that while returning home that same evening they saw "a luminous object hanging over a field."

The air force's report in the files of Project Blue Book states that all the witnesses are considered to be sincere, intelligent, and trustworthy people. Following the investigation conducted by the military authorities, and the local publicity on the case, Mr. S. declared:

> I hope what I did see would add to the national interest or national information that would maybe help understand these things a little better. I do know that they exist, now that I have seen it myself. I am not saying that it was a flying saucer, I don't know. I do know there are at least such things now as UFO's.

ABOUT AN IRON BRIDGE

A French observation made only two days after the Loch Raven Dam case, in strikingly similar conditions, was parallel to it in many ways. First, let us emphasize the fact that the Loch Raven case received no publicity in the United States and that this is the first time it has been published in detail; hence there was no possibility that the French public knew about it only two days later.

The report was made by Jean Boyer, of Beylon-de-Montmaur, who was returning home on October 28, 1958, at the time of the incident. Some of the details have appeared in the *Dauphine Libere* of October 30, 1958, but most of the information we have obtained was the result of a direct investigation.

I had reached the area of Pont-la-Dame and was ready to climb the stretch of road called "Cote des Egaux," when I saw in the sky, right above Pont-la-Dame, in the valley of the Grand Buech river, a motionless and luminous "disk." I stopped the car and got out. The time must have been 7:55 P.M.

I looked at the "disk," which resembled two plates glued together; I believe it was about 200 to 400 meters above the ground. Suddenly, after two or three minutes, some sparks flew as the object rose vertically at a dizzying speed, leaving first a fiery trail, then a faint glow, which vanished. At the same time, I felt a current of air that rocked my station wagon.

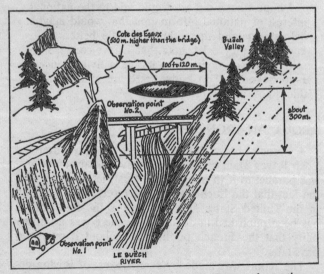

FIG. 33.—The scene of the Pont-la-Dame observation, October 28, 1958 (after a sketch by a witness).

Boyer was about 600 to 700 meters from the bridge (*see* Figures 33 and 34) when he saw, above the railroad bridge, a sharply defined oblong shadow swaying to the left and to the right very gently. He got out of his station wagon, *but not before he had driven the car up to the bridge, in order to place himself exactly below the "disk."* This is an essential part of the report, because it establishes that the witness was indeed observing a real object with a precise position in space. He saw a perfectly circular machine, with a second, smaller circle inside the large one; from this smaller circle short sparks of a dark red color were emitted. As he had left the headlights of his station wagon on, he walked back to the car and turned them off. As he was reaching the vehicle, the object emitted a formidable stream of blinding sparks, similar to those of burning magnesium, and vanished *instantaneously* in the sky. At the same time there was a very strong air displacement.

There are two interesting differences with the Loch Raven Dam case: first, no noise was heard in connection with the departure of the object; second, no interference with the ignition of the car was noted. There were five other witnesses (187), most of them motorists driving along the same road.

These two observations give us the occasion to summarize our earlier remarks about the systematic, scientific approach necessary in the study of the UFO phenomenon. In the first place, they indicate very plainly that any investigation restricted to the limits of one country would be practically worthless. The obvious interest of the two cases is their occurrence at a forty-eight-hour interval in sparsely populated areas on two continents, at a time when UFO's were not a popular theme in the newspapers.

Second, these two reports are typical of cases describing objects whose physical parameters—diameter, thickness, total radiated energy, electric charge, etc.—could be computed. The duration of both sightings is,

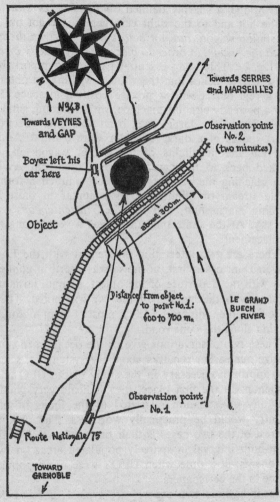

FIG. 34.—Map of the Pont-la-Dame observation.

to say the least, remarkable, and the witnesses' distance from the energy source can be precisely computed in both cases. The type of the automobile is known in both cases. The cause of the interference with ignition, or its absence, can be sought experimentally. The same goes for some thirty or forty reports of the same type in the files.

Microscopic analysis of the photographic evidence contained in some reports can add to these physical indications. While no photograph that proves beyond question the existence of the UFO's as machines exists, at least ten photographs of disks and an equivalent number of movie films showing circular images, alone or in formation, are available, not to mention a large number of films that have recorded only vague luminous spots; all these documents could yield luminosity profiles and isophotes, even those that seem worthless on superficial analysis. Of course, in the absence of good standardization, the indications thus secured would remain general in nature. But they would at least provide an idea of the distribution of the luminosity over the area, and this would be one way of approaching the study of the energy that gives rise to this luminosity.

In our opinion, cases like the Loch Raven Dam sighting present a serious problem of methodology. It is one thing to compute statistics and to talk philosophically about illusions and percentages; it is another to find the courage to study such reports with an open mind. As scientists, we cannot escape our responsibility to study these cases with perfect sincerity; we must give the public an answer that satisfies its need to understand and to know. The number and reliability of the witnesses, the excellence of their observations, and the remarkably complete official investigation into the Loch Raven Dam case and many others show that the UFO sightings are not and never have been a subject fit for ridicule or a matter of vague, unverifiable rumors. The reports accumulated over nearly twenty years *do* offer a solid foundation for research.

CONCLUSION

THE SOLUTION IS WITHIN REACH

THE CAREFUL STUDY of the UFO phenomenon may contribute to our knowledge of human psychology and sociology and to our understanding of the universe in which we live. The only proper way to conduct research on the phenomenon is to centralize all the files, both official and private, and to initiate the necessarily long and difficult work of classification, indexing, and information-gathering under the aegis of an international scientific commission.

We recommend the creation of a team whose members would encourage discussion, debate, or even controversy; regularly publish their findings and investigations; and possess immediate investigative capability through local scientific groups instructed in data-gathering methods in all parts of the world. The members of this commission should be chosen on the basis of their ability to draw up original methods of research based on the latest scientific ideas. They should be given this task as a full-time project.

We have presented here a picture of the situation of

the UFO problem as it can be observed today. We have seen that two avenues of research, opposite in spirit and application, could be followed in studying the phenomenon. The first of these is based on the desire to reach a speedy explanation of the reports and holds that the testimony of a pilot or a technical person is necessarily to be preferred to that of the ordinary witness. It seeks to arrive at the definition of a limited sample comprising only such cases deemed worthy of being submitted to the attention of committees of scholars who examine each sighting in detail in the light of their individual specialties. This method is, in our view, erroneous for at least four main reasons:

1. It masks entirely the psychosociological phenomenon that is the supporting context of the UFO reports and thus presents each case without reference to the conditions that surround it. The psychological component of the phenomenon is ignored.

2. It leads to the arbitrary constitution of a "typical list" of cases that will represent the UFO phenomenon in all subsequent studies. This list results from a selection from the mass of the original sightings; its criteria are predetermined in a biased, subjective way and are not deduced by objective analysis from the body of the observations treated as a whole.

3. It falsifies the relative proportions of the different types of reports, eliminating some entirely (Type I) and masking others by misclassification (Type II). It distributes the weight or reliability index of the sightings in such a way that certain groups of witnesses are favored, even though only certain types of sightings correspond to these groups: if a great deal of weight is given to observations by astronomers, the Type I sightings, which astronomers have little chance to witness, are depreciated.

4. By lifting each sighting out of its context, it overlooks the global nature of the phenomenon and blocks every avenue of investigation into the distribution pattern of the sightings and the fluctuation of the phe-

nomenon in time; it restricts the discussion to a mere weighing of probabilities.

Our objective in this work has been to explore an entirely different channel of research, based upon the idea that, in the absence of any plausible physical theory, the UFO phenomenon can only be defined by the set of its manifestations. We have considered the *totality* of the sightings reported by human witnesses, *all* of which involve a certain degree of uncertainty, varying as a function of the time of sighting, the training of the observer, his age, his social environment, etc.

Abandoning the attempt to interpret every individual case, a task for the professional physicist, we declare useless any explanation that applies only within certain limits of time or space, or within certain strict boundaries, or for only a reduced sample of cases. Since experience has shown that a strong psychological component is present in periods of intense activity of the phenomenon, we have made it a principle not to reject sightings on the mere basis of their "fantastic" interpretation by the witness; for certainly even the today well-understood and recognized physical phenomenon of comets was once viewed in a fantastic and even extravagant context. Just as the fifteenth-century chronicles described comets as "the hand of God holding a bloody sword," today we are confronted with fantastically distorted accounts of real, physical events. *It is the duty of the scientist to analyze the reports, separating those elements that are the work of the imagination.*

Upon this basis, then, our objectives have been: (1) to identify the various components of the phenomenon and to introduce a descriptive language, viewing the reports, in turn, from the point of view of psychology and that of the exact sciences; (2) to present statistical studies based on the most general sample we were able to gather, without seeking to decide between the various theories subjectively; on the contrary, we have tried to delineate as clearly as possible the assets and liabilities of all the hypotheses put forward to explain the phenomenon; (3) to open the way for a full-scale, global study by reviewing some of the methods that could be used if such a study were to be entrusted to a scientific commission.

This book is intended to be a basis of reference and a general survey of the present state of the UFO problem and associated ideas. The adherents to widely diverging theories can (as we have seen in the case of the correlation with Mars) interpret our results as supporting their particular view. A more positive approach would be to go beyond the methods surveyed here and to look for original means of deciding exactly what the physical nature of the UFO phenomenon is.

A RESEARCH PROPOSAL

The possible lines of research that could be followed fall into two groups.

1. If the phenomenon continues to be observed on the surface of the globe, its nature may be ascertained by establishing carefully selected sighting stations (or by supplying existing scientific or military stations with a precise set of instructions in the event of a UFO sighting in their vicinity) to secure spectrographs and good photographs of the objects with some means of standardizing them. It would be advisable for every police station to have at least one squad car with adequate photographic equipment. Similarly, the official investigators should have at their disposal mobile units supplied with magnetic and photographic recording instruments. The time required to transmit and process UFO reports that originate at military bases and radar stations throughout the world should be drastically reduced by the use of on-line computing facilities, providing immediate investigative capability.

2. The efforts of reliable groups of sincere amateurs to be of intelligent and helpful assistance in the official investigation should not be ignored. These groups

should be encouraged to pursue independent work in the area of historical research, documentation of past cases, field study of current sightings, etc.

3. The possibility that traces of civilizations, or even entities and artifacts of non-human origin, may be encountered during space exploration should be faced quite frankly and without further delay. It is possible that the expeditions toward the planets, in the coming years or decades, will provide us with the means of deciding between the main theories of the UFO problem. But we should not be satisfied to await this answer passively, for a series of crucial decisions will have to be made at the critical moment if the evidence points to extraterrestrial intelligence as the cause of the phenomenon.

If nothing is met with in space that can be related to this problem, and if no trace of civilization is found on other planets, then the responsibility of analyzing the mass of documentation accumulated in these recent years falls to the psychologist. If, in the meantime, an adequate explanation for all the facts is found in a new physical phenomenon, then the immediate study of its manifestations will be of the utmost importance; all the data gathered on the past sightings will be of value. And if the exploration of space reveals that extraterrestrial civilizations do exist, then the ideas that we shall have formed as to the degree of advancement of their technology, their level of social and moral maturity, and the relations they may have had with our planet in the past will be the deciding factors in our attitude toward them.

The "UFO phenomenon," with all its disturbing aspects, presents a most unwelcome challenge to the physical and philosophical conceptions of the universe painstakingly formed in the course of many centuries of civilization on this planet. But it is there; we cannot forever refuse to study it. And it could well be that, in the final analysis, our own existence will be dependent upon the sincerity with which we conduct this research.

APPENDIX I

COMPUTATION OF THE GREAT CIRCLES

THE CONVENTIONS we have used in the computation of the great circles are as follows: the *node* is defined as the point where a moving body traveling along this great circle in the direction of the earth's rotation (from west to east) would cross the equator in passing from the southern hemisphere to the northern hemisphere. The longitude of this point and the inclination (angle of the great circle with the equator at the node) are the two quantities that define completely the track of the great circle on the planisphere. All coordinates are referred to the Greenwich meridian and expressed in decimal degrees.

In order to compute a table of values that would allow us to trace easily the great circle on a planisphere or a local map, we determined, for each latitude x (which varies by steps of one degree), the longitudes of the four points of the great circle that have as their latitude either $+x$ or $-x$. When more than three sightings are used in the actual computation, it is natural to fit the great circle to their coordinates by least squares. We have described such a method in detail in (16), and Menzel has proposed a generalization of our formulas that is better adapted to the case of the American observations (whose longitude may

235

be close to 90°, introducing a distortion of the weights of the various points). These techniques ensure greater precision.

These computations when performed by hand, with a table of logarithms or a desk calculator, are extremely cumbersome; the time required to achieve some degree of accuracy is considerable and intricate questions of precision arise. We reduced these problems through the use of digital computers of several types. About one-half dozen great circles were first computed and tabulated by hand. Later, the majority of the calculations were performed on an IBM 1620 computer. The program read the coordinates of the observations directly from the catalogue and the operator could, by changing a switch on the console, obtain a tabulation with a step of one degree or a finer tabulation with ten points per degree.

These calculations were done in France in 1962. The time required to compute and print out a great circle was provided by the formula $t = 20 + 12\,i$, in seconds, with i being the value of the inclination in degrees. At a later stage, the least-squares technique was used and all the alignments were recomputed on a larger machine. The results did not show any variation of great significance to the discussion of the orthotenic theory.

As an illustration, we give below the tabulation of the Bayonne-Vichy line, with a step of one degree, except in the interval between 47° and 49°, where we have ten points per degree.

TABULATION OF THE BAYONNE-VICHY LINE

1.0	41.4915	—137.1335	—138.5085	42.8665
2.0	40.8034	—136.4454	—139.1966	43.5546
3.0	40.1143	—135.7563	—139.8857	44.2437
4.0	39.4236	—135.0656	—140.5764	44.9344
5.0	38.7309	—134.3729	—141.2691	45.6271
6.0	38.0355	—133.6775	—141.9645	46.3225
7.0	37.3369	—132.9789	—142.6631	47.0211
8.0	36.6347	—132.2767	—143.3653	47.7233
9.0	35.9281	—131.5701	—144.0719	48.4299
10.0	35.2166	—130.8586	—144.7834	49.1414
11.0	34.4997	—130.1417	—145.5003	49.8583
12.0	33.7766	—129.4186	—146.2234	50.5814
13.0	33.0468	—128.6888	—146.9532	51.3112

14.0	32.3096	—127.9516	—147.6904	52.0484
15.0	31.5643	—127.2063	—148.4357	52.7937
16.0	30.8101	—126.4521	—149.1899	53.5479
17.0	30.0463	—125.6883	—149.9537	54.3117
18.0	29.2720	—124.9140	—150.7280	55.0860
19.0	28.4865	—124.1285	—151.5135	55.8715
20.0	27.6888	—123.3308	—152.3112	56.6692
21.0	26.8780	—122.5200	—153.1220	57.4800
22.0	26.0530	—121.6950	—153.9470	58.3050
23.0	25.2127	—120.8547	—154.7873	59.1453
24.0	24.3561	—119.9981	—155.6439	60.0019
25.0	23.4818	—119.1238	—156.5182	60.8762
26.0	22.5885	—118.2305	—157.4115	61.7695
27.0	21.6747	—117.3167	—158.3253	62.6833
28.0	20.7389	—116.3809	—159.2611	63.6191
29.0	19.7794	—115.4214	—160.2206	64.5786
30.0	18.7942	—114.4362	—161.2058	65.5638
31.0	17.7814	—113.4234	—162.2186	66.5766
32.0	16.7386	—112.3806	—163.2614	67.6194
33.0	15.6635	—111.3055	—164.3365	68.6945
34.0	14.5531	—110.1951	—165.4469	69.8049
35.0	13.4045	—109.0465	—166.5955	70.9535
36.0	12.2142	—107.8562	—167.7858	72.1438
37.0	10.9783	—106.6203	—169.0217	73.3797
38.0	9.6925	—105.3345	—170.3075	74.6655
39.0	8.3516	—103.9936	—171.6484	76.0064
40.0	6.9500	—102.5920	—173.0500	77.4080
41.0	5.4809	—101.1229	—174.5191	78.8771
42.0	3.9366	—99.5786	—176.0634	80.4214
43.0	2.3077	—97.9497	—177.6923	82.0503
44.0	.5832	—96.2252	—179.4168	83.7748
45.0	—1.2502	—94.3918	178.7498	85.6082
46.0	—3.2094	—92.4326	176.7906	87.5674
47.0	—5.3152	—90.3268	174.6848	89.6732
47.1	—5.5348	—90.1072	174.4652	89.8928
47.2	—5.7562	—89.8858	174.2438	90.1142
47.3	—5.9794	—89.6626	174.0206	90.3374
47.4	—6.2044	—89.4376	173.7956	90.5624
47.5	—6.4312	—89.2108	173.5688	90.7892
47.6	—6.6600	—88.9820	173.3400	91.0180
47.7	—6.8907	—88.7513	173.1093	91.2487
47.8	—7.1233	—88.5187	172.8767	91.4813
47.9	—7.3580	—88.2840	172.6420	91.7160
48.0	—7.5947	—88.0473	172.4053	91.9527
48.1	—7.8335	—87.8085	172.1665	92.1915
48.2	—8.0744	—87.5676	171.9256	92.4324

48.3	—8.3175	—87.3245	171.6825	92.6755
48.4	—8.5629	—87.0791	171.4371	92.9209
48.5	—8.8105	—86.8315	171.1895	93.1685
48.6	—9.0604	—86.5816	170.9396	93.4184
48.7	—9.3126	—86.3294	170.6874	93.6706
48.8	—9.5673	—86.0747	170.4327	93.9253
48.9	—9.8245	—85.8175	170.1755	94.1825
49.0	—10.0842	—85.5578	169.9158	94.4422
49.1	—10.3464	—85.2956	169.6536	94.7044
49.2	—10.6114	—85.0306	169.3886	94.9694
49.3	—10.8790	—84.7630	169.1210	95.2370
49.4	—11.1494	—84.4926	168.8506	95.5074
49.5	—11.4226	—84.2194	168.5774	95.7806
49.6	—11.6987	—83.9433	168.3013	96.0567
49.7	—11.9778	—83.6642	168.0222	96.3358
49.8	—12.2600	—83.3820	167.7400	96.6180
49.9	—12.5453	—83.0967	167.4547	96.9033
50.0	—12.8339	—82.8081	167.1661	97.1919
51.0	—15.9176	—79.7244	164.0824	100.2756
52.0	—19.4521	—76.1899	160.5479	103.8101
53.0	—23.6445	—71.9975	156.3555	108.0025
54.0	—28.9422	—66.6998	151.0578	113.3002
55.0	—36.8707	—58.7713	143.1293	121.2287

APPENDIX II

SIMULATION OF ORTHOTENIC NETWORKS

THE COMPUTATION of the great circles and the critical
examination of the orthotenic networks present five basic
problems: (1) to compute the parameters of the great
circle joining two points on the earth; (2) to compute by
least squares the great circle that "best" represents a number of points; (3) to compute the orthogonal distance
between a point and a great circle; (4) to tabulate a great
circle whose parameters are known; and (5) to compute
the distance between two points whose coordinates are
known.

In order to simulate the networks we apply these simple
techniques to distributions of points that do not represent
actual sightings but are chosen at random. Various methods for generating such random numbers are available
commercially. We have used the following:

Given an odd number n_0 between 1 and $2^{46} - 1$, the
terms of the sequence: $n_i = n_{i-1} \cdot 5^{13} \pmod{2^{46}}$ are
positive integers whose value is in the same range as n_0.

$$x_i = n_i \cdot 2^{-46}$$

we obtain random numbers between zero and one. Statistical tests have been made on samples of such numbers and the method has been found satisfactory (*see* Control Data Corporation publications).

To simulate the area of France we first distributed points randomly inside a square, then transformed this figure into a rectangle ABCD, with length AC = 4 b and width AB = 2 a (Figure 35). We fixed the proportions of the rectangle so that $a = b\sqrt{3}$. A hexagon that would be contained within a circle of radius $2b$ was defined by tracing the two horizontal lines $y = b$ and $y = -b$ as shown on Figure 35.

If we set $z = |y|/\sqrt{3}$ and $w = |x|$, we reject all points that lie outside this hexagon by retaining only the pairs (x,y) that verify: $w \leq AB - z$

A better simulation can easily be derived from the case of the hexagon if we reject the points that fall in the following domains:

$$x \text{ negative and } y > 3\,b/2$$
$$x < -\tfrac{1}{2}a \text{ and } y > b$$
$$x < -\tfrac{1}{2}a - y(a/b) \text{ and } y \text{ positive} < \tfrac{1}{2}b$$
$$x < -\tfrac{1}{2}a \text{ and } y \text{ negative}$$

and if we keep, on the other hand, the points that verify:

$$x > \tfrac{1}{2}\,a \text{ and } y \text{ negative} > -3b/2$$

The contour finally obtained is shown in Figure 35.

We now set the dimensions of this area by assuming that BD = 1,000 kilometers, thus achieving a suitable geometric representation of the region under study. The equations that determine the region's linear boundaries are easy to handle on a computer. To approximate even more closely the problem conditions, the coordinates of the points were transformed so that the longitude would vary between +5° and −8° and the latitude between 42° and 51°.

When we had carefully produced this set of random points, the operations to be executed were as follows:

1. Calculate, for each pair of points in the distribution, the parameters of the great circle that joins them.

2. Calculate the orthogonal distances of all the remain-

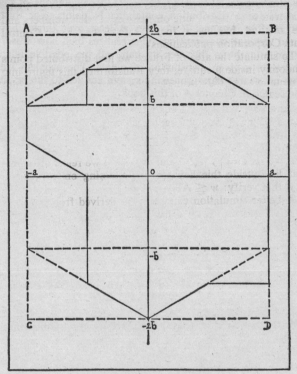

FIG. 35.—Geometric contour simulating the area of France.

ing points to this great circle and make a list of those that lie within a constant distance of the great circle.

3. If this list is void, abandon the alignment in question and return to problem (1).

4. If the list is not void, recalculate the parameters of the great circle, using all the points in the list, by the least-squares method.

5. Compute the maximum error, the mean error, and the standard deviation.

6. Record all the data relative to this great circle, then return to problem (1) until all possible pairs have been considered.

The method leads to $N(N - 1)/2$ calculations of great

circles and to $N(N-1)(N-2)/2$ calculations of distances for a distribution containing N points. For thirty points, for instance, it involves at least over thirty thousand distance computations. One realizes then how illusory is an attempt to discover by hand all the possible alignments in a given distribution of points. The problem was run on a large data-processing system and led to the results presented in Chapter 4 of this book.

APPENDIX III

A CATALOGUE OF 500 OBSERVATIONS

THIS CATALOGUE in machine-readable form was prepared in 1961–62 to serve as a source of coordinates for the computation of the great circles. A new catalogue, much more extensive and using an improved codification system (*see* Appendix IV) has now been developed, but space does not permit us to publish it here. The coding scheme for the catalogue presented here has been described in detail in another publication (203).

№	Longitude	Latitude	J	M	An	H	Min			Location		Ref
001	−013.74333	36.68223	18	06	1845				10	NAV.VICTORIA P.SYR		SY102 438F
002	+027.01444	05.78333	22	03	1870				30	MER.—LADY OF LAKE		AT151 44 F
003	−007.11459	43.72200	23	03	1877				60	VENCE		F 111 F
004	−053.18333	26.43333	15	05	1879					GOLFE PERSIQUE		GP1027 9F
005			30	07	1880				03	ST PETERSBOURG		U 153 F
006			20	08	1880					*FRANCE		F 111 F
007			17	11	1882				02	*GREENWICH OBS.ASTR.		GB 151 F
008	−170.00000	37.00000	24	02	1885					INNERWICH—NAVIRE		PF1017 9F
009	+057.00000	37.65000	19	03	1885					EN MER		AT 152 F
010	+001.26300	51.73000	31	08	1887					*OXFORD		GB 0011 F
011	−090.00000	61.43000	30	06	1895					*PODKAM.TUNGUNSKA		U 181 249G
012	−005.40000	43.29000			1908					MARSEILLE		F 2011 G
013	−002.70733	45.13500		04	1921					COL DE SERRES		F 0011 5G
014			08	06	1947					MUROC-FIELD		X 156 G
015			12	06	1947					WEISER IDAHO		X 152 G
016			21	06	1947					—DALH.(MAURY ISLAND)		X 155 22 E
017			24	06	1947	14	59	1		MONT RAINIER		X 159 05 G
018			04	07	1947					SANTA MONICA CALIF.		X 151 4G
019			04	07	1947	13	05	1		PORTLAND—OREGON		X 159 G
020			08	07	1947	10	00	1		MUROC—FIELD CAL.		X 153 G
021			01	01	1948					JACKSON MISSISSIP.		X 151 05 G
022			07	01	1948					—FT.—KNOX.MADISONV.		X 3018019G
023			20	02	1948					EMMETT IDAHO		X 151 G
024			05	04	1948					MANILA PHILIPINES		PC151 G
025			08	04	1948					ASHLEY OHIO		X 151 D
026				07	1948	20	00	1		DENVER COLORADO		X 151 G
027	−003.93900	44.3835	08	07	1948					CONCOULES GARD		F 12 A
028	−006.87276	44.70300	14	07	1948					ST—VERAN.HTES—ALPES		F 12 G
029			20	07	1948					ARNHEIM—LA HAYE		NL151 G
030			23	07	1948	20	45	1		ATLANTA BOSTON		GQ151 055G

#	J	M	A	H	Mn	N	Lat.	Long.	Lieu	Réf.
031	24	07	1948	01	55	2			ROBINS FIELD GEORG.	X 151 D
032	24	07	1948	02	45	1			MONTGOMERY ALABAMA	X 1512055G
033	01	09	1948	21	00	4			MOSCOU	U 151 9G
034	19	10	1948			120			*FARGO (BASE)	X 1511220G
035	07	10	1948	15	30	220			JAPON	J 151 053G
036	18	11	1948						*LOCKBOURNE OHIO	X 151 A
037	23	11	1948	22	00	1			ANDREWS FIELD	X 151 G
038	05	12	1948	21	05	1			FURSTENFELDBRUCK	D 151 G
039	13	12	1948						LAS VEGAS N.MEXICO	X 18 E
040	21	12	1948	21	29	1	43.04700	—004.82000	AVIGNON	X 18 G
041	14	03	1949						STUTTGART ARKANSAS	F 18 G
042	20	04	1949	22	15	1			*WHITE—SANDS N.MEX.	X 151205 E
043	29	08	1949						*LAS CRUCES N.MEXICO	X 1521 0G
044	06	08	1949	10	12	1			WHITE—SANDS N.MEX.	X 1511 G
045	01	09	1949	17	00	1			SUISSE	X 151 9G
046		10	1949						MOUNT HOPE VIRGINIE	CH 151 4G
047	18	01	1950						*WHITE SANDS	X 141 4G
048	08	02	1950	06	07	1			TEBESSA (DPT BONE)	X 0011440G
049	09	02	1950	15	00	1			BERTHELOT (ORAN)	AG 151 G
050	28	02	1950						SAN LEANDRO CALIF.	AG 153 G
051	07	02	1950				41.93500	—002.28000	VICH (ND BARCELONE)	X 159 R
052	11	03	1950	04	00	2			CIUDAD REAL	E 151 R
053	16	03	1950						GOERING NEBRASKA	E 151 R
054	17	03	1950	17	30	1			PUNTO ARENAS	X 151 3G
055	21	03	1950						DALLAS TEXAS	RH 151 0G
056	21	03	1950						MEXICO	X 151 0G
057	21	03	1950	03	00	1			CORDOBA	MX 151 5G
058	23	03	1950	13	30	1			GAINCHURIZQUETA	RA 151 G
059		03	1950	15	00	2			MIRANDA DEL EBRO	E 152 R
060		03	1950						EL MOUZINE	MA 151 G

No.	Long.	Lat.	D	M	Year	H	Min	N	Place	Code
061				04	1950				JUNEAU —ALASKA	X 0081 1 G
062			10	04	1950				AMARILLO —TEXAS	X 0011 0G
063			19	04	1950				CLARENDON,DALLAS—FD	X 111 G
064	—004.70400	47.30580	01	05	1950	12	15	1	*SOMBERNON	F 1512 G
065			20	05	1950	07	15	1	*FLAGSTAFF (LOWELL)	X 151 4E
066	—002.07198	48.77280	23	07	1950	23	30	1	—GUYANCOURT —S+O	F 0221 2G
067			09	01	1951	21	48	1	ROUIBA	AG 151 G
068			29	01	1951	15	00	3	WONSAN—COREE	EO 180 00 G
069	+001.02870	44.79840	25	03	1951				LIGNAN P.BORDEAUX	F 301 E
070			29	05	1951				*DOWNEY	X 1593 G
071			25	08	1951				—LUBBOCK	X 159327 G
072					1952				HASSELBACH	D 0212 3G
073	—004.71150	47.83500	01	05	1952	17	00	1	COLOMB BECHAR	AF1510 E
074	+001.42470	46.66900	08	05	1952	14	00	1	VANVEY—GREY	F 151 G
075			14	05	1952	18	00	1	LA ROCHE SUR YON	F 151 G
076			27	05	1952	24	20	3	BRESIL	BR 151 G
077			28	05	1952	23	30	004	ALJARAQUE	E 151 D
078			29	05	1952	05	00	1	SAIGON	EO 151 G
079	+000.88200	47.06100		06	1952	24	00	3	CHOLET	F 301 G
080	—002.27610	48.99150		06	1952				EAUBONNE	F 151 D
081				06	1952				MORMON MESA —CALIF	X 0311 G
082			03	06	1952				ATHENES—GRECE	GR 11 G
083			30	06	1952				(ENID—OKLAHOMA)	X 0011 8L
084			04	07	1952	03	00	1	COLOMB BECHAR	AF 301 E
085	—005.43330	47.53980	18	07	1952	18	00	1	POUILLY/VINGEANNE	F 1206 5D
086			20	07	1952	00	30		DAI EL AOUAGRI	MA 001122 G
087			29	07	1952				*MONTANA	X A546 E
088	—002.83500	50.43240	01	08	1952	21	30	101	LENS	F 1511 D
089			03	08	1952	12	24	104	DIJON-MONTCHAPET	F 152 D
090	—002.56230	55.79200	03	08	1952	22	59	1	ARBRET (GARE)	F 3012 D

No.	Long.	Lat.	DD	MM	YYYY	HH	MM		Place	Code	
091	—001.39383	43.63560	13	08	1952	14	20	110	BLAGNAC	F 1545	D
092			19	08	1952	20	00	2	WEST PALM BEACH	X 011132	H
093			22	08	1952	23	40	1	MIAMI—FLO.37 M.	X 204	U
094			12	09	1952				FLATWOOD —VIRGINIE	X 011642	G
095	—003.60621	43.99200	15	10	1952	19	10	1	LE VIGAN —GARD	F 021	4G
096	—004.34781	43.84620	15	10	1952	19	50	1	NIMES—P.AEROD.	F 021	4G
097	+000.60938	43.18740	17	10	1952	15	00	2	*OLORON STE MARIE	F 129 41	D
098	—001.89711	43.90200	27	10	1952	16	00	1	*GAILLAC —TARN	F 129	D
099	—005.21730	43.43400	27	10	1952	21	00	1	MARIGNANE AEROPORT	F 0011	2C
100			16	11	1952				(CASTEL-FRANCO)	I 0011	G
101					1954				RAUCH	RA 001	V
102	—005.21730	43.43400	04	01	1954				MARIGNANE AEROPORT	F 0011	G
103				04	1954				*EDWARD USAF BASE	X 005	G
104			20	05	1954				(BRUTON—SOMERSET)	GB 0011	4G
105			30	05	1954	23	55	115	+BUFFON( )ST REMY	F 1516	D
106			23	06	1954	15	45	103	BRETIGNY	F 1511	E
107	—004.07790	48.29940	21	07	1954	16	00	1	TROYES	F 1516	D
108			07	08	1954	16	15	1	ZURICH	CH 301	A
109	—005.49619	47.09250	12	08	1954	24		2	DOLE —JURA—	F 11	A**
110	—005.49619	47.09250	19	08	1954	00	45	1	DOLE —JURA	F 11 2	C**037
111			20	08	1954				OEYDALEN P.MOSJOEN	N 0012	3I
112	—003.41730	47.73600	23	08	1954				(VARENNES P.DIGES)	F 001	G
113	—001.48131	49.09320	23	08	1954	01	00	145	*VERNON—EURE	F 1253	C 025
114	—002.10222	49.05000		09	1954	15	30	205	* PONTOISE	F 1313444E	
115	—002.47770	50.00400	07	09	1954	07	15	105	*(CONTAY—SOMME)	F 0012444C	049
116	—001.92600	45.61650	10	09	1954	20	30	105	MOURIERAS —CORREZE	F 0111 2C	058
117	—003.61530	50.39640	10	09	1954	22	30	105	*QUAROUBLE —NORD	F 021133 C	*064
118	—004.09230	49.91940	13	09	1954	00	30	1	HIRSON GARE TRIAGE	F 301	A
119	+000.96938	46.72800	14	09	1954	17	00	130	SIGOURNAIS.ST PRT	F 121744	C 030
120	—004.85721	45.66600	15	09	1954	23	20	105	(FEYSIN—ISERE)	F 0011	C 073

No.	Lat	Long	D	M	Yr	H	Mn	Z	Station	Ctry	Cat.	Obs	Ref
121			17	09	1954	16	45	1	PITIGLIANO	I	3012	C	081
122			17	09	1954	16	45	196	*ROME—CIAMPINO AER.	I	301901	C	079
123	46.71900	—000.53730	17	09	1954	22	30	105	VOUNEUIL / VIENNE	F	0111442C		084
124			18	09	1954	20	15	101	CASABLANCA	MA	0011441C		088
125	45.68400	—003.78630	19	09	1954	16	30	101	COL DU BEAL	F	3016	C	090
126	46.34100	—002.59821	19	09	1954	17	00	202	MONTLUCON—ALLIER	F	1516	C	091
127	49.27500	—006.59610	19	09	1954	21	15	101	OBERDORFF	F	0111	4C	091
128			20	09	1954	23	00	1	*SANTA MARIA—ACORES	F	0111	2E	091
129	38.00000	037.00000	21	09	1954				*ACORES—AU LARGE	AT	109700	A	
130			21	09	1954	21	15	130	FLEURANDERIE—INDRE	F	301	A	
131	48.84840	—003.23271	22	09	1954				REBAIS	F	151	C	100
132	48.45060	—002.62611	22	09	1954	20	00	130	FONTAINEBLEAU,N7	F	1271	C	*096
133	48.53700	—002.53071	22	09	1954	20	30	1	PONTHIERRY—ESSONNES	F	11.4	C	096
134	47.13660	—002.40390	23	09	1954	22		1	LE JOU P. BOURGES	F	0014	C	105
135	47.73600	—003.39750	24	09	1954				—DIGES P. AUXERRE	F	0011	I	—
136	45.09900	—003.49461	24	09	1954				LANGEAC	F	151	C**	114
137	45.04500	—003.88521	24	09	1954				LE PUY	F	151	C**	114
138			24	09	1954				SIERRA GARDUNHA	P	021	G	*
139	43.49100	001.47356	24	09	1954	15	00	205	BAYONNE	F	3037	C**	119
140	46.11900	—003.43300	24	09	1954	15	00	201	VICHY	F	1517	C**	117
141	44.10216	000.40761	24	09	1954	21	00	1	(LENCOUACQ—LANDES)	F	0011	C**	115
142	45.54719	—002.30895	24	09	1954	22	00	1	USSEL—CORREZE	F	001322	C**	118
143	45.25997	—001.74994	24	09	1954	23	00	102	*TULLE	F	151144	C**	445
144	44.90100	—005.01930	26	09	1954	14	30	1	CHABEUIL —DROME	F	011122	C**	131
145	45.54900	—005.98851	26	09	1954	17	15	2	CHALLES	F	151100	C**	130
146	44.28000	—004.15250	27	09	1954	02	00	199	FOUSSIGNARGUES	F	001744	C**	135
147	38.12000	037.36000	27	09	1954	03	20	1	AVION NY—LISBONNE	AT	1017	E	
148	44.60850	—002.02851	27	09	1954	08	40	1	FIGEAC —LOT	F	011	A	
149	42.68700	—002.90431	27	09	1954	15	00	2	PERPIGNAN—NE.	F	0211	C**	140
150	48.87000	—002.39121	27	09	1954	19	57	101	PARIS—EST	F	3012	C**	137

No.	Long.	Lat.	D	M	Year	Time	N	Station		
151	—006.02730	46.46340	27	09	1954	20 30	1	PREMANON —S.MOREZ	F 011441	C *143
152	—002.33721	48.87000	27	09	1954	21 30	2	PARIS SACRE—COEUR	F 3014	C**138
153	—004.77171	45.10980	27	09	1954	22 15	145	LEMPS	F 11 644	C**141
154	—007.40421	47.75000	27	09	1954	24 00	2	RIXHEIM HT—RHIN	F 1293	C**148
155	—003.29130	47.84400	28	09	1954	20 30	101	SENS —YONNE	F 0012	C**151
156	—002.47590	46.76400	28	09	1954	22 30	1	BOUZAIS —CHER	F 031133	C**157
157	002.07270	47.64600	28	09	1954	23 00	201	AUTUN—REGION (ST NICOLAS REDON)	F 0012	C 152
158			29	09	1954				F 0011	G
159	—004.96467	48.49920	29	09	1954	06 00	1	WASSY	F 151	C**154
160	—002.94642	42.67800	29	09	1954	20 00	101	CABESTANY	F 151	C**154
161	—006.30621	47.47950	29	09	1954	20 00	101	MONTAGNEY	F 1517	C**154
162	—004.62591	47.14920	29	09	1954	20 00	101	PAINBLANC	F 151144	C**155
163	—006.17661	47.38950	29	09	1954	20 00	201	RIGNEY	F 1511	C**155
164	—003.08331	46.91700	29	09	1954	21 00	2	LANGERON	F 1511	C**157
165	—003.23271	48.84840	29	09	1954	22 00		REBAIS	F 151	C**154
166	—003.27240	48.79800	30	09	1954			*(JOUY/MORIN)	F 0011	3G
167	—000.53730	47.04660	30	09	1954	16 30	1	—MARCILLY / VIENNE	F 016	2I
168			30	09	1954	20 00	1	BREST.AU LARGE.	F 101	A
169	—000.99891	49.35960	30	09	1954	22 00	130	GD—COURONNE P.ROUEN	F 301	A
170	—001.67121	50.76900	01	10	1954			(COMINES)	F 001	A
171			01	10	1954			DHUBRI —INDE	IN 0	A
172	—004.39551	46.69200	01	10	1954	13 00	1	*MONTCEAU LES MINES	F 0017	I
173	—000.33900	44.30300	02	10	1954	20 30	1	AIGUILLON	F 154	C**170
174	—004.20100	45.37100	02	10	1954			AUREC/LOIRE.HTE—L.	F 304	C**185
175	—003.30000	48.56000	02	10	1954			PROVINS	F 151	C**185
176	—003.03900	48.77100	02	10	1954			MAUPERTHUIS	F 151	C**185
177	—005.21721	46.66500	02	10	1954			LOUHANS	F 001	C**175
178	—004.82000	43.04700	02	10	1954			AVIGNON	F 151	C**170
179	—003.81300	45.13700	02	10	1954			ST PAULIEN	F 154	C**185
180	—004.03000	44.21700	02	10	1954			LA GD COMBE	F 151	C**170

#	Long	Lat			Year	Hr	Min	No	Name	F	C
181	−005.22600	46.20400	02	10	1954				BOURG	F 151	C**170
182	−001.16700	46.21500	02	10	1954				MAGNAC—LAVAL	F 151	C**170
183	−002.20200	46.56200	02	10	1954				CHATEAUMEILLANT	F 151	C**170
184	−005.46900	45.67500	02	10	1954				MORESTEL	F 151	C**170
185	−007.31900	47.58500	02	10	1954				WILLER	F 151	C**170
186	004.10200	48.01500	02	10	1954				QUIMPER	F 151	C**170
187	−003.43300	46.11900	02	10	1954				VICHY	F 151	C**170
188	002.76100	48.51000	02	10	1954				(SAINT—BRIEUC)	F 001	C**170
189	002.75400	47.65700	02	10	1954				VANNES	F 151	C**170
190	000.88200	47.06100	02	10	1954				CHOLET	F 151	C**170
191	−004.78300	47.50700	02	10	1954				PELLEREY	F 12	C**170
192	−002.79700	47.18700	02	10	1954				RIANS	F 12	C**170
193	−003.58920	47.82600	02	10	1954			105	(JONCHES.AUXERRE)	F 021	G
194	−006.06000	46.48500	02	10	1954	15	45	1	LES ROUSSES	F 1117	C**184
195	−002.73051	49.54050	02	10	1954	18	15	1	RESSONS/MATZ—OISE	F 001122	E
196	−001.80900	47.07000	02	10	1954	19	00		VATAN—INDRE	F 11	C**184
197	−004.76181	47.49750	02	10	1954	19	40	160	PONCEY/L IGNON CDO	F 11 2	C**176
198	−006.67530	48.49260	02	10	1954	21	00	160	BLANCHE—EGLISE	F 0013	C**168
199	−006.80500	48.87000	02	10	1954	21	00		BASSING	F 001	C**168
200	−000.15921	45.64800	03	10	1954				ANGOULEME	F 1512	C**220
201	000.20672	46.41300	03	10	1954				SAINT—MAIXENT	F 151	C**220
202	−000.48402	44.85150	03	10	1954				BERGERAC —DORDOGNE	F 0012	2C**220
203	−002.27710	48.99150	03	10	1954				*EAUBONNE—S+O	F 0013	E
204	000.44190	46.83420	03	10	1954	06	00	202	BRESSUIRE.4KM.ESE	F 0111	2C**221
205	−001.83096	50.31360	03	10	1954	18	45	103	LIGESCOURT—SOMME	F 0112	2C *198
206	−003.20940	50.61150	03	10	1954	19	20	1	(CHERENG—NORD)	F 0012	G
207	+000.52470	45.94500	03	10	1954	20	00		ST—JEAN D ANGELY	F 301	A
208	−006.78870	48.84840	03	10	1954	20	17	115	BIDESTROFF P.DIEUZE	F 0016	C**169
209	−002.09430	48.89700	03	10	1954	20	30		ST.GERMAIN EN LAYE	F 301	A
210	−003.17430	50.12100	03	10	1954	20	30	1	MARCOING P.CAMBRAI	F 301	C 186

211	—005.04200	47.32200	03	10	1954	20	45	101	DIJON	F 151	C**208
212	—002.92770	50.52960	03	10	1954	20	45	1	ANNOEULLIN	F 0011	I *
213	—003.07000	45.77400	03	10	1954	20	55	101	CLERMONT—FERRAND	F 151	C**211
214	—002.94606	46.89000	03	10	1954	21	00	101	LA CHAPELLE HUGON	F 301	C**214
215	—003.93471	47.06550	03	10	1954	21	05	105	CHATEAU—CHINON	F 1313	3C *192
216	—002.25720	50.02740	03	10	1954	21	05	107	(HERISSART—SOMME)	F 301	C**214
217	—006.80490	47.51100	03	10	1954	21	05	105	MONTBELIARD	F 301	C**214
218	—006.97617	47.53800	03	10	1954	21	05	105	GRANVILLARS	F 0013	C 194
219	—001.64800	50.29200	03	10	1954	21	10	1	(QUEND—SOMME)	F 152144	C 205
220	—002.51721	48.81150	03	10	1954	21	30	1	*CHAMPIGNY/MARNE	F 1512	C**217
221	—001.65861	46.52370	03	10	1954	21	30	101	POMMIERS	F 3014	C**206
222	—002.40200	48.40200	03	10	1954	21	30	102	MILLY LA FORET	F 1412	C *196
223	—002.71125	50.39460	03	10	1954	21	30	103	ABLAIN ST NAZAIRE	F 1416	C *195
224	—002.76740	50.42160	03	10	1954	21	30	105	(LIEVIN—P DE C)	F 1513	C**222
225	—000.77661	46.50840	03	10	1954	22	45	201	LEIGNES—FONTAINE	F 001122	C 220
226	—000.24930	45.47700	03	10	1954	22	45	101	RONSENAC —CHARENTE	F 3015	C**222
227	—001.12114	46.43550	03	10	1954	23	00	2	P.LUSIGNAN—VIENNE	F 001222	C**222
228	000.59768	46.36800	03	10	1954	23	30	201	BENET—NESSIER—VEND	F 0012	C**172
229			03	10	1954	23	30	1	GUEBLIN —MOSELLE	F 301	A
230	—001.07730	49.41900	03	10	1954	24	00	2	ROUEN	F 0012	3C**235
231	—002.59641	43.09880	04	10	1954			1	LAGRASSE —AUDE	F 0011	A
232	—000.93060	45.50760	04	10	1954				CHALAIS—DORDOGNE	F 001	E
233	—001.25721	45.85050	04	10	1954				LIMOGES	F 0111	C**234
234	—004.72761	49.63500	04	10	1954	18	40	1	VILLERS LE TILLEUL	F 0017	C**224
235	—004.36200	46.67400	04	10	1954	19	00	101	*MONTCEAU—LES—MINES	F 0012221	C**224
236	—004.76181	47.49750	04	10	1954	20	00	1	*PONCEY/L IGNON	F 001	233
237	002.18438	48.56940	04	10	1954	20	00	2	(TREGON SW DINARD)	F 0011334C	233
238	—006.67071	47.06100	04	10	1954	20	30	170	VILLERS LE LAC	F 1516	C**235
239	+003.44100	48.81600	04	10	1954	20	30	101	PERROS—GUIREC	F 0211	2C 236
240	002.26178	48.37500	04	10	1954	22	00	102	(MEGRIT SW DINAN)		

No.	Longitude	Latitude	d	mo	yr	h	m	N	Locality		Num	Code
241	−005.70861	43.27560	05	10	1954				CUGES—LES—PINS	F	001	G
242	−004.90311	48.43260	05	10	1954				MERTRUD—HTE MARNE	F	011	3G
243			05	10	1954				MANTOUE,PROV.DE	I	—	G
244	004.17428	47.83500	05	10	1954	04	00	1	—LOCTUDY—FINISTERE	F	0011	2I
245	−004.86630	48.10820	05	10	1954	07	15	1	VOILLECOMTE H—MARN	F	001	A
246	001.06028	46.77840	06	10	1954				MOUCHAMPS—VENDEE	F	001	G
247	−003.36321	49.66200	06	10	1954	21	30	1	CASERNE LA FERE	F	0024	2E
248	−001.50030	46.64700	07	10	1954				CHASSENEUIL —INDRE	F	301	A
249	−001.66941	46.45710	07	10	1954				SAINT PLANTAIRE	F	151	C**143
250	+001.62278	49.63950	07	10	1954				CHERBOURG	F	153	C**241
251	−005.54031	43.21620	07	10	1954				CASSIS	F	151	C**141
252	−000.99351	44.62020	07	10	1954				BOURNEL	F	3012	C**242
253	−002.06721	46.57680	07	10	1954				MONTLEVICQ—INDRE	F	110	C**242
254	−003.68343	47.25900	07	10	1954				CORBIGNY—NIEVRE	F	122	C**242
255	−000.18495	45.61200	07	10	1954				PUYMOYEN—CHARENTE	F	001 22	C 242
256	+000.52478	45.27000	07	10	1954	02	00	1	MARCILLAC DE BLAYE	F	1511	C**237
257	−004.20021	49.35600	07	10	1954	02	00	1	ISLES SUR SUIPPES	F	0111222C	238
258	−000.52191	44.34930	07	10	1954	02	00	2	MONTPEZAT D AGENAIS		151	C**238
259	004.42322	47.80800	07	10	1954	02	00	1	(PLOZEVET—FINISTER)	F	0016	C 237
260	−000.20691	46.56600	07	10	1954	04	00	1	BERUGES W.POITIERS	F	0011	2C 239
261	−000.14121	48.15000	07	10	1954	06	20	105	LE MANS	F	001	C 240
262	−000.69921	47.79000	07	10	1954	06	20	2	ST JEAN D ASSE	F	301133	C**239
263	−004.99761	44.03520	07	10	1954	07	00	1	LAVENAY	F	1514	C**241
264	−004.03520	48.49200	07	10	1954	14	30	1	MONTEUX—VAUCLUSE	F	0011332C	244
265	−004.11381	48.50280	07	10	1954	19	30	1	ARCIS/AUBE.5KM.SSW	F	003	C
266	−004.10661	49.19400	07	10	1954	19	30	1	ST ET.SS.BARBUISE	F	003	C 249
267	−001.46511	49.74940	07	10	1954	20	00	2	HENNEZIS SE.ANDELYS	F	0212	C 249
268	−007.36371	47.59740	07	10	1954	24	00	1	JETTINGEN—HT RHIN	F	0011	2C**243
269	−002.93301	42.73110	07	10	1954	24	00	1	BOMPAS PY.ORIENT.	F	0011	1C 250
270			08	10	1954	20	00	2	MUZKA AER.,EGYPTE	ET	301	A

No.	Long.	Lat.	D	Mo	Yr	N	H	M	Location	Ref
271			09	10	1954				HUY—BELGIQUE	B 001 A
272	−002.59821	46.34100	09	10	1954				MONTLUCON—ALLIER	F 151 C 263
273	−002.94930	48.66000	09	10	1954				TRILPORT	F 301 A
274	−001.34181	48.84300	09	10	1954				DREUX.12KM.NORD.	F 0012 G
275	000.57068	45.37440	09	10	1954	1	16	00	SOUBRAN CHAR.—MAR.	F 001 C *263
276	−002.34963	43.20900	09	10	1954	105	18	30	(CARCASSONNE—AUDE)	F 0211 A
277	−006.15501	49.02120	09	10	1954	3	19	00	POURNOY LA CHETIVE	F 0134442C *262
278	000.30788	48.60900	09	10	1954	1	19	00	(BEAUVAIN—ORNE)	F 0011 4C 260
279	000.52677	46.59660	09	10	1954	2	20	00	LAVOUX E.POITIERS	F 301144 C *262
280	−007.59500	51.96300	09	10	1954	1	20	30	(MUNSTER)	D 0411 I—
281	−001.91421	43.74900	09	10	1954	1	22	15	BRIATEXTE—TARN	F 0210 3C 264
282			09	10	1954				BEYROUTH —LIBAN	RL 001 I—
283	−000.21690	54.54600	10	10	1954				*ST.GERM.DE LIVET	F 301 A
284			10	10	1954				BIRMANIE—SIAM—ETC.	SM 002 A
285	−004.15971	47.50380	10	10	1954				EPOISSES—TOUTRY	F 0012 2G
286	001.00358	47.96280	10	10	1954	1	06	30	RTE MERAL—ST POIX	F 001 2G
287	−005.83101	48.62700	10	10	1954	2	20	10	CHARMES LA COTE MM	F 001 A
288			10	10	1954		21	00	YAOUNDE—KAMERUN	AF 301 A
289	006.17130	54.57000	10	10	1954	199	24		*METZ	F 301 C 265
290	−006.63921	48.71880	10	10	1954	1			MONCOURT SSW DIEUZE	F 001 22 I—
291	−002.53593	46.35900	11	10	1954				DOMERAT	F 151 C**273
292	−002.88621	48.96000	11	10	1954				MEAUX	F 151 C**273
293	−002.83221	48.45870	11	10	1954				MACHAULT	F 151 C**273
294	−002.59821	46.34100	11	10	1954				MONTLUCON—ALLIER	F 151 C**273
295	−001.17981	49.17060	11	10	1954				ACQUIGNY	F 001 C 273
296	003.89258	47.99250	11	10	1954				ELLIANT—FINISTERE	F 001 I—
297	−004.20030	44.27100	11	10	1954				ST AMBROIX—GARD	F A
298	−003.11661	45.89280	11	10	1954	2	02	00	*RIOM—PUY DE DOME	F 1232 C 271
299	000.64358	49.03200	11	10	1954	1	04	15	(BAUQUAY—CALVADOS)	F 0011 C**274
300	−004.32621	45.89600	11	10	1954	101	04	15	FONFREDE	F 151133 C**267

No.	Long.	Lat.			Year				Location			
301	−004.56390	47.07630	11	10	1954	04	20	1	(LACANCHE W.BEAUNE)	F	001133	C *269
302	−007.23951	47.57400	11	10	1954	06	00	2	HEIMERSDORF HT—RH	F	0014	1C**272
303	−003.51936	47.46060	11	10	1954	06	00	1	CLAMECY—CORBIGNY	F	031333	C *268
304	001.00448	45.67500	11	10	1954	19	30	110	(TAUPIGNAC NWROYAN)	F	0413	C**269
305	−000.82521	45.87300	11	10	1954	20	00		SAILLAT/VIENNE	F	001	C 273
306	000.06128	45.56160	11	10	1954	21	30	1	BIRAC—CHARENTE	F	0013	G
307	−003.69621	43.51500	11	10	1954	22	00	1	MONTBAZIN—HERAULT	F	001	—
308	−002.22831	44.47800	11	10	1954	22	00	102	MONTBAZENS—AVEYRON	F	0016332C	275
309	001.31678	47.65500	11	10	1954	22	30	1	ERBRAY—LOIRE ATL.	F	011	C**271
310	−002.92716	44.35560	12	10	1954				GAILLAC	F	151	C**283
311	−004.84821	46.78650	12	10	1954				CHALON			C**
312	−001.23471	43.59960	12	10	1954				LEGUEVIN HT—GARONNE	F	001	—
313			12	10	1954				LA CROIX—DAURADE	F	00122	A
314	−002.59821	46.34100	12	10	1954				MONTLUCON—ALLIER	F	011	C *283
315			12	10	1954				MAMORA—FORET	MA	161	A
316	−006.53031	47.13120	12	10	1954				ORCHAMPS—DOUBS	F	3012	C *283
317			12	10	1954				TEHERAN—IRAN	IR		C —
318	001.14578	46.16100	12	10	1954	19	10	1	(LA ROCHELLE C.MAR)	F	001	C**283
319	−004.69521	46.77300	12	10	1954	21	30	1	JAMBLES	F	151	C**285
320	006.19101	46.37200	12	10	1954	22	45	1	(DOMPIERRE—TILLEUL)	F	3012	G
321	−006.16221	46.85670	12	10	1954	22	45	1	FRASNE	F	301244	C**283
322	−002.09241	43.62120	12	10	1954	23	30	1	VIELMUR—TARN	F	031	C *283
323	001.40121	43.59600	13	10	1954				TOULOUSE HTE—GAR.	F	0113	2G
324	−004.20030	44.27100	13	10	1954				ST AMBROIX—GARD	F	167	A
325	−004.87251	45.96480	13	10	1954	16	50	101	(RANCE—ENE TREVOUX)	F	3011	C 285
326			13	10	1954	19	35	1	BOURRASOLE	F	161	A
327	−004.83921	47.00250	14	10	1954				BEAUNE	F		C**
328			14	10	1954				THAILANDE	SM	001	G
329	−002.90431	42.68700	14	10	1954				PERPIGNAN	F	011	A
330	−005.13351	43.91100	14	10	1954	12	30	180	*FONTAINE—VAUCLUSE	F	151700	C**300

No.	Long.	Lat.	D	M	Year	H	Min	N	Place		
331	001.40318	46.40940	14	10	1954	18	00	2	(ANGLES—VENDEE)	C**298	F 301
332		46.33200	14	10	1954	18	00	1	CHEMIN LONG TOULON	A	F 011
333	—005.13036	46.20240	14	10	1954	18	13	101	*MONTREVEL	C**299	F 1517
334	—005.20621	43.62660	14	10	1954	18	13	101	*BOURG	C**299	F 1517
335	—007.10001	46.80840	14	10	1954	18	15	1	BIOT P.ANTIBES A.M.	3I	F 0011
336	—004.86171	46.63260	14	10	1954	18	20	1	CHARDONNAY	C**289	F 15 12
337	—005.21730	47.00250	14	10	1954	18	30	101	*LOUHANS S>LOIRE	C**290	F 1512
338	—004.89699	46.96560	14	10	1954	18	31	105	MEURSANGES	C**290	F 1416
339	—004.97943	45.79100	14	10	1954	18	35	101	CHEVIGNY/VALLIERES	C**291	F 151
340	—005.75721	45.61100	14	10	1954	18	40	1	POLIGNY	C**292	F 1511
341	—004.42701	46.60200	14	10	1954	19	10	2	BROSSES—TILLOTS	C**293	F 301233
342	—004.30821	46.56870	14	10	1954	19	20	105	CIRY LE NOBLE	C**293.	F 1511
343	004.08771	66.60200	14	10	1954	19	30	1	(BOIS DE CHAZEY)	C**294	F 001233
344	000.61191	46.75320	14	10	1954	19	35	101	GUEUGNON	C**294	F 151233
345	—005.24331	47.96100	14	10	1954	20	00	2	(S.GERMAIN DU BOIS)	C**292	F 0011
346	000.97928	49.74930	14	10	1954	20	00	210	MERAL—MAYENNE	C**295	F 011133
347	—001.93041	51.53200	14	10	1954	20	10	1	THIEULOY LA VILLE	E	F 001133
348	—000.72000	47.68830	15	10	1954				SOUTHEND —ESSEX	C**306	GB 0011
349	—002.62899	50.91300	15	10	1954				GIEN	C**312	F 151
350	—001.90251	48.87000	15	10	1954	03	40	102	ST P.HALTE—CALAIS	3C**304	F 0011
351	—002.39121		15	10	1954	14	40	1	PARIS	C**305	F 154
352			15	10	1954	15	00		PO DI GNOCCA		I 0016223
353	—002.44970	50.61960	15	10	1954	20	00	2	ISBERGUES—P.DE C.	C**305	F 0011
354	—002.73771	47.99700	15	10	1954	20	30	2	MONTARGIS	C**305	F 1511
355	004.01138	47.89530	15	10	1954	21	00	2	FOUESNANT—FINIST.	C**305	F 0021
356	—007.50463	47.70000	15	10	1954	21	00	2	NIFFER—KEMPS	C**306	F 131
357			16	10	1954				P.VARESE		I 301
358			16	10	1954				MIRAFIORI P.MILAN	A	I 301
359	—003.24540	45.50040	16	10	1954				ISSOIRE—LE—BROC	A	F 301
360			16	10	1954				LIVRY SUR SEINE	A	F

ID	Longitude	Latitude							Place	Code
361	−002.15721	48.98700	16	10	1954	21	00	2	HERBLAY S+O	F 011144 G
362	−001.43721	49.79340	16	10	1954	21	30	1	BAILLOLET. SEINE—MAR	F 014133 G
363	−002.41650	48.73500	16	10	1954	21	30	1	*ORLY	F 301 A
364	−001.93221	51.90300	16	10	1954	21	45	1	*(BELESTA—ARIEGE)	F 0033 G
365			16	10	1954				DOMPIERRE	F 0012 4E
366			17	10	1954				ILE DE CAPRI	I 0411 2G
367	−005.71221	43.18200	17	10	1954				ST CYR/MER —VAR	F 011 G
368	−006.21621	47.83500	17	10	1954				(VARIGNEY HT—SAONE)	F 0016 G
369			17	10	1954	22	30	1	ARMIGNY	F 0011 E
370	000.87668	45.82800	18	10	1954				PONT ABBE ARNOULT	F 001 A
371	−002.70711	45.79200	18	10	1954				CISTERNES—FORET	F 0012 I
372	−002.76471	45.77130	18	10	1954	17	30	101	*GELLES—PUY DE DOME	F 0011332C**335
373			18	10	1954	17	30		COHEIX P.GELLES	F 0011333G
374	−003.40191	45.14850	18	10	1954	18	00	1	ST—CIRGUES.HT—LOI.	F 302744 C 324
375	000.79928	45.70200	18	10	1954	21	00	2	SAINTES.WNW.N150	F 042244 C 326
376	−006.31083	46.80000	18	10	1954	22	45	102	VEZENAY—DOUBS	F 031122 C**332
377	+003.05460	48.65500	19	10	1954				TREVEREC C.DU N.	F 001 A
378			20	10	1954				RTE P.MERS—SOMME	F 001 44 G
379			20	10	1954				ST VALERY —MERS SOM	F 121 G
380	−004.28121	48.26700	20	10	1954				LUSIGNY—FORET	F 0011333G
381	−007.10721	48.56400	20	10	1954				TURQUENSTEIN—MOSEL	F 001133 G
382	−007.25583	47.90333	20	10	1954				ISSENHEIM—HT RHIN	F 001 G**
383	−006.82821	48.34800	20	10	1954	03	00	1	ST REMY NW ST DIE	F 0111 I
384	000.42128	45.99000	21	10	1954				POUZOU—GC20—CH.M	F 001233 G
385	+004.47750	48.39300	21	10	1954	10	00	2	BREST	F 301 A
386			21	10	1954	21	30	1	RTE SERIFERE—PAILLE	F 301 G
387	−004.30821	46.60200	22	10	1954	15	30	1	CIRY LE NOBLE	F 144 E
388	+000.66150	46.47240	23	10	1954				ST—HILAIRE—DES—LOG.	F 301 A
389	000.00278	46.66050	23	10	1954				CHALAMBRAY—VIENNE	F 0011 A
390			23	10	1954	22	15	1	PARIS—BD PEREIRE	F 301 A

No.	Long.	Lat.	D	M	Yr	H	Min	N	Place	Ref
391	−006.29721	48.83400	24	10	1954				PLAGE AIN EL TURCK	AG 301 G
392	+002.59407	48.17700	25	10	1954				ARRAYE ET HAN MM.	F 001 2I
393	−002.14821	45.99000	25	10	1954				PLEMET—C.DU NORD	F A
394			26	10	1954				LA VAUREILLE—CREUSE	F 011122 G
395			26	10	1954			1	ANGOULEME.18KM.	F 001 3A
396	−007.53840	47.97000	26	10	1954	06	00	1	HEITEREN	F 0011 E
397	−002.20221	50.34600	27	10	1954	21	30		*(LINZEUX P.DE C.)	F 001233 C *341
398	−004.71411	49.76370	27	10	1954	05	15	1	*MEZIERES	F 001 E
399	−002.35521	46.43100	29	10	1954				(MESPLES—ALLIER)	F 001244 G
400	−001.97901	50.04000	31	10	1954	20	00		LONG—SOMME	F 0013 2E
401	−001.71990	50.27760	31	10	1954			1	ARRY—SOME	F 001 E
402			01	11	1954				POGGI DI AMBRA	I 0211222G
403	−004.12380	45.14400	05	11	1954	21	00	1	YSSINGEAUX	F 301 A
404			05	11	1954				LA COROGNE	E 001 A
405	−000.04221	47.94300	08	11	1954	06	00		LOUPLANDE—SARTHE	F 0011333I
406			09	11	1954			1	COULSOU	F 0011 E
407			13	11	1954				CURITIBA.V.FER.PR.	BR 0311 G
408	−001.27521	49.57560	13	11	1954				INTER.RN28—RN319	F 001133 G
409			14	11	1954				ISOLA P.LA SPEZZIA	I 031133 G
410	−003.53421	50.44400	24	11	1954				TOURNAI.ENVIRONS.	B 001133 G
411	−001.57590	49.63140	27	11	1954	22	50	102	*LA BELLIERE.N.15	F 151144 E
412			01	12	1954	15	15	175	MOSCOU	U 11 E
413	−000.24561	43.58250	02	12	1954	06	30		BASSOUES—GERS	F 0011 0E
414			07	12	1954	14	11	160	*CEUTA	MA 151 01 E
415			13	12	1954				(FONTLAND—CHER)	F 001 3G
416			19	12	1954				(CAMPINAS.S.PAULO)	BR 001 44 G
417	−001.59741	50.42700	13	12	1954	05	00	1	*BERCK—AEROD.	F 0011 4E
418			19	12	1954	06	00	1	YGRANDE—ALLIER	F 0016 2D
419			05	01	1955	20	00		SAN SEBASTIAN	E 001 2G
420			22	03	1955			1	(BARIKA P.SETIF)	AG 001 G

No.	Long.	Lat.	Day	Mo.	Year	Hr	Min		Name	Code
421	−002.04651	45.79200	31	05	1955	11	00	120	PUY ST GULMIER	F 0011442I
422	−001.84221	50.14080	18	07	1955	03	30	1	*PLESSIEL AER.SOMME	F 0011 3E
423	−004.95981	49.42800	05	08	1955	14	30	1	*BUZANCY—ARDENNES	F 0052 E
424			25	08	1955				GREENHILLS	X 011 G
425			15	01	1956				LOS CARACAS	VZ 101 G
426			09	02	1956				CALIFORNIE—COTE	X 101 2G
427				04	1956				SALINE ARICAO—SALTA	RA 11 V
428				04	1956				DRAKENSBERG(AF.SUD)	ZA 001 G
429			07	04	1956	23	45	1	ELBEUF—L OURAIL	F 0016 3E
430			13	04	1956	01	20	1	CALIFORNIE—AU LARGE	PF 101 G
431			29	06	1956	18	00	1	BUENOS AIRES	RA 11 A
432	−003.00000	43.18560	17	08	1956	22	00	1	NARBONNE—AUDE	F 001 I
433			09	09	1956				DERBY—ULSTER	GB 001 1G
434			16	09	1956				PUY DE DOME	F 021 G
435			25	11	1956	21	10	1	SALTA.ENVIRONS.	RA 001 44 G
436			12	02	1957				—ANTOFAGASTA—ANDES	RH 11 G
437	−143.50000	31.25000	19	04	1957	15	00	1	JAPON—PARAGES.	PF 102 G
438			25	06	1957	01	00	1	CHERBOURG—AU LARGE	F 101 G
439			05	07	1957				URIMAN	VZ 021 G
440	−004.04181	49.25700	05	10	1957				REIMS—MARNE	F 011 2G
441			05	10	1957				COTE DU NORD	F 021 G
442			10	10	1957				QUEBRA—COCO	BR 071 444G
443			30	10	1957	21	00	1	CASPER.WYOM.13M.N.	X 001233 U
444			02	11	1957	22	50	1	*LEVELLAND—TEXAS	X 0017335U
445			03	11	1957				MUROC — LOUISIANE	X 001 G
446			03	11	1957	03	00	1	LEVELLAND—ENVIR.	X 001 U
447			03	11	1957	19	00	1	SIBBALD—E.ALBERTA	X 001133 U
448			03	11	1957	20	00	1	LEVELLAND—250 M.E.	X 001 U
449			04	11	1957	03	15	1	*ELMWOOD PK ILL.	X 001333 U
450			04	11	1957	13	13	1	RTE 84 SW.SITE A	X 0011 U

ID	Long.	Lat.	Day	Mo	Year	H	M	N	Location	Code
451			04	11	1957	22	00	1	MONROE—LOUISIANE	X 0014 1U
452	—005.92911	46.45800	04	11	1957	24	00	1	LONGCHAUMOIS—JURA	F 001 G
453			05	11	1957				WABASH—70M.SSW.	X 0013 U
454			05	11	1957	17	00	1	KEARNEY—NEBRASKA	X 061122 U
455			06	11	1957	00	04	1	SANTA FE—NV—MEXIQ	X 001233 U
456			06	11	1957	01	00	1	MACON—ATLANTA	X 0015 U
457			06	11	1957	06	30	1	KNOXVILLE—TENNESSEE	X 041144 U
458			06	11	1957	18	00	1	EVERITTSTOWN,N.J.	X 112 U
459			06	11	1957	21	00	1	LAKE BASKALONG	CN 001433 U
460			07	11	1957				MERIDIAN—MISS	X 031 G
461			07	11	1957	07	25	102	HONSE—MISS.ENVIR.	X 031244 U
462			07	11	1957	20	40	1	LANSFORD—PENNS.	X 031244 U
463			07	11	1957	23	30	1	MONTVILLE—OHIO	X 0011443U
464			08	11	1957				WATERLOO—IOWA	X 0211 U
465			09	11	1957	02	00	1	NY—SLOANVILLE	X 001 5U
466			09	11	1957	19	15	1	WHITE SANDS	X 001333 U
467			10	11	1957	01	25	1	MADISON—OHIO	X 001133 U
468			16	11	1957	22	30	1	BAGES CITY	BR 001 G
469			23	01	1958	04	01	2	SMARZEDZ —POLOGNE	PL121
470			09	02	1958				GENERAL PICO	RA 11 A
471	—007.33491	43.70760	02	03	1958	01	55	2	BEAULIEU /MER	F 11 G
472			08	08	1958	24	27	1	*RTE UNSUE—BOLIVAR	RA 001134 V
473	—001.36071	43.08120	27	09	1958	21	00	160	MAZ D AZIL ARIEGE	F 11 G
474			03	10	1958				BIARRITZ—REGION	F 11 G
475			03	10	1958	03	10	1	ROSSVILLE—INDIANA	X 004 3G
476	—003.09321	45.77850	20	12	1958	16	00	1	CL.FERRAND	F 001 224G
477	—021.58500	53.06700	20	03	1959	17	30	1	OSTROLEKA—POLOGNE	PL E
478			20	05	1959	17	30	1	TRES LOMAS—PAMPA	RA 0012221V
479			01	04	1960				—MOZAMBIQUE	AF 001 A
480			26	04	1960				CHERBOURG—AU LARGE	F 101 A

No.	Lat	Long	DD	MM	YYYY	HH	MM	Dur	Location	Code
481	44.66250	001.17278	01	09	1960	03	00	1	ARCACHON	F 001 A
482	49.30740	—000.94491	12	11	1960				LA LONDE	F 001 A
483			01	11	1961				*VUKOVAR CROATIA	JU 151 38 E
484			03	11	1961	16	30	1	EYRES MONSELL	GB 1513 E
485			11	12	1961	10	00	1	+SOUTHPORT	GB 3021 E
486				01	1962				(CENTRE FRANCE)	F 001 E
487			02		1962				(TUCUMAN—B.AIRES)	RA 002333 E
488				04	1962				MILAN	I 301 14E
489			12	05	1962	04	10	1	+ROAD 35,KM 72,PAMPA	RA 0013 5E
490			14	05	1962	10	00	2	+SANTA ROSA	RA 156 E
491			14	05	1962	24	00	2	PUERTO BELGRANO	RA 151 E
492			20	05	1962	20	20	140	CANAL ROAD,DEFIANCE	X 151 E
493			23	05	1962				BAHIA—BLANCA	RA E
494			22	05	1962				BRISTOL	GB 151 00 E
495			15	06	1962			320	OLAVARIA,PR.B.AIRES	RA 1517 E
496			15	06	1962	24	00	2	+PR.OF WALES ISLAND2	AU 001 E
497			19	06	1962	18	08	1	LONDON	GB 1511 E
498			07	07	1962	23	10	103	CAPE HALLETT	NZ 151 E
499			08	08	1962				MADRID,ALCAZAR,	E 151 E
500	45.86000	—002.92000	29	08	1962	13	45	110	VAURIAT,P.DE DOME	F 1543 E

APPENDIX IV

AN ANALYSIS OF UFO ACTIVITY

CLASSIFICATION SYSTEM

WE HAVE SEEN that reports of unusual aerial phenomena are classified mainly according to their described *behavior*, because this characteristic is least likely to be affected by the witness' lack of experience as an observer or by the loss of information that occurs when the reports are obtained through the newspapers. The definitions of the various types are given in Chapter 3. In this section we will indicate the changes that have been made in the various categories since the system was introduced in 1961. *Type I, Classes A, B, C, and D:* The general definition remains unchanged, but Class A is the set of observations reporting objects on or near the ground ("tree height" maximum). In Class B are cases reporting objects near or over an open body of water. Class C gathers cases reporting craftlike objects whose occupants displayed interest in the witness by gestures or luminous signals. In Class D are cases reporting objects "scouting" a terrestrial vehicle (Monticello, Exeter, etc.). *Type II, Classes A, B and C:* The definitions remain the same as those given in Chapter 3. We have introduced Class C for cases reporting "cloud-cigars" among a number of secondary objects, without generation or reintegration (Oloron, Gaillac, Lemps).

Type III, Classes A, B, C, D, and E: These are objects seen in flight whose trajectories show at least one point of discontinuity. Class A covers cases reporting vertical, up-and-down motion, a "dead-leaf" trajectory, or a pendulum motion. In Class B cases the continuous flight trajectory is interrupted as the object halts, without a change of altitude, for some time before resuming its flight. Class C cases report the object as stopping and altering its physical appearance while hovering: suddenly changing luminosity, releasing a smaller object, etc. Class D cases describe "dog fights," where several objects seem to participate in an aerial dance, or the peculiar behavior of a single object. In Class E are cases reporting an object altering its trajectory to fly very slowly above a certain point, or circling, or suddenly changing course.

Type IV, Classes A, B, C, and D: The general definition ("continuous flight") is retained. It applies best to Class A. Three new classes are defined: in an observation of Class B, the behavior, trajectory, or physical appearance of the object is said to be affected by a nearby conventional aircraft. In Class C, several objects are reported "in formation." In Class D are descriptions of objects in continuous flight whose trajectory is compared to that of a wave or a "zigzag."

Type V, Classes A, B, and C: Reports of this type involve less definite objects that do not, either because of unfavorable observing conditions or by the very nature of the phenomenon, appear as material or solid in structure. In Class A are cases of peculiar aerial phenomena of extended apparent diameter not described as material objects and cases of "nocturnal meandering lights," excluding point sources. In Class B are reports of starlike objects motionless for periods of long duration. In Class C are the cases of point sources rapidly crossing the sky: borderline objects that cannot be identified as meteors, artificial satellites, or high-flying planes because of their peculiar trajectory or velocity (cf. "The Case of the Crooked Bolides," Chapter 1).

CODING OF SECONDARY CHARACTERISTICS

The code we use to describe the reported phenomena compactly is a very simple one, contained in two "words" of six characters (a letter or a number). The first word gathers the "external" features of the sighting, i.e., those conditions that guide us in our estimate of the reliability and significance of the report, as distinguished from those characteristics indicative of the phenomenon itself, which are expressed by the second word.

The following data are treated as "external" features: (1) the country where the sighting took place (two letters); (2) the number of witnesses (one number); (3) the general observation conditions (one letter); (4) the physical effects associated with the phenomenon (two letters).

The following data are considered "internal": (5) the type of the observation (a number from 1 to 5); (6) the class (a letter from A to E); (7) the number of objects (one number); (8) the shape (one letter); (9) the reported color (one letter); (10) the dimensions: greatest diameter (one number).

To show the number of witnesses (2), the number of objects (7), and the dimensions (10) of the objects in meters, we use the following code:

CODE	NUMBER OF WITNESSES	NUMBER OF OBJECTS	DIMENSIONS (IN METERS)
o	observation by automatic instrument	not applicable	less than 1
1	1	1	1–2
2	2	2	2–5
3	3	3	5–10
4	4	4	10–20

CODE	NUMBER OF WITNESSES	NUMBER OF OBJECTS	DIMENSIONS (IN METERS)
5	5	5	20–30
6	about 10	6	30–60
7	dozens	7	60–100
8	hundreds	8	about 100
9	thousands	9	very large
+	several (precise no. unknown)	several (precise no. unknown)	not applicable
×	not applicable	very large no.	

CODE FOR GENERAL OBSERVING CONDITIONS (3):

A observations by trained technical personnel
I sighting by non-technical witnesses using an optical instrument
O observation made during a thunderstorm
P observation made by pilots in flight
R radar observation
S simultaneous air-visual and ground-radar sighting
T observation confirmed by material traces
V sighting by witnesses inside a vehicle on the ground

CODE FOR PHYSICAL OBSERVATIONS (4): TWO LETTERS

First Letter

A halo or diffuse glow
B flipping motion
D separation into several parts
E emission of sparks
F emission of smoke
H emission of lightning
M appendages
O horizontal oscillations

Second Letter

A sudden changes of altitude
B vertical disappearance
C emission of heat
D sudden changes of direction
F group flight behavior
H high velocity
I object seen stationary

P beam of light
R odor
S spin
T honeycomb structure
K secondary effects in general
M electromagnetic effects
N noise

P inhibition of motion in witness
Q heat felt by witness
R radioactivity
S erratic trajectory
V sudden accelerations

At this point we should remark that the code is mainly oriented toward information-retrieval applications, not toward a physical study-in-depth of the reports. The categories introduced here are the product of an empirical, trial-and-error process in the assignment of the codes, as more and more sightings were studied. Its objective is merely to make possible a broad description of the statistical condition of the sightings. On this basis, it would be desirable to develop a more formal system.

CODE FOR THE SHAPE (8) AND COLOR (9):

A triangle — bright, silvery
B half-sphere with "filaments" — blue
C tube or cylinder — variable
D disk — two colors
E point source — blinding white
F cone with base down — fiery, incandescent
G "mushroom" — metallic appearance
H half-sphere
I complexity of structure
J — yellow
K crescent — blinking light
L light without precise shape — light source only
M "haystack" — multicolored
N cloud-shaped — dark
O oblong, cigar-shaped — orange
P changing shape — phosphorescent
Q "cauldron" — gray
R wheel, ring, torus — red
S sphere, globe — fluorescent, luminescent

T	top-shaped	flat white, dull
U	composite object	blinding
V		green
W		violet
X	craftlike	transparent, translucent
Z	"immaterial"	gold

Here again, we are not trying to define the object within a spectrum of possible shapes or colors; for the moment we want only *to reflect the terminology used by the witnesses themselves* by using the expressions most popular among the authors of the reports.

In the last column of the card we punch a letter that indicates whatever special interest the sighting might have:

E the object vanished suddenly
F a photograph has been secured
M the sighting is of military or strategic significance
P the sighting has some physical peculiarity
R a recurrent sighting
T the witness is a known personality
C the case is interesting for several of these reasons

RELIABILITY (WEIGHT) OF THE SIGHTINGS

The "weight" given each sighting necessarily reflects the personal judgment of the person who compiles the catalogue. We have always used the utmost care, not only in attributing a weight to a sighting but also in following consistent rules in distributing weights to large numbers of reports, when fatigue or personal bias might have altered the homogeneity of the process. This "weight" is entirely independent of the code itself; it is not only a measure of the reliability of the witness, it seeks to determine to what degree each report is important in a study of the phenomenon and to what degree a theory of the phenomenon should account for this observation, or at least not contradict it.

Thus a star (*) denotes the sightings that must be accounted for in any global theory of the phenomenon, either because of the strong evidence obtained or because of the large number or scientific competence of the witnesses (assuming favorable observing conditions).

A plus sign (+) indicates significant cases where we feel that sincerity of the witnesses cannot be questioned, and where the reported phenomenon is representative of the problem under study.

No weight is given (the space is left blank) when the report is an ordinary one.

An equals sign (=) denotes doubtful cases where the report can be interpreted, on the basis of the data presented, by a borderline conventional phenomenon.

A minus sign (−) calls attention to those reports that, in our view, have nothing to do with the UFO phenomenon, but have to be catalogued because of the effect they have had on the general rumor, at least on a local scale.

DEFINITION OF UFO ACTIVITY

The frequency of past and current reports is often studied to find if it can be correlated with some known effect or if its future variation can be predicted. Most students of the phenomenon approach this study on a yearly or monthly basis. In the study reported here, we have used the number of sightings per week as an indication of the level of activity. However, the *number* of cases is not necessarily in correlation with the *quality* of the reports; sometimes newspapers give unusual publicity to vague and uninteresting observations simply because UFO's are "in the news," and the number of reports thus reflects more public interest in the problem. Obviously this artificial momentum must be eliminated.

Let us consider once again our classification into types and our system of weights. Should we say that the activity is at the same level if one week we receive six observations of "nocturnal meandering lights" and the next week we get one Type II observation made by competent witnesses and five reports of objects seen on the ground? Certainly not.

Whatever the nature of the phenomenon we are studying, we need some notation system that will allow us to extract the true significance of the reports so that ten doubtful cases will not introduce artificial correlations with external effects. We have experimented with such systems, and we present an example of a possible rating scheme in the following table. It will be observed that all observations with weight (−), as well as most cases of weight (=), vanish, while Type V cases, meandering lights and point sources, play only a very minor role. The weights are scaled from zero and ten, with the highest number corresponding to the most stable and complex phenomenon, that of Type II-B.

DEFINITION OF THE ACTIVITY INDEX

Type	Class	*	+	blank	=	−
				Weight		
I	A	8	6	4	0	0
	B	8	6	4	0	0
	C	8	6	3	0	0
	D	5	3	1	0	0
II	A	8	7	4	1	0
	B	10	9	5	2	0
	C	8	7	4	1	0
III	A	7	5	3	1	0
	B	7	5	3	1	0
	C	8	6	4	1	0
	D	8	6	3	1	0
	E	6	4	2	0	0
IV	A	6	3	2	0	0
	B	6	3	2	0	0
	C	6	3	2	0	0
	D	6	3	2	0	0
V	A	5	2	1	0	0
	B	2	1	1	0	0
	C	2	1	1	0	0

APPENDIX V

CIVILIAN UFO GROUPS IN THE UNITED STATES

THE MOTIVATION for this survey was provided by the sociological context of the rumors associated with UFO reports. The possible correlations between the activity of local and national groups, the number of sightings reported in the area they influence, and the theories or beliefs of their members have been noted on many occasions.

There are in the United States two professionally presented and distributed publications that devote a great deal of attention to the UFO problem. They are:

(1) *Fate,* published by Clark Publishing Company, 500 Hyacinth Place, Highland Park, Illinois 60035. Monthly, 40¢ a copy on newsstands, $4.00 per year. In 1965, *Fate* printed a monthly average of about 133,000 copies, and total paid circulation was about 93,000.

(2) *Flying Saucers,* published by Palmer Publications, Inc. C-137 Hickory, Mundelein, Illinois. Edited by Ray Palmer, Box AD, Amherst, Wisconsin 54406. Bimonthly, 35¢ a copy, $2.00 for six issues (one year).

Both publications were started by Ray Palmer, a gifted science-fiction writer who was originally the managing editor of *Amazing Stories* in 1938. Palmer attained fame by launching the tale of "The Shaver Mystery" in 1944 and by his early collaboration with Kenneth Arnold, whose story he published in the very first issue of *Fate* (spring, 1948). His new magazine, *Flying Saucers,* took its present name and pocket-size format in the spring of 1961; it has been published since June, 1957, under a slightly different presentation. Palmer is no longer connected with the preparation of *Fate* magazine, which specializes in occultism, astrology and spiritualism but carries at least one article on UFO's every month. The history and presentation of both magazines are discussed in a most entertaining manner by Menzel and Boyd in their book *The World of Flying Saucers.*

There are a very large number of UFO groups throughout the United States; the major ones issue regular periodicals. In our efforts to establish a survey of these groups we were surprised to find that more than two hundred had been formed in the United States since 1947; and this estimate, which does not include informal discussion groups and clubs formed by students, must be regarded as a conservative one. A majority of our questionnaires missed their targets, either because groups had dissolved or because their addresses had been changed. Of the groups active at the time of the survey and reached by the questionnaire, more than thirty gave answers sufficiently detailed for inclusion here. Names and addresses were compiled from the following sources: (1) private correspondence and knowledge of researchers with whom we were in contact; (2) file of personalities active in the field of UFO research and list of UFO periodicals of the United States Air Force, Dayton, Ohio; (3) list of "saucer clubs" published by AFSCA (*see* below); and (4) *International Flying Saucer Directory* of James Rigberg, New York.

A questionnaire, accompanied by a letter stating its purpose and that answers would be used for partial publication, was sent to 96 groups in January, 1965. Groups 97 to 217 received the material in March. The survey was closed in August, 1965. The groups that answered our questionnaire are listed below. A brief statement of each group's history, the name of the publication it issues, and its address are provided. Groups are listed randomly.

LIST OF CIVILIAN UFO ORGANIZATIONS
IN THE UNITED STATES (AS OF AUGUST, 1965)

1. *Interplanetary Intelligence of Unidentified Flying
   Objects (IIUFO)*
   3005 West Eubanks, Oklahoma City, Oklahoma
   William F. Riefer, Director; Hayden C. Hewes, Associate Director
   > Created in August, 1958, for the purpose of investigating the UFO mystery. Claims free, worldwide membership of 4,500. Believes UFO's are real, but has reached no conclusion as to their nature and origin. State offices in almost all fifty states under nine district representatives. Fifteen foreign representatives.

   Publication: *Interplanetary Intelligence Report,* bimonthly, $3.00 yr.

2. *American UFO Committee (AMUFO)*
   2875 Sequoyah Drive N.W., Atlanta, Georgia
   Ricky Hilberg, Dale Rettig, Allen Greenfield, Executive Directors
   > Formed October, 1963, through merger of two older organizations. Affiliated with the UFO group union, the United Ufological Association. Participant in the Congress of Scientific Ufologists. No conclusion regarding nature and origin of UFO's. 500 members.

   Publications: *UFO Sighter* and *American UFO Committee Review*

3. *National Investigations Committee on Aerial
   Phenomena (NICAP)*
   1536 Connecticut Avenue N.W., Washington 6, D.C.
   Major Donald E. Keyhoe, Director; Richard H. Hall, Acting Director
   > History and objectives are stated in the report *UFO Evidence* published by the group in May, 1964. This document summarizes the files and activities of the organization. Formed in 1956 by T. T. Brown; claims membership of 5,500. Works under the "definite hypothesis that UFO's are real, apparently controlled, from an extraterrestrial source." Charges the U.S. Air Force with practicing an "intolerable degree of secrecy." Local investigations

are carried out by subcommittees. Membership dues $5.00 annually.

Publication: *UFO Investigator,* scheduled bimonthly

4. *Aerial Phenomena Research Organization (APRO)*
   3910 E. Kleindale Road, Tucson, Arizona
   Leslie J. Lorenzen, Director

   Oldest organization in the field, created in January, 1952. Tries to gather responsible and rational researchers rather than a large number of enthusiastic followers. Present membership of 800 includes many teachers, technicians, scientists, etc. Majority of APRO members feel that the facts indicate an interplanetary source of UFO's, possibly a colony established on Mars by an advanced civilization. APRO is the best informed American organization on foreign sightings. Has documented many accounts of "landings" and given publicity to the theory of "UFO hostility." Foreign correspondents include Aime Michel (France), Olavo Fontes (Brazil), Peter Norris (Australia), Eduardo Buelta (Spain).

   Publication: *A.P.R.O. Bulletin,* bimonthly, $3.50 yr.

5. *National Investigation Commission on Aerial Phenomena (NICAP)*
   5108 South Findlay Street, Seattle 18, Washington
   Robert J. Gribble, Director

   Similar initials and situation in Washington (city in one case, state in another) create a confusion between this group and organization No. 3. The two groups are distinct. This is a commission of six members with no open membership, created on January 1, 1955. It has been active since that date, but under several different names. Believes that the authorities have evidence but that they maintain a policy of official secrecy. Concludes that "a high percentage of UFO's are coming from another world."

   Publication: *NICAP Reporter,* $1.50 yr.

6. *Flying Saucer News Club of America (FSNCA)*
   119 East 96th Street, New York 28, New York
   James Rigberg, Editor

   Formed March, 1955. Believes authorities have obtained evidence of the nature or origin of the UFO's and keep it secret.

Publication: *Flying Saucer News*, 25¢ per copy

7. *Amalgamated Flying Saucer Clubs of America (AFSCA)*

2004 N. Hoover Street. Los Angeles, California 90027

Gabriel Green, Founder-President

Formed January, 1959, the group has 2,500 members. Believe many UFO's are in reality extraterrestrial spaceships piloted by crews of men and women from advanced races on other planets.

Publication: *UFO International,* bimonthly, $3.00 yr.

8. *Saucer and Unexplained Celestial Events Research Society (SAUCERS)*

P.O. Box 163, Fort Lee, New Jersey 07024

James W. Moseley, Editor

4,000 members in group. Created July, 1954. Believe UFO's are probably extraterrestrial "though there is no proof as yet of their origin."

Publication: *Saucer News,* $2.00 for six issues

9. *The Aetherius Society*

674 Crenshaw Blvd., Los Angeles, California 90005

George King, Founder-President

Created in November, 1960, the Society keeps its membership confidential. "The orientation of the Aetherius Society is a spiritual one, since it is definitely known that the Mission of the Flying Saucers and their crews to Earth is a spiritual mission."

Publication: *Aetherius Society Newsletter*

10. *Cleveland Aerial Phenomena Investigations Club (CAPIC)*

3132 West 142nd Street, Cleveland, Ohio 44111

Created in June, 1964. 19 members. Believes UFO's are interplanetary spaceships and authorities may have obtained evidence. No publication.

11. *Aerial Phenomena Investigations Committee (APIC)*

P.O. Box 87, Rugby Station, Brooklyn, New York 11203

Eugene R. Steinberg, Director; Kenneth J. Alpert, Associate Director

Created as a local group in February, 1959, is now international in scope with 2,000 members. The group feels that an extraterrestrial origin of UFO's is more likely to be correct than any other solution offered thus far.

Publication: *UFO Reporter*, quarterly. Stopped publication in 1965, when purchased by *Saucer News* (8, above)

12. *Civilian Flying Saucer Investigations Bureau (CFSIB)*
    6101 Sturgeon Creek Parkway, Midland, Michigan
    The general attitude of the group, formed in October, 1963, is that UFO's are interplanetary space vehicles under intelligent control, probably from a planet outside the solar system.
    Publication: *CFSIB Newsletter*

13. *The Planetary Space Center (formerly Interplanetary Foundation)*
    24720 Carlysle Street, Dearborn, Michigan 48124
    Laura Mundo (Marxer), Connie Grish, Carmella Falzone
    Created in December, 1954. No membership or dues. Reaches about 1,000, main list of 300. Feels the UFO's are spaceships of more advanced, friendly human beings.
    Publication: *Interplanetary News*

14. *The Christian Zion Advocate*
    P.O. Box 48, Neah Bay, Washington
    Active under various names since 1953, the group has arrived at the definite conclusion that UFO's are "The Lord's Angels which He has sent before Him" (Matt. 24:31–32) and that authorities have not obtained evidence of their origin.
    Publication: *Humanitarian*

15. *Long Beach Interplanetary Research Group*
    1227 E. 2nd Street, Long Beach, California 90802
    A. Rowe, Secretary
    Created about 1957. Has no conclusion on the UFO problem but thinks authorities have considerable evidence.
    Publication: *Understanding*

16. *Solar Cross Foundation*
    5132 Lincoln Avenue, Los Angeles, California 90042
    Robert Short, Director; James Jordan, Editor
    Created in July, 1957, the group had 876 members in 1964. It believes that the facts are "beyond our concepts at this time."
    Publication: *Inter-Galaxy News*

17. *Tucson Science Club*
    5350 E. Ft. Lowell, Tucson, Arizona 85716

Informal discussion group. Regular meetings since 1958. The group has few members and only one conclusion: "There is no simple, single answer." Publication discontinued.

18. *Houston UFO Bureau (HUFOB)*
3302 Askew, Houston, Texas 77017
Gary Kitpatrick, President
Created August, 1964. Twenty members. The group "has obtained confidential evidence" and withholds other comments.
Publication: *UFO Mystery,* irregularly published

19. *School of Thought*
P.O. Box 458, Independence, California 93526
Hope Troxell, Founder and Director
Created February, 1960. The group has 250 members and concludes that a higher race has populated the universe and uses other dimensions that we are not able "to see or to understand."
Publication: brochures and courses

20. *UFO Magazine Publications*
3403 West 119th Street, Cleveland, Ohio 44111
Ricky Hilberg, Editor
Created April, 1963. Average number of members in 1964: 323. No definite conclusion arrived at. Hilberg is one of the executive directors of AMUFO (*see* 2, above).
Publication: *UFO Magazine* (combined with *Saucer Album*), published twice yearly, $1.00

21. *Philadelphia Investigation Committee on Aerial Phenomena (PICAP)*
6100 Belden Street, Philadelphia, Pennsylvania 19149
Group created in May, 1964. Twenty members. Feels authorities have obtained information, keep it secret for fear of scaring the American public. No publication.

22. *Morse Fellowship*
P.O. Box 72, Alamogordo, New Mexico 88310
Louise Morse
Incorporated in 1957. Has several hundred members and has sent thousands of its publications (sample lessons on "soul growth") to all states and twelve foreign countries. States that UFO's come from planets of higher frequencies of light.

Publications: *Through the Portals,* plus 250 separate lessons

23. *Controversial Phenomena Bulletin (CPB)*
48 Great Brook Valley Ave., Worcester, Massachusetts 01605
Armand A. Laprade, Editor; Joseph L. Ferriere, Co-Editor
> Created in summer, 1963. Has 300 members. The group does not offer definite conclusions, but feels that descriptions of UFO "operators" should be taken very seriously. The *Bulletin* is one of the most informative publications in the field.

Publication: *Controversial Phenomena Bulletin,* bi-monthly, $2.00 yr. Published under the name of *Probe* since September, 1965

24. *New England UFO Study Group*
20 Buckingham Road, Norwood, Massachusetts 02062
George D. Fawcett, private UFO researcher
> Created by Fawcett in November, 1959, group took present name in 1964. The majority of the 175 members believe that "flying saucers" are in reality intelligently controlled machines from outer space conducting a scientific study of our planet for purposes as yet unknown. Accepts "operators" as authentic.

Publication: meeting reports

25. *Dr. Rudolf Steiner Research Foundation, Inc.*
533 Lincoln So., Salem, Oregon
M. Gordon Allen, Director
> This is a research foundation, not a UFO organization. States that the UFO problem is that of dealing with alien intelligences who can project material devices into our material world from some other plane of existence. No publication.

26. *Universal Research Society of America (URSA)*
118 Oberreich St., La Porte, Indiana
Orvil R. Hartle, Director; Harry F. Koch, Research Director; Prof. Charles A. Maney, Chairman, Board of Advisors
> Created May 15, 1965. The group feels that in spite of the enormous amount of evidence in support of UFO reality, it is still insufficient to determine its nature and origin. Periodical publication contemplated.

27. **The Little Listening Post (LLP)**
    4811 Illinois Avenue N.W., Washington 11, D.C.
    Publication, founded in January, 1954, sent by subscription only. Circulation figures private. Sixty issues of the magazine have been published until 1965.
    Publication: *Little Listening Post,* $3.00 for six issues
28. *UFO Research Organization (UFORO)*
    739 75th Avenue No., St. Petersburg, Florida 33702
    E. R. Sabo, President
    The group has 75 active members. Organized in October, 1964, it has concluded that UFO's are some form of spacecraft under intelligent control, probably extraterrestrial. Rejects contactee claims and believes an independent, non-governmental scientific group should be organized for the analysis of the problem.
    Publication: *UFO Researcher,* monthly, $10.00 yr.
29. *Flying Saucer Investigating Committee (FSIC)*
    P.O. Drawer G, Akron, Ohio 44305
    Americo E. Candusso, Co-Chairman and Editor; Larry Moyers, Co-Chairman
    Created on October 28, 1961. Believes that the possibility that UFO's are extraterrestrial has much evidence in its favor, but definite proof has not yet been presented. FSIC presents itself as an objective, science-minded organization, and there is not necessarily a common belief among its members on the many facets of the UFO problem.
    Publication: *FSIC Bulletin,* bimonthly, $2.00 yr. The information and observations in the *Bulletin* reflect fine investigation on the part of group members. Many first-hand reports, well documented.

ADDITIONAL INFORMATION ON DEFUNCT GROUPS

Among organizations that have now ceased their activity are:

1. *Grand Rapids Flying Saucer Club*
   Created in 1951, this group has published a periodical called *Uforum* and organized lectures with attendances as high as 750. The questionnaire indicated how the group died:

"The group was split between the scientifically-minded investigators and the so-called esoteric lunatic fringe. As far as I know the scientists still do not have an acceptable answer, while the esoterists 'knew' the answer right from the beginning (The Brothers sent to watch over us)."

2. *North Jersey UFO Group*

   Created in 1954, the group published 13 issues of the *UFO Newsletter* (Lee R. Munsick, Editor). It was generally felt that UFO's were intelligently controlled vehicles, not from this planet; that government secrecy was due to bureaucratic automatic censorship; and that contactee claims should be rejected.

3. *Ufology Bulletin*

   In Ventura, California. Twenty-four issues of the *Bulletin* were published in two years. It was, to a degree, an outgrowth of the Ventura UFO Study Group. It died when it fell in the hands of the believers in "contactee" stories.

4. *Civil Commission on Aerial Phenomena (CCAP)*

   The group ceased to operate about 1960.

5. *Decatur UFO Group*

   Founded in 1957. Former members continue to discuss the subject informally. They feel authorities of several countries, including the U.S., have obtained evidence of the nature and origin of the UFO phenomenon and have definitely made every possible attempt to keep this information secret. But they are not in complete disagreement with the policy of secrecy, and "recognize that any information and educational program would have to be presented to the people in a slow and gradual manner to avoid all sorts of fear and panic that might otherwise occur."

6. *Flying Saucers International (FSI)*

   Did not answer our questionnaire. Published the well-known magazine *Saucers* from 1953 to 1959, with Max Miller as editor.

7. *Civilian Research, Interplanetary Flying Objects (CRIFO)*

   The group was created by Leonard Stringfield in Ohio and published a magazine, *Orbit*, from 1954 to 1957.

8. *The Saucerian Bulletin*

   This was the first magazine published by Gray Barker, who now manages the Saucerian Publications, Box

2228, Clarksburg, West Virginia 26302. Its first issue appeared in March, 1956. It was absorbed by *Saucer News* in 1960. In November, 1965, Barker released the first issue of a new publication, *Spacecraft News*.

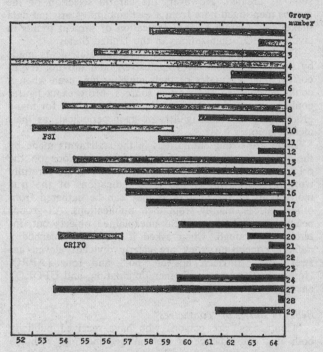

FIG. 36.—American UFO organizations active on January 1, 1965.

ANALYSIS OF
THE RETURNED QUESTIONNAIRES

The above list by no means constitutes an exhaustive description of the activity in the U.S. today. Much redundancy and duplication are present, and many organizations, including some important ones, have probably been forgotten. It is meant to be a sampling of the groups active in "UFO research" rather than a complete picture. Also, many local clubs are composed of members of various larger national groups. Sudden interest in one particular sighting (such as that at Socorro in 1964) brings about the formation of associations, many of which die almost as soon as created. However, the careful selection of the groups mentioned here from a vast amount of original data makes this sample a good indication of present trends in civilian UFO organizations in the United States.

Throughout our survey we used the statements made by the groups themselves exclusively and did not try to correct their estimates of their membership, even when it could be checked from other sources. More exact figures could be given if such corrections were applied, for many groups give the mailing lists of their periodicals as their membership.

There are strong similarities in the statements made by the various groups concerning their conclusions on the origin and nature of UFO's. These statements are carefully worded and obviously are poor indications of the true motivations of the leaders as they can be gathered from other sources, mainly from their publications. All groups believe that UFO's are real unexplained objects but, interestingly enough, when asked if they have reached a *definite* conclusion, they are clearly divided: eleven answer "yes," thirteen answer "no," and four (APRO, Houston UFO Bureau, Steiner Foundation, and UFORO) answer "yes" with reservations (*see* Table I).

Belief in stories of "contactees"

"Contactees" are persons who have received publicity both as a consequence of their alleged meetings with the "occupants" of the "saucers" and the revelation given them of the origin and purpose of the "saucers." Such stories must be totally separated from two other classes of reports, accounts of "operators" described by witnesses who do not claim they have received a message and accounts of meetings with messengers interpreted as religious miracles; although many aspects of the generation of such reports and their propagation follow the patterns observed in the UFO phenomenon, the occasion of these accounts is never a flying object described as a machine (the Fatima phenomenon, for example, falls in this category).

In Table I we have classified the degree of acceptance or rejection of various types of reports by the different groups, using the following very simple scale: A means a report of this type is *rejected* by the group; B: it is investigated as other reports are; C: it is considered as possibly true; D: it is believed under certain conditions; E: it is generally accepted.

The question "Do you think the 'contactees' should be believed?" has brought the following answers: Nine groups reject these reports absolutely and three treat them as any other report in their investigation. Four think there is a possibility of truth in them, eight accept them under certain conditions, and four (Nos. 6, 7, 19, and 22, Flying Saucer News Club, AFSCA, School of Thought, and Morse Fellowship) attach definite credence to them.

It is interesting to correlate the acceptance of "contactee" stories with answers to the first question, "Have you reached a definite conclusion?" Not all who think "contactees" might be sincere have a definite conclusion. Of twelve groups that believe at least some of the "contactee" stories, seven have a definite answer, three do not, while two are hesitant. Although it is true that most groups (nineteen out of twenty-eight) are willing to consider the truth of such accounts a possibility, very few take all "contactee" stories for granted. Among these, some may have made no distinction between "contact" stories of the Adamski type and "landings with operators"; this would introduce a considerable bias in the interpretation of their answers.

Belief in descriptions of "operators".

The replies to the question on belief in reports of "operators" illustrated a sharp difference in spirit between APRO and NICAP. Keyhoe's group gave the same uncommitted answer as to the previous question: such incidents "should be investigated." Does this mean that since 1956 the group has not even reached a working hypothesis on these two subjects?

APRO answers that some accounts of "operators" should be taken seriously, but certainly not descriptions made by the "contactees," as "they deal with emotionally inspired projections and sometimes are merely the product of people who are attempting to benefit monetarily from the UFO mystery."

A few other answers are significant:

Group No. 7:

"Hundreds of detailed accounts of landings have been made. If Flying Saucers do exist at altitudes of a few hundred feet, why can't they land?"

Group No. 17:

"The 'non-communicating' ones where humanoid forms were seen but fought and ran, and the observers did not subsequently go on lecture tours, should be taken seriously. Numerous countries have reported similar events."

Group No. 20:

"The facts seem to point to there being a small biped associated with UFO landings. They may or may not be the pilots of the craft."

The acceptance of the dwarflike "operator" seems fairly general. Only one group (No. 14, which believes "contactee" stories) specifically rejects all accounts of landings of "little men."

TABLE I

SUMMARY OF ANSWERS TO THE QUESTIONNAIRE

Group No.	Definite Conclusion*	Belief in "Contactees"	Official Evidence	Official Secrecy	Belief in "Operators"	Name or Initials of Group
1	No	C	Yes	Yes	C	IIUFO
2	No	A	Poss.	Some	C	AMUFO
3	No	B	Yes	Yes	B	NICAP (Keyhoe)
4	(Yes)	A	Yes	Yes	E	APRO
5	Yes	D	Yes	Yes	E	NICAP (Gribble)
6	No	E	Yes	Yes	E	FSNCA
7	Yes	E	Yes	Yes	E	AFSCA
8	Yes	A	Poss.	Yes	E	SAUCERS
9	Yes	D	Yes	Yes	E	Aetherius Society
10	Yes	C	Poss.	Yes	D	CAPIC
11	No	C	Poss.	Yes	C	APIC
12	No	B	Yes	Yes	B	CFSIB

Group No.	Definite Conclusion*	Belief in "Contactees"	Official Evidence	Official Secrecy	Belief in "Operators"	Name or Initials of Group
13	Yes	C	Yes	Yes	D	Planetary Space Center
14	Yes	D	No	Yes	A	Christian Zion Advocate
15	No	D	Yes	Yes	E	Long Beach Interp. Res. Group
16	Yes	D	Yes	"Distortion"		Solar Cross Foundation
17	No	A	Yes	Yes	E	Tucson Science Club
18	(Yes)	D	No	Yes	D	HUFOB
19	Yes	E	Yes	Yes	E	School of Thought
20	No	A	Yes	Yes	E	UFO Magazine Publications
21	No	A	Yes	Yes	E	PICAP
22	Yes	E	Yes	Yes	E	Morse Fellowship
23	No	D	Yes	Yes	E	CPB
24	Yes	A	Poss.		E	New England UFO Study Group
25	(Yes)	D	Yes	Yes	E	Steiner Foundation
26	No	B	No		B	URSA
28	(Yes)	A	Yes	Yes	E	UFORO
29	No	A	No	Some	E	FSIC

* Yes, with reservations

Correlation between belief in "contactees" and in accounts of "operators" in general

Most of the groups that accept "little men" stories reject the "contactee" claims, as APRO does. The reverse is also true in certain cases: a group of "contactee" believers accepts accounts of "pilots" only if "they look like you and I" (sic). The most conservative group is AMUFO (No. 2), which rejects "contactee" stories and considers cautiously the possibility of the "operators."

Six groups reject absolutely "contactee" claims and definitely accept the "operators": No. 4 (APRO), No. 8 (SAUCERS), No. 17 (Tucson Space Club), No. 20 (UFO Magazine Publications), No. 28 (UFORO), and No. 29 (FSIC).

Recommended writers and books

Another question was: "What are the books on UFO's your organization recommends?" It led to the following frequencies:

TABLE II

Keyhoe	15	Gray Barker	1
Ruppelt	12	Carl Jung	1
Michel	9	Leslie	1
UFO Evidence	8	Le Poer Trench	1
Coral Lorenzen	7	Waveney Girvan	1
Jessup	6	Trevor James	1
Fry	5	Stranges	1
Adamski	4	Laura Mundo	1
Maney and Hall	3	Menger	1
Max Miller	2	Angelucci	1
Charles Fort	2	*A Dweller on Two Planets*	1
Van Tassel	2	*India to Planet Mars*	1
Harold Wilkins	1	The Bible	1

These answers show that the ideas expressed by Keyhoe still had, in 1965, the strongest influence on the leaders of UFO organizations in the U.S. The low rating of Charles Fort should, in our view, be interpreted as a lack of interest in the historical perspective. Even more striking and disturbing is the fact that APRO stands alone in its reference to Jung's book. Michel and Jung are the only non-English writers of all contemporary authors in the list. The trends noticeable here were confirmed by answers to the next question.

Most significant sightings

Table III gives the frequencies associated with each sighting. Out of sixty-three answers, forty-nine were relative to American observations.

A total of twenty-six sightings, of which thirteen are given several times, are indicated. Interestingly enough, no "contactee" sightings are found in the list of repeated cases. Only one group (No. 13) mentions Adamski's account, although several groups answered "yes" to the question "Do you think 'contactees' should be believed?" and four groups recommend his books.

The most frequently named case was Socorro, New Mexico, which was by far the best known case in 1964. Next in popularity come the Washington incident (1952), Trindade Island, Arnold, and Mantell.

TABLE III

Socorro	9	Alpert (photo)	1
Washington	8	Red Bluff	1
Trindade	5	Captain Sperry	1
Kenneth Arnold	4	BOAC crew	1
Mantell	4	Rome	1
Southwest, 1957	4	New Jersey, 1964	1
Kinross Case	3	Chiles & Whitted	1
Personal sightings	3	100% pure magnesium	1
Rapid City, S.D.	2	McMinneville	1
Lubbock Lights	2	Adamski's sighting	1
Nash & Fortenberry	2	Star of Bethlehem	1
Father Gill	2	Lady of Fatima	1
Fort Itaipu	2	Angel Moroni	1

The most striking character of this list is what it *does not include:* the Kelly landing, the Bismarck case, the Walesville incident, and the Loch Raven Dam sighting seem to be totally unknown. Similarly, it is remarkable not to find any mention of "cloud-cigar" observations or any of the classical landings (except Socorro), although many groups are familiar with Michel's work.

The sightings are ranked practically in the order of the publicity they have received, regardless of their intrinsic value or their convincing character. The sentimental attachment for such cases as the dramatic Mantell accident or the "Lubbock Lights" is very evident. Clearly, the groups take it for granted that the most publicized cases are the most convincing, when even a small amount of research would have brought to light an entirely different type of reports. Again, APRO is the most original group in this respect: it lists three foreign sightings out of five (Trindade, Father Gill, and the BOAC incidents). NICAP also gives evidence of careful consideration of the question, although it lists only American cases. They are: Nash and Fortenberry; Red Bluff; Captain Sperry; Southwest, 1957; and Socorro. Neither Washington, nor Arnold, nor Mantell is listed by APRO or NICAP among the most significant cases. However, the groups were asked to select only five sightings, which was a strong restriction.

Geographic distribution of believers in "contactee" stories

If we come back for a moment to the question of "belief in contactees," we see that we can narrow our classification down to two categories: the strong "contactee" believers are groups in classifications D and E; all others either reject them or consider them with some skepticism. On Figure 37 we have represented the locations of the strong "contactee" believers as a man waving his arm, and other groups as open circles.

The geographic effect is fairly obvious: ten contactee believers out of twelve are located west of a line from Seattle to Houston. Fourteen out of sixteen of the others are located east of this line.

H. Taylor Buckner, of the Berkeley campus of the University of California, noted in a paper given before a meeting of the American Sociological Association that in 1953 and 1954 ten books claiming contact with the saucers were published. The people who believed them were, in the main, people already functioning in the world of the occult. The same researcher added that 80% of the "saucer club" audiences are usually older women, single or widowed. They do not have a great deal of formal education, Buckner said, and they believe "seeing things" is a mark of special sensitivity.

Fig. 37.—Distribution of twenty-eight civilian UFO groups in the U. S.

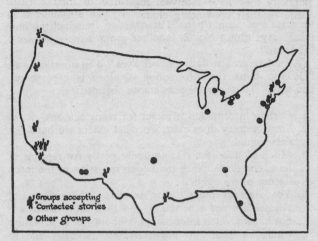

We feel that Buckner's geographical location puts him at the focal point of every extravagance in the field of superstition and false science and that it is unfair for him to generalize his results to the entire field of research into unusual aerial phenomena. His findings, however, are informative for those still sentimentally attached to the claims of such "contactees" as Adamski, Daniel Fry, George van Tassel, and Truman Bethurum. Adamski, for instance, before becoming a prominent figure in "UFO research," was the head of a mystical cult called the Royal Order of Tibet. The generalization of these indications by a professional sociologist is of great interest.

Belief in government secrecy

Of the twenty-nine groups studied here, only one believes that authorities have obtained no evidence whatsoever concerning the nature and origin of the UFO phenomenon; this is group No. 14, whose doctrine is that UFO's are direct emissaries from God. Another group (No. 18) indicates that government investigators have probably obtained no evidence, "but at least 80 to 85% are on the right track. . . ." Group No. 18, we should keep in mind, has received confidential evidence and withholds other comments (they believe in Bender's theory of "the three men in black").

Five groups see a strong possibility that evidence is in the hands of authorities. "The question is: which authorities?" says group No. 2. Another group simply answers: "Hmmm!"

All other groups flatly answer "yes." The question was, "Do you think the information obtained is kept secret, and why?" These are the answers we obtained:

1. Certain information is secret for many reasons.
2. Some secrecy does exist. To what extent we have not determined.
3. Much of it is (secret), no doubt partly for reasons of bureaucratic thinking and underestimation of the intelligence of the public.
4. Yes. Because the ultimate answers—who, why—and whence are not a certainty, and their motivations are not known. Such information, without *full* information would be disastrous politically, economically and to some extent, emotionally for all the people of the world.
5. Yes. The world's monetary system and religions.
6. Yes. To protect manufacturers of our rockets and satellites—may hamper their production.
7. Yes. Several reasons. Introduction of revolutionary new forms of power would make present power sources obsolete and jeopardize our economy. As throughout history, special interest groups feeling their power and financial status threatened by introduction of new knowledge, oppose progress.
8. If the Air Force has significant information that the public does not have, it is kept secret for what they consider to be security reasons.
9. Yes. Official recognition would result in loss of government power and influence.
10. Yes. Maybe because they are scared of UFOs or because of what public reaction might be.
11. Yes. AFR-200-2 and JANAP 146 demand secrecy for unsolved cases. Fear of panic, economic collapse or other reasons might justify secrecy in the event they know what UFOs are.
12. Yes. Air Force directives and their policy of withhold-

ing information seems to indicate this. *The Flying Saucer Conspiracy* best outlines this.

13. If they consider possibilities, at all, who are Earthman that is, fearing panic on part of people, by religions . . . only angels "up there" . . . and monsters by writers.

14. Yes. Because they can't understand it.

15. Yes.

16. Not secret, but distorted! Due to religious views, those who would panic, and advanced military devices.

17. Yes. Each country is trying to discover the secrets of the saucers, especially their advanced technology, and trying to prevent other countries from profiting from his evidence and getting there first.

18. Yes. I think in some cases, the truth may cause mass hysteria.

19. Yes, kept under cover. The truth would upset our economy, religions, education and military ego.

20. Yes, it is hard to say why. They may think some sort of panic could come from a disclosure that there are UFOs. However, it seems that bureaucracy plays an important role in UFO suppression.

21. Yes. They are afraid of scaring the American public.

22. Yes. The materialists have no explanation for the realm of spirit which is reality.

23. No answer.

24. Yes. Refer: AFR 200-2, CIRVIS Reports, Holloman Air Force orders, etc. Panic. Time to duplicate Saucers for own space arsenal, etc.

25. Yes. Because it contains a whole new conceptive idea unknown to conventional science—that of *Emergence* into our plane of existence, intelligently directed.

26. We feel that governmental security policy is such that unless this UFO phenomenon is interpreted as a threat to National Security, there is no use to make a public explanation.

27. No answer.

28. Yes, probably in the knowledge that what *is* known would be difficult for the public to accept. Also, it is likely they do not have the most important facts: origin, purpose, etc. Without satisfactory answers to these questions, the emotional consequences would be disastrous, as well as the results politically and economically.

29. To some extent, but mostly from lack of knowledge.

It is difficult to extract the basic elements in these statements because of the differences in wording. We should probably have asked the question in a more direct form to obtain answers easier to classify. In trying to summarize the reasons given for official secrecy, we found the following frequencies: eight groups mention fear of panic, mass hysteria; six, economic disaster; four, collapse of religious faith; four, loss of political power; three, space industry would become obsolete; three, officials are unable to understand; two, bureaucratic thinking; two, still insufficient conclusions; two, hope to be the first discoverer of the "secret."

CONCLUSIONS

Since this survey was made, a wave of new sightings has developed over the area under study, undoubtedly favoring the generation of new groups. Therefore we present these conclusions as indicative of *trends* in American "Ufology," not as definite results.

We think our survey indicates that the leaders of the UFO movement in the U.S. are: (1) *conservative:* Mantell and Keyhoe remain their typical symbols while Father Gill and Professor Jung are practically ignored; (2) *suspicious* of foreign observations: the main waves that have taken place outside the United States (New Guinea, Australia, Scandinavia, Europe) have had no impact on their ways of thinking; and (3) *unscientific:* the role of these groups is limited to the dispersion and documentation of reports; none of them has the equipment, training, staff, or funds for effective scientific research.

Yet an objective analysis of their motivations and theories gives a somewhat brighter picture than is generally believed. It is true that many of the groups are irrational in their thinking. An even larger number consider "Ufology" a hobby that brings a touch of mystery and science fiction into uneventful lives. But most are undoubtedly open minded, as we have seen. We feel that a serious effort on the part of scientific investigators to bring the UFO problem into the open would be supported by most of the groups and that most would be willing to admit the weakness of all present theories, including their own.

The current attitude of these civilian organizations toward the alleged official secrecy should perhaps be brought to the attention of the responsible agencies. Their distrust of the air force investigating procedure, for instance, is complete, and this cannot be explained simply by the popularity of Keyhoe's books.

Many of the groups surveyed here give evidence of sincerity and dedication. They certainly do not (if we exclude a few extremists) deserve the term "charlatans," which is often applied to them.

The next step, of course, is to repeat this survey on a global scale. To this effect, we ask all groups engaged in research in this field anywhere in the world to address replies to the questions presented in this Appendix, and if possible a sample of their publications, to Vallee, c/o Henry Regnery Company, 114 W. Illinois St., Chicago, Illinois 60610.

BIBLIOGRAPHY

1. HYNEK, J. A. Definition of "Unidentified Flying Objects," *Encyclopaedia Britannica*, 1963 Edition.
2. RUPPELT, E. J. *The Report on Unidentified Flying Objects*. New York: Doubleday, 1956.
3. MENZEL, D. H. *Flying Saucers*. Cambridge, Mass.: Harvard University Press, 1954.
4. WILKINS, H. T. *Flying Saucers on the Attack*. New York: Citadel Press, 1954.
5. MICHEL, A. *Mystérieux Objets célestes*. Paris: Arthaud, 1958.
6. ————. *Flying Saucers and the Straight Line Mystery*. A translation of (5) with an Appendix by A. MEBANE on the U.S. 1957 wave. New York: Criterion Books, 1958.
7. SIMONS, A. *Platillos Volantes*. Barcelona: G. P., 1961.
8. GARREAU, C. *Alerte dans le Ciel*. Paris: 1954.
9. FONTES, O. "Brazil under UFO Survey," *Flying Saucer Review*, VII, 2 (March-April, 1961), 10.
10. MICHEL, A. "Saucers over Europe," *Fate*, August, 1957.
11. RIBERA, A. "BAVIC in the Iberian Peninsula," *F.S.R.*, IX, 5 (September, 1963), 30.
12. MICHEL, A. "Global Orthoteny," *F.S.R.*, IX, 3 (May, 1963), 3.

293

13. VALLEE, J. F. "Towards a Generalization of Orthoteny," *F.S.R.*, VIII, 2 (March, 1962), 3.

14. MENZEL, D. H. "Do Flying Saucers Move in Straight Lines?" *F.S.R.*, X, 2 (March, 1964), 3.

15. MICHEL, A. "Where Dr. Menzel Has Gone Wrong," *F.S.R.*, X, 2 (March, 1964), 8.

16. VALLEE, J. F. "Recent Developments in Orthotenic Research," *F.S.R.*, IX, 6 (November, 1963), 3.

17. ———. "The Menzel-Michel Controversy," *F.S.R.*, X, 4 (July, 1964), 4.

18. MICHEL, A. "Éloge du Sorite," *Satellite* (Paris).

19. QUINCY, G. List of 1,027 UFO sightings. Personal communication.

20. ———. Annotated catalogue of landings. Personal communication.

21. FORT, C. *The Book of the Damned*. Paris: Boni and Liveright, 1919; New York: Holt, 1941.

22. WEBB, T. W. *Celestial Objects for Common Telescopes*. 1859.

23. KEYHOE, D. E. *The Flying Saucers Are Real*. New York: Fawcett, 1950.

24. ———. *Flying Saucers from Outer Space*. New York: Holt, 1953. French translation: *Le Dossier des Soucoupes volantes*. Paris: Hachette, 1954.

25. ———. *Flying Saucers: Top Secret*. New York: Putnam, 1960.

26. MICHEL, A. *Lueurs sur les Soucoupes volantes*. Paris: Mame, 1954. American edition: *The Truth About Flying Saucers*. New York: Criterion Books, 1956.

27. RIBERA, A. *Objetos desconocidos en el Cielo*. Barcelona: Argos, 1961.

28. BUELTA, E. *Astronaves sobre la Tierra*. Barcelona: Oroni, 1955.

29. VOGT, C. *El Misterio de los Platillos Voladores*. Buenos Aires: La Mandragora, 1956.

30. RIBERA, A. "Platillos Volantes," *Gaceta Ilustrada*, 1962.

31. MENZEL, D. H., and BOYD, L. G. *The World of Flying Saucers*. New York: Doubleday, 1963.

32. "CODOVNI Report of 1962." Personal communication.

33. *Project Blue Book Special Report No. 14*. Aerospace Technical Intelligence Center (ATIC).

34. Collections of the large French daily newspapers, including *Figaro, Franc-Tireur, Libération, Combat, Paris-Presse, La Croix.*

35. The authors wish to thank the many researchers who kindly made available their personal collections, in particular A. Michel, C. Vogt, R. Veillith, C. Garreau.

36. Collections of specialized journals, including *Flying Saucer Review, Australian Flying Saucer Review, Lumières dans la Nuit,* etc.

37. RIETTI, A. Article on the Bahia-Blanca, Salta, and Cordoba sightings, *La Razon* (Buenos Aires), May 24, 1962.

38. "Météores autour de la Terre," *Franc-Soir,* August 26, 1954.

39. "Les Soucoupes volantes au Siècle passé" (Memoires de la Société d'Emulation du Jura), *Le Parisien,* September 29, 1954.

40. NOLAN, J. "Those Flying Saucers: Are or Aren't They?" *New York Times,* April 9, 1950.

41. *Les Soucoupes volantes.* Paris: La Table Ronde, January, 1955.

42. "La Controverse des Savants italiens sur les Soucoupes volantes," *Le Monde, October* 29, 1954.

43. GUIEU, J. *Les Soucoupes volantes viennent d'un autre Monde.* Paris: Fleuve Noir, 1954. English edition: *Flying Saucers Come From Another World.* London: Hutchinson, 1956.

44. OBERTH, H. Statement on the UFO Problem, *L'Aurore,* August 3, 1954.

45. HEUYER, G. Statement on UFO's before the French Academy of Medicine. *See* French papers of November 17 and 18, 1954.

46. SAGAN, C. Statement on UFO visits in prehistoric times, *Los Angeles Times,* November 16, 1962.

47. HYNEK, J. A. "Flying Saucers I Have Known," *Yale Scientific Magazine,* April, 1963.

48. *Dictionnaire Général des Communes de France.* Paris: Albin Michel.

49. DAVIS, M. "A Problem of Orthoteny," *F.S.R.,* VIII, 6 (November, 1962), 20.

50. MANEY, C. A. "An Evaluation of Aimé Michel's Study of the Straight Line Mystery." Lecture given

     at Akron, Ohio, March 14, 1959. Published in *F.S.R.,* V, 6 (November-December, 1959), 10.

51. RIBERA, A. "Spanish Orthotenies in 1950," *F.S.R.,* VII, 6 (November, 1961), 9.

52. ———. "UFO Survey of Spain," *F.S.R.,* IX, 1 (January, 1963), 14.

53. "Les premières Photographies des Soucoupes," *L'Oise-Matin,* October 2, 1954.

54. "Recrudescence de Soucoupes dans le Ciel de la France," *L'Oise-Matin,* September 24, 1954.

55. "Une Soucoupe volante à St-Crépin-Ibouvillers?" *L'Oise-Libérée,* October 9, 1954.

56. "Un mystérieux Objet lumineux dans le Ciel de Provence," *Ouest-France,* November 18, 1959.

57. "More Reports of Phenomena in Night Skies," *Wellington Evening Post,* November 9, 1959.

58. "Un Phénomène lumineux a fortement intrigué les Habitants de Veauche," *Dépêche de St.-Étienne,* October 30, 1959.

59. "Boule de Feu dans le Ciel dauphinois," *Le Dauphiné Libéré,* January 31, 1960.

60. "Un Objet lumineux dans le Ciel de Toscane," *Dernière Heure Lyonnaise,* October 26, 1959. See also *Le Maine Libre,* October 26, 1959.

61. "Flying Object Awed and Frightened Invercargill Men," *Wellington Evening Post,* November 4, 1959.

62. "Soucoupe volante sur une Voie ferrée en Seine-Maritime," *Le Maine Libre,* November 19, 1960.

63. "Etrange Phénomène météorologique sur Authéon," *Le Maine Libre,* November 15, 1960.

64. "Mystérieux Phénomène à Authéon," *Nice-Matin,* November 15, 1960.

65. "Un mystérieux Objet volant observé au-dessus d'Innsbruck," *Le Soir,* October 20, 1959.

66. "Un Objet lumineux dans le Ciel de Laval," *Ouest-France,* November 26, 1960.

67. "El Artefacto que cruzo el Cielo al amanecer del 20 de Febrero era un Platillo volante?" *Pamplona Diario de Navarra,* March 16, 1960.

68. "Une Soucoupe volante à Gazinet?" *Sud-Ouest,* September 3, 1960.

69. "La Soucoupe volante de Saint-Omer," *Paris-Presse,* August 6, 1960.

70. "Phénomène dans le Ciel," *Dépêche de St.-Étienne,* June 14, 1960.

71. VUILLEQUEZ. L'Observation du 13 novembre 1960 à La Londe. Personal communication.

72. "Soucoupes volantes dans la Région de Saint-Omer," *Dépêche de St.-Étienne,* August 12, 1960.

73. "Another 'Strange Object,'" *Advertiser* (Australia), April 9, 1959.

74. "Lens Caught This 'Saucer,'" *Adelaide News,* April 30, 1959.

75. "Un Objet lumineux dans le Ciel roussillonnais," *Dépêche du Midi,* February 21, 1960.

76. "Un Mystérieux 'Véhicule Cosmique,'" *Dépêche du Midi,* February 21, 1960.

77. LE MONNIER, H. "Mars se rapproche de la Terre, les Soucoupes apparaissent," *Le Dauphiné Libéré,* May 9, 1960.

78. "An Object has Landed in Mozambique," *Times of India* (also Portuguese Agency "Lusitania"), May, 1960.

79. "Le Soleil aurait 'dansé' dans le Ciel portugais," *Dépêche de St.-Étienne,* May 21, 1960.

80. "Strange Objects That Cross the Sky Have Once More Been Seen in Jujuy," *La Razón,* March 10, 1959.

81. "A Strange Object in the Sky of Cordoba," *La Razón,* February 28, 1959.

82. "Another Strange Phenomenon in the Sky of the Pampas," *La Razón,* April 26, 1959.

83. "A Flying Saucer in the Jujuy Province," *La Razón,* October 30, 1960.

84. "Official Probe: Tasmanian Parson's Story," *Tasmanian Truth,* October 12, 1960.

85. "Les 'Soucoupes volantes' ont-elles fait une Apparition dans le Ciel girondin?" *Sud-Ouest,* November 16, 1959.

86. "Dos Extranos Objetos Sobre el Ciel de Totana," *Diario de Africa,* October 22, 1960.

87. THIROUIN, M. "Marius Dewilde n'a pas menti," *Ouranos,* No. 24 (1959), p. 11.

88. "Cigare volant sur le Gers," *Sud-Ouest,* August 20, 1959.

89. "Un Objet étrange observé dans le Ciel à l'Est du Labrador," *Le Figaro,* September 24, 1959.

90. "Une Soucoupe volante dans le Ciel d'Aubagne?" *Le Petit Provençal,* October 3, 1959.

91. "Un 'Objet mystérieux' dans le Ciel de Bari," *Libre Belgique,* May 22, 1959.

92. Tees-Side UFO Research Group. *Quarterly News Bulletin,* I, 5 (March, 1959).

93. "Air Pilots See Lights," *New York Herald Tribune* (Paris Edition), September 7, 1959.

94. "Engin mystérieux aperçu dans le Ceil," *Dernières Nouvelles d'Alsace,* August 28, 1959.

95. "A Celestial Phenomenon Observed Again in the Mal Paso Sky," *La Razón,* October 18, 1958.

96. "Flying Saucers in the Sky of the Capital," *La Razón,* October 19, 1958.

97. "Strange Sight in the Pehuajó Sky," *Noticias,* November 26, 1958.

98. "Soucoupe volante sur la Forêt Noire," *Tribune de St.-Étienne,* March 9, 1959.

99. "Était-ce une Soucoupe volante?" *L'Oise-Matin,* October 3, 1956.

100. "Objet non identifié dans la Région roannaise?" *Le Progrès,* October 14, 1956.

101. LEE, Y. W. *Statistical Theory of Communications.* New York: Wiley & Sons, 1950.

102. TUKEY, J. W. *The Sampling Theory of Power Spectrum Estimates: Symposium on Applications of Autocorrelation Analysis to Physical Problems.* (NAVEXOS-P-375.) Woods Hole: Off. of Nav. Res., June 13, 1949.

103. BLACKMAN, R. B., and TUKEY, J. W. *The Measurement of the Power Spectra from the Point of View of Communication Engineering.* Dover: 1959, and *Bell System Technical Journal* (January, 1958, and March, 1958).

104. BROUWER, D. "A Study of Changes in the Rate of Rotation of the Earth," *Astronomical Journal* (1952), pp. 125–46.

105. COUFFIGNAL, L. "La Méthode de H. Labrouste pour la Recherche des Périodes," *Ciel et Terre,* No. 66 (1950), pp. 78–86.

106. BUELTA, E. "La Constante de Frecuencia," *Boletin del Centro de Estudios Interplanetarios,* No. 9 (October, 1961).

107. VALLEE, J. M., and VALLEE, J. F. "The Study of the

Periodicity of the UFO Phenomenon in Its Correlation with the Oppositions of Mars," *F.S.R.*, VIII, 5 (September, 1962), 5.

108. FONTES, O. "Note" on the Periodicity of the UFO Phenomenon. *APRO Bulletin*, January, 1963.

109. TROENG, I. "Venus Observed," *F.S.R.*, VIII, 5 (September, 1962), 12.

110. JUNG, C. G. *Ein Moderner Mythus.* French Translation: *Un Mythe moderne.* Paris: NRF, 1961. English Translation: *Flying Saucers—A Modern Myth of Things Seen in the Skies.* London: Routledge, Kegan Paul, 1959. New York: Harcourt, 1959.

111. TISSERAND. "Notice sur les Planètes intramercurielles," *Annuaire du Bureau des Longitudes* (Paris).

112. BUSCO, P. *L'Évolution de l'Astronomie au XIXe Siècle.* Larousse, 1912.

113. RUDAUX, L. *La Lune et son Histoire.* Nouvelles éditions latines, 1947.

114. HYNEK, J. A. "Unusual Aerial Phenomena," *Journal of Optical Society of America*, April, 1953.

115. MARTIN, C. N. *Les Satellites artificiels.* Collection *Que Sais-Je?* Paris: P.U.F., 1958.

116. *L'Astronomie*, Bulletin Societé Astronomie de France. Collection.

117. Collections of *Sky and Telescope, Observatory, Scientific American, Monthly Notices, Popular Astronomy*.

118. GIRVAN, W. *Flying Saucers and Common Sense.* London: Frederick Muller, 1955. New York: Citadel Press, 1956.

119. HEARD, G. *Is Another World Watching?* New York: Harper, 1950.

120. LE POER TRENCH, B. *The F.S.R.'s World Round-Up of UFO Sightings and Events.* New York: Citadel Press, 1958.

121. For the opinions of E. Sänger and J. Gauzit, see *Science et Vie*, No. 403 (April, 1951), p. 216.

122. For the opinion of E. Schatzman, see *Libération*, October 2 and 5, 1954.

123. For the opinion of André Danjon, see *Le Figaro Littéraire*, December 5, 1953.

124. For the opinion of P. Guérin on theoretical possibility of extraterrestrial life, see *Conférences de l'Union Rationaliste* (Paris).

125. For the opinion of A. Kazantsev, *see* his article in *Tekhnika Molodyëzh* (Moscow), September, 1958.

126. SAGAN, C. Address to American Rocket Society, 1963.

127. MISRAKI, P. (PAUL THOMAS). *Les Extraterrestres*. Paris: Plon, 1962.

128. "Une Soucoupe volante à Genève en 1814," *Tribune de Genève* (Geneva, Switzerland), November 9, 1954.

129. "Les Soucoupes volantes au XVe Siècle," *La Croix*, November 20, 1954.

130. "Soucoupes et Cigares sont-ils les Miracles d'un Siècle sans Foi?" *Combat,* October 9, 1954.

131. "L'Église et le Problème des Martiens," *Paris-Presse,* September 17, 1954.

132. For the statements by the German theologian Dessauer, see *Franc-Tireur,* October 15, 1954.

133. "Les Cigares volants remontent à 1034," *France-Soir,* October 27, 1954.

134. On UFO sightings in Communist countries, see *Paris-Presse,* October 27, 1954.

135. RIBERA, A. "UFO Waves Follow a Certain Pattern," *F.S.R.,* V, 9 (May, 1959), 12.

136. ———. "Two More Facts for the UFO File," *F.S.R.,* VIII, 4 (July, 1962), 14.

137. On "flying saucers" and theology, see *Franc-Tireur,* July 29, 1954, and *Le Monde,* July 30, 1954.

138. *Globe Democrat* (St. Louis), April 28, 1897.

139. "Des Spirites avaient annoncé l'arrivée d'une Soucoupe volante," *France-Soir,* September 8, 1954.

140. MANAS, J. H. *Flying Saucers and Space Men*. New York: Pythagorean Society, 1961.

141. RAVON, G. "La Solution de Rechange," *Le Figaro,* September 15, 1964.

142. KLEIN. "Sur l'Existence des Soucoupes," *Tribune de Genève,* November 18, 1954.

143. CUSIN, R. "Non, il n'y a pas de Martien à grosse Tête," *L'Aurore,* September 15, 1954.

144. For reports of the object seen in Kansas City, Chicago, etc. in 1897, see *Popular Astronomy,* 5-55; *New York Sun,* April 2; *New York Herald,* April 11. For the photographs taken in Chicago, see *New York Herald,* April 12. *See also* references (138) and (331).

145. For the observations of Professor Swift, see *Astron. Journal* (September 20, 1896), 17–18; 103.

146. For the observations of "L'Astre-Cherbourg," see *Journal des Débats,* April 4, 1905; *Bull. Soc. Astr. de France,* 1905; *Le Figaro,* April 13, 1905.

147. For the so-called messages from Mars received by Marconi aboard "Electra," see *New York Tribune,* September 2, 1921.

148. For an observation at Córdoba (Argentina) observatory, see *Scientific American,* CXV, 493.

149. For declarations of the Astronomer Royal, Sir Richard Woolley ("Space travel is utter bilge"), *see Austr. F.S.R.,* No. 5, 1961.

150. On the declarations of F. Halstead ("I feel that we have had visitors from space"), *see Austr. F.S.R.,* No. 1.

151. For the declarations of Admiral R. F. Hillenkoetter, former CIA Director, see *UFO Investigator,* May, 1960. ("Unknown objects are operating under intelligent control. It is imperative that we learn where the UFOs come from and what their purpose is.")

152. MILLER, W. *Looking for the General.* New York: McGraw Hill, 1964.

153. LE POER TRENCH, B. *The Sky People.* London: Neville-Spearman, 1961.

154. ———. *Men Among Mankind.* London: Neville-Spearman, 1962.

155. *La Dépêche de Constantine,* July 22, 1955.

156. "Une Soucoupe volante observée le 10 octobre 1954 à Brazzaville," report of the Director of Meteorological Services. Communiqué of *Agence France-Presse,* Spécial Outre-Mer.

157. *The Fitzgerald Report.* UFO Research Committee of Akron, Ohio. December 1, 1958.

158. "Une Soucoupe à l'Heure du Thé?" *Sud-Ouest,* December 23, 1958.

159. "Les Équipages de deux Navires suédois observent un Objet mystérieux dans le Ciel," *L'Espoir,* December 9, 1958.

160. KEYHOE, D. "U.S. Air Force Censorship of UFO Sightings," *True,* January, 1965.

161. GARREAU, C. "L'Objet lumineux aperçu dans notre Région le 24 juin n' était pas une Météorite," *Bourgogne-Republicaine,* July 26–27, 1958.

162. "Un Objet répandant une vive Lumière a traversé le Ciel de Chanteau," *République de Centre*, December 6–7, 1958.

163. "Un curieux Phénomène lumineux a eté observé de nuit sur la Route de Montpellier à Lunel," *Midi Libre*, November 17, 1958.

164. "Un Objet mystérieux observé dans le Ciel de Rio par trois Astronomes brésiliens," *Le Figaro*, July 15, 1959.

165. "Une Soucoupe volante visite-t-elle Madagascar?" *Fandrosoam-Baovao*, January 21, 1955.

166. "Engins mystérieux," *La Dépêche de Constantine*, September 23, 1955.

167. "Disques volants au-dessus de Batna," *La Dépêche de Constantine*, March 25, 1955.

168. "Réapparition des Soucoupes?" *Radar* (Paris), January 29, 1956.

169. "Un Cigare volant dans le Ciel d'Oyonnax?" *Le Progrès*, February 8, 1956.

170. "Une Soucoupe filante sur la Crau," *Franc-Tireur*, August 3, 1955.

171. "Strange Light Over Suva on Sunday Night," *Fiji Times*, October 27, 1957.

172. "Près de Laval un Automobiliste a aperçu un Engin mystérieux," *Ouest-France*, September 5, 1958.

173. "Soucoupes volantes dans la Gironde," *Sud-Ouest Dimanche*, August 24, 1958.

174. "Engin mystérieux dans le Ciel de Bonn," *France-Soir*, June 21, 1959.

175. "Objets mystérieux dans le Ciel danois?" *Libre-Belgique*, June 25, 1959.

176. "Dans le Ciel des Basses-Pyrénées . . . ," *Dépêche du Midi*, January 8, 1959.

177. LISS, JEFFREY. "UFO's That Look Like Tops," *Fate*, November, 1964, p. 66.

178. OSBORN, RICHARD D. "UFO Over Toledo," *Fate*, November, 1964, p. 31.

179. DRAKE, W. RAYMOND. "UFO's in Ancient Times," *Fate*, December, 1964, p. 62.

180. EVANS, GORDON. "Flying Saucers Propulsion and Relativity," *Fate*, December, 1964, p. 67.

181. FULLER, CURTIS. "A Summer Full of UFO Sightings," *Fate*, January, 1965, p. 35.

182. "UFO Hoax at Glassboro?" *Fate*, January, 1965, p. 66.

183. *Saucer News*, XI, 4 (December, 1964).

184. VEILLITH, R. Personal communication, May 21, 1957.

185. MICHEL, A. Personal communication.

186. *Dépêche du Midi* (November 11, 1957 and November 13, 1957).

187. Mr. R. Borale, Personal communication.

188. "Dix Soucoupes volantes survolent la Belgique," *Le Soir Illustré* (Brussels), No. 1681 (September 10, 1964).

189. WATTS, ALAN. "An Experiment on the Effect of an External Magnetic Field on the Ignition Coil of a Car," *BUFORA Journal*, I, 2 (Autumn, 1964).

190. "Remarkable UFO Sighting in New Zealand," *Australian F.S.R.* (Victorian Edition), No. 2 (October, 1964).

191. "Wonthaggi Sighting Report," *Austr. F.S.R.* (Victorian Edition), No. 1 (May, 1964), p. 1.

192. "Unusual Cloud Formations," *Austr. F.S.R.* (Victorian Edition), No. 1 (May, 1964), p. 10.

193. STRUVE, OTTO. "What I Don't Know About Flying Saucers," *Western Amateur Astronomical Convention* (Berkeley), August 19, 1952.

194. "The New Zealand Flap of 1909," *New Zealand SPACEVIEW*, May–June, 1964.

195. RIBERA, A. "UFO's and the Sea," *F.S.R.*, X, 6 (November–December, 1964), 8.

196. CREIGHTON, GORDON W. "What the Soviet Press is Saying," *F.S.R.*, X, 6 (November–December, 1964), 31.

197. JESSUP, M. K. *The Case for the UFO*. New York: Citadel Press, 1955.

198. ARNOLD K., and PALMER, R. A. *The Coming of the Saucers*. Amherst, Wisconsin: Privately printed, 1952.

199. *Fate*, I, 1 (Spring, 1948).

200. PALMER, R. A. "An Open Letter to Paul Fairman," *Other Worlds Science Stories*, June, 1952, pp. 151–56.

201. HYNEK, J. A., and SUMMERSON, H. E. *Project 364 Final Report*. April 30, 1949.

202. RIGOLLET, R. "A New Method for the Photographic

Observation of Meteors of Cosmic Origin," *Journal des Observateurs*, XLV, 8 (1962). In French.

203. VALLEE, J. F. "How to Classify and Codify UFO Sightings," *F.S.R.*, IX, 5, 9–12.

204. JONES, HUNTON, GREGORY and NELMS. "Delta Wing Configuration for the Supersonic Transport," *Astronautics*, June, 1963.

205. KASH, S. W., and TOOPER, R. F. "Active Shielding for Manned Spacecraft," *Astronautics*, September, 1962, pp. 68–75.

206. LEVY, R. H. "Radiation Shielding of Space Vehicles by Means of Superconducting Coil," *ARS Journal*, Vol. XXXI (1961), pp. 1568–70.

207. PENNINGTON, J., and BRISSENDEN, R. "Visual Capability in Rendez-Vous," *Astronautics*, February, 1963, pp. 96–99.

208. BAALS, D., and POLHAMUS, E. "Variable Sweep Aircraft," *Astronautics*, March, 1962.

209. BEISHER, D. E. "Human Tolerance to Magnetic Fields," *Astronautics*, March, 1962.

210. BARNOTHY, T. M. "Biological Effects of Magnetic Fields," *Medical Physics*, Vol. III (O. Glasser, Editor.) Chicago: Year Book Publishers, Inc., 1960.

211. EISELEIN, T. E.; BOUTELL, H. M.; and BIGGS, N. W. "Biological Effects of Magnetic Fields—Negative Results," *Aerospace Medicine*, XXXII, 5 (1961), 383–86.

212. BEISHER, D. E. "Biological Effects of Extremely Strong Magnetic Fields," *Proceedings of International Conference on High Magnetic Fields* (Cambridge, Mass.), 1961.

213. ROW, P., and FISHEL, J. "X-15 Flight-Test Experience," *Astronautics*, June, 1963, p. 25.

214. LEWIS, H. W. "Ball Lightning," *Scientific American*, March, 1963.

215. ATIC special investigation on the Loch Raven Dam case.

216. FINCH, B. E. "The Saucer, a Flying Plasma," *F.S.R.*, VII, 4 (July–August, 1961).

217. KRASSOVSKIY. "Astronautics and Extraterrestrial Civilizations," *Izvestiya*, May 4, 1961.

218. HAFFNER, H. "Les Soucoupes volantes sont une Manifestation de la Foudre," *Combat*, September

15, 1954. See also *Le Parisien* and *France-Soir*, September 16, 1954.

219. MEURES, J. "L'Hystérie des Soucoupes volantes est un Signe de notre Temps." See *Combat* and *Franc-Tireur*, October 6, 1954.

220. BRÉGUET, LOUIS. "Pourquoi Pas?" *Franc-Tireur*, October 6, 1954.

221. MONTALAIS, J. DE. "Soucoupes volantes et Science-fiction," *Combat*, September 16, 1954.

222. BREUIL, D. "Shall We See More Flying Saucers?" *Combat*, September 25, 1954. In French.

223. For D. Fletcher's opinion regarding UFO's, *see* the French press, October 6, 1954.

224. For H. Oberth's opinion on UFO's and their origin, *see* the French press, October 4 and 5, 1954.

225. LAMARRE, L. "Non, il n'y a pas de Soucoupes, etc.," *L'Aurore*, October 1, 1954.

226. NICOLLIER, J. "How Far Have We Got as Regards the Enigma of the Flying Saucers?" *Gazette de Lausanne*, August 8, 1954. In French.

227. On the failure of the Canadian UFO tracking station, see *Le Figaro*, September 1, 1954, and *La Croix*, September 3, 1954.

228. VALJEAN, J. "Les Soucoupes volantes," *L'Humanité*, September 16, 1954.

229. "Les Soucoupes volantes sont des Objets réels," *La Croix*, September 3, 1954.

230. "Serons-nous libérés de la Pesanteur?" *Combat*, November 8, 1954.

231. DEROGY, JEAN. *Libération*, October 14, 1954.

232. For the attitude of the British Air Ministry, see *Franc-Tireur*, October 15, 1954.

233. FONTAINE, Y. For the sightings in Brittany, see *La Croix*, October 16, 1954.

234. EULA, A. "Les Martiens sont forcément très différents de nous," *Franc-Tireur*, October 18, 1954.

235. For questions asked about UFO's in the French Parliament, *see* the French press, October 19 and 20, 1954.

236. VENAISSIN, G. "Le Problème de l'Accueil," *Combat*, October 20, 1954.

237. Statement by the Italian Air Minister: *Le Monde* and *La Croix*, October 26, 1954, *Le Figaro*, October 25, 1954.

238. SWOBODA, G. "Un Savant nie l'Existence des Soucoupes volantes," *Paris-Presse*, October 25, 1954.

239. "The Flying Cigars in 1034," *France-Soir*, October 27, 1954.

240. For the explanation of flying saucers as balloons carrying anti-Communist leaflets, see *Combat*, November 3, 1954.

241. GOLOSNITSKY. *Life on Other Worlds*. Moscow: 1955.

242. BARABASHEV. *Life in the Universe*.

243. GUIEU, J. "Les Soucoupes volantes, Visiteurs ou . . . Ravisseurs extraterrestres?" *Satellite*.

244. For the statements of Dr. Russell, see *Austr. F.S.R.*, I, 1 (1960).

245. For the statements of Dr. Bracewell ("Artificial Satellites From Other Stars May Already be Orbiting Within Our Solar System"), see *Nature*, May 28, 1960.

246. For the statements of Dr. F. Segal ("Beings From Other Planets Could Already Be Making Flights Into Space"), Radio-Moscow broadcast of September 30, 1959.

247. For the statements of Dr. Walter Riedel, see *Austr. F.S.R.*, I, 1.

248. For the statements of Dr. Naugle of NASA ("Further UFO Investigations May Lead to New Scientific Discoveries"), see *UFO Investigator*, II, 9.

249. For the statements of Dr. W. Howells of Harvard ("Intelligent beings abound in the universe and most of them far older than we are"), see *Austr. F.S.R.*, I, 1 (January, 1960).

250. On the "ball-lightning" theory, see *Monthly Weather Review*, 34–17. Quoted by Fort in *op. cit.* p. 284.

251. WILKINS, H. T. *Flying Saucers Uncensored*. New York: Citadel Press.

252. MICHEL, A. "Three Genuine Photographs—Why They Are Authentic," *F.S.R.*, VII, 1 (January-February, 1961), 13–14.

253. VEILLITH, R. Conclusions published in *Tribune de St.-Étienne*, January 24, 1957.

254. "Une Soucoupe volante au-dessus de la Gare de Beauvais," *L'Oise Libérée*, March 4, 1953.

255. MENZEL, D. "Global Orthoteny," *F.S.R.* X, 4 (July–August 1964), 3–4.

256. LEWIS, F. J.; VALLEE, J. F.; and SHIMIZU, T. "Re-

spiratory Mechanics Following Major Surgery," *Digest of the International Conference on Medical Electronics and Biomedical Engineering* (1965), p. 497.

257. VALLEE, J. *Anatomy of a Phenomenon.* Chicago: Regnery, 1965.

258. ———. "A Moment of History," *F.S.R.* X, 4 (July–August, 1964), 30.

259. KEYHOE, D. "U.S. Air Force Censorship of UFO Sightings," *True,* January, 1965.

260. Personal communication.

261. CIEO, *Proceedings* of the meeting of October 3, 1959. Personal communication.

262. TACKER, L. J. *Flying Saucers and the U.S. Air Force.* Princeton, New Jersey: D. Van Nostrand Co., 1960.

263. KRAUS, E. B. "Flying Saucer?" *Weather,* November, 1954.

264. REED, R. J. "Flying Saucers Over Mount Rainier," *Weatherwise,* IX (1958), 43.

265. SCULLY, F. *Behind the Flying Saucers.* New York: Holt, 1950.

266. SARSON, P. B. "Aircraft Condensation Aura," *Meteorological Magazine,* LXXXV (1956), 217.

267. *Johannesburg Star,* April 14, 1958.

268. CRIFO. *Orbit,* Vol. II (March 2, 1956).

269. *Detroit Times,* February 25, 1959.

270. BARKER, G. "Chasing the Flying Saucers," *Flying Saucers,* July, 1959, p. 24.

271. KIRSCH, F. A. "Air Force Right on Killian 'Saucer'?" *Flying Saucers,* August, 1960, p. 17.

272. "Report on Unidentified Objects Observed February 24, 1959, by American-United Airline Pilots." Compiled by UFO Research Committee, Akron, Ohio. February, 1960.

273. "Smithsonian Astrophysical Observatory," *SAO News,* 1, 6 (November, 1961).

274. LEY, W., and VON BRAUN, W. *The Exploration of Mars.* New York: Viking Press, 1956.

275. WHIPPLE, F. L., and HAWKINS, G. S. "Meteors," *Handbuch der Physik,* LII (1959), 519–69.

276. ROBEY, D. H. "An Hypothesis on the Slow Moving Green Fireballs," *Journal of the British Interplanetary Society,* XVII (1959–60), 398–411.

277. O'KEEFE, J. A. "Tektites and the Cyrillid Shower," *Sky and Telescope*, XXI (1961), 4.

278. FESENKOV, V. G. "Cloudiness of the Atmosphere Produced by the Fall of the Tunguska Meteorite of June 30, 1908," *Meteoritika*, VI (1949), 8.

279. OLIVIER, C. P. "Tables of Hourly Rates Based Upon American Meteor Society Data" (Interim Report No. 28), Harvard University Radio Meteor Research Program, May, 1958.

280. JACCHIA, L. G. "The Descent of Satellite 1957 Beta One," *Smithsonian Astrophysical Observatory Special Report No. 15*, July 20, 1958.

281. VALLEE, J. "Sur le Passage d'un Satellite artificiel," *L'Astronomie*, January, 1958.

282. BARKER, G. *They Knew Too Much About Flying Saucers*. New York: University Books, Inc., 1956.

283. "Radar Objects Over Washington," *Air Weather Service Bulletin*, September, 1954, pp. 52–57.

284. MENZEL, D. H. "Why Flying Saucers Show Up on Radar," *Look*, September 9, 1952.

285. KEYHOE, D. E. "What Radar Tells Us About Flying Saucers," *True*, December, 1952, p. 25.

286. WITHROW, S. R. "Angels on Radar Scopes," *Air Weather Service Bulletin*, September, 1954, pp. 48–51.

287. LETELLIER, C., and VALLEE, J. *Report on the Theoretical Study of the Palmier G Radar Antenna*. Paris: Thomson-Houston Co., October, 1962 (Classified).

288. HARPER, W. G. "Angels on Centimetric Radars Caused by Birds," *Nature*, CLXXX (1957), 847.

289. LIDGA, M. G. H. "Radar Observations of Blackbird Flights," *Texas Journal of Science*, December, 1958.

290. CADE, C. M. "Thunderbolts as the X-Weapon," *Discovery*, XXIII (1952), 23–28.

291. KAPITSA, P. L. "The Nature of Ball Lightning," *Dokl. Acad. Nauk SSSR*, CI, 2 (1955), 245–48 (Translated in 292).

292. RITCHIE, D. L. *Ball Lightning*. A collection of Soviet research in English translation. New York: Consultants Bureau, 1961.

293. SCHMIDT, R. O. "The Kearny Incident," *Flying Saucers*, October, 1959, p. 31.

294. "The Case of the Radio-active UFO," *Flying Saucers,* February, 1958, p. 30.

295. *Electromagnetic Effects Associated With Unidentified Flying Objects.* Washington, D.C.: NICAP, June, 1960.

296. CRAMP, L. G. *Space Gravity and the Flying Saucer.* New York: British Book Centre, 1955.

297. MAC DOUGALL, C. D. *Hoaxes.* New York: Ace Books, 1958.

298. FRY, D. W. *The White Sands Incident.* Los Angeles: New Age Publishing Co., 1954.

299. BETHURUM, T. *Aboard a Flying Saucer.* Los Angeles: De Vorss & Co., 1954.

300. VAN TASSEL, G. W. *I Rode a Flying Saucer.* Los Angeles: New Age Publishing Co., 1952.

301. CAHN, J. P. "Flying Saucers and the Mysterious Little Men," *True,* September, 1952.

302. MENGER, H. *From Outer Space to You.* Clarksburg, West Virginia: Saucerian Publications, 1959.

303. "Have We Visitors From Outer Space?" *Life,* April 4, 1952.

304. FONTES, O. T. "The Brazilian Navy UFO Sighting at the Island of Trindade," *Flying Saucers,* February, 1961, p. 27.

305. MANEY, C. A., and HALL, R. *The Challenge of Unidentified Flying Objects.* Washington, D.C.: 1961.

306. *O Cruzeiro.* Rio de Janeiro: May 17, 1952.

307. LORENZEN, C. E. "The Reality of the Little Men," *Flying Saucers,* December, 1958, p. 26.

308. NASH, W. B., and FORTENBERRY, W. H. "We Flew Above Flying Saucers," *True,* October, 1952.

309. "Flying Saucers, the Enigma of the Skies," *Armstrong Circle Theatre TV Script,* January 22, 1958.

310. LORENZEN, C. E. "The Psychology of UFO Secrecy," *Flying Saucers,* October, 1958, p. 12.

311. DAVIDSON, L. "An Open Letter to Saucer Researchers," *Flying Saucers,* March, 1962, p. 36.

312. *The Fitzgerald Report.* The UFO Research Committee of Akron, Ohio, 1958.

313. "Nine Saucers Flying 1200 mph Sighted.—But What Are They?" *Los Angeles Times,* June 26, 1947.

314. "Many Report Seeing Flying Saucers," *Los Angeles Daily News,* June 29, 1947.

315. *Los Angeles Examiner,* July 4 and 5, 1947.

316. "F-51 and Captain Mantell Destroyed Chasing Flying Saucer," *Louisville Courier,* January 7, 1948.

317. "Flying Saucer Sets Off Explosion?" *Omaha Herald,* February 18, 1948.

318. *Los Angeles Times,* April 8 and 27, 1949.

319. SHALETT, S. "What You Can Believe About Flying Saucers," *Saturday Evening Post,* April 30, 1949.

320. *Los Angeles Times,* July 25, August 21 and 31, and September 16, 1949.

321. "New Theory Hinted. Flying Saucers are Really Real," *Los Angeles Daily Mirror.*

322. SCULLY, F. "One Flying Saucer Lands in New Mexico," *Variety* (New York), October 12, 1949.

323. *Los Angeles Daily Mirror,* October 31, 1949.

324. SCULLY, F. "Flying Saucers Dismantled, Secrets May Be Lost," *Variety* (New York), October 23, 1949.

325. "Flying Saucers Ideas Blasted by Air Force," *Hollywood Citizen News,* December 28, 1949.

326. SCULLY, F. "Air Force Asked Twenty Questions," *Variety* (New York), January, 1950.

327. *Kansas City Times,* January 20, 1950.

328. LITTLE, C. "D.U. Students Hear Weird Tale of Midget Disk Pilots Landing," *Denver Post,* March 9, 1950.

329. "Disk Reports Start Jitters," *Chicago Daily Times,* March 10, 1950.

330. BOORSTIN, DANIEL. *The Image.* New York: Harper, 1964.

331. CLARK, JEROME. "A Contact Claim," *F.S.R.,* XI, 1, 30–32.

332. OPIK, ERNST. *Physics of Meteor Flight in the Atmosphere.* New York: Interscience Publishers, 1958.

333. "Flying Saucer Fans in Occult World," *Chicago American,* September 2, 1965.

334. RADAU, R. *Sur les Petites Planètes.* A brochure giving the details of ancient observations of intramercurial planets, 1861.

335. TISSERAND. "Notice sur les Planètes intramercurielles," *Annual Bureau des Longitudes,* 1882.

336. *Natal Daily News,* February 21, 1951.

337. *Nairobi Sunday Post,* February 25, 1951.

338. LEWIS, RICHARD. "Mystery of Flying Saucers—Why No Solution?" *Chicago Sun-Times,* March 14, 1965.

339. SAGAN, C. "Exobiology: A Critical Review," Life Sciences and Space Research II, Fourth International Space Science Symposium. Warsaw: June 3–12, 1961.

340. ———. "Unidentified Flying Objects," *Encyclopedia Americana*, 1963.

341. HARRISON, BROWN. "Planetary Systems Associated with Main Sequence Stars," *Science*, CXLV (September 11, 1964), 177–81.

342. FREUDENTHAL. *LINCOS: Design of a Language for Cosmic Intercourse*. Amsterdam: North Holland Publishing Co.

343. *Journal de Lausanne*, July 23, 1951.

344. *Sunday Express*, October 1, 1951.

345. *Le Figaro*, March 28, 1951.

346. *L'Astronomie* (1951), p. 474.

347. *Le Figaro*, September 13, 1951.

348. MANEY, CHARLES A. "Donald Menzel's UFO. A Critical Report," *Fate*, April, 1965, p. 64.

349. HARTLE, ORVIL H. *A Carbon Experiment?* La Porte, Indiana: Privately printed, April, 1963.

350. SEEVIOUR, PETER M. "Foundations of Orthoteny," *F.S.R.*, XI, 2 (March–April, 1965), 10–12.

351. "The Air Force Intimidates Witnesses," *The UFO Investigator*, III, 1 (March–April, 1965), 1.

352. "Controverse sur L'Existence des M.O.C." (correspondence between Mrs. P. Neirinck and R. Veillith), *Lumières dans la Nuit*, No. 74 (March–April, 1965).

353. VERVISCH, ROGER. "Une Soucoupe volante photographiée en Belgique?" *Le Soir Illustré*, June 16, 1955.

354. BOOHER, JAKE. "Policeman Recalls Night Which Changed His Life," *El Paso Times*, April 24, 1965.

355. "Saucers Not Hostile," report of the Scientific Panel on UFO's (released by U.S. Air Force, April 9, 1958), *Flying Saucer News*, August, 1965.

356. TERRENCE, ARTHUR. "Con Man Nets 300 G by Scaring Thousands Into Believing Venus is Going to Invade the Earth," *National Enquirer*, October 25, 1964, pp. 10–11.

357. MANEY, CHARLES A. "Scientific Measurement of UFO's," *Fate*, June, 1965, p. 31.

358. COHEN, DANIEL. "Should We Be Serious About

UFO's?" (Review of [257], *Anatomy of a Phenomenon*), *Science Digest*, June, 1965.

359. MENZEL, DONALD H. "Orthoteny. A Lost Cause," *F.S.R.*, XI, 3, (May–June, 1965), 9–11.

360. MICHEL, A. "Reflections of an Honest Liar," *F.S.R.*, XI, 3 (May–June, 1965), 11–14.

361. "Un ONI est aperçu dans le Ciel de la Vallée du Buech," *Dauphiné Libéré*, October, 1958.

362. FIRSOFF, V. A. *Life Beyond the Earth*. New York: Basic Books, Inc., 1963.

363. DENEAULT, HAROLD H. "UFO's Return to Washington," *Fate*, July, 1965.

364. "Saucer Info Needed," *San Antonio Light*, August 1, 1965.

365. KLECKNER, ROBERT S. "An Astronomer Calls Flying Saucers Serious Business," *Chicago Sun-Times*, August 8, 1965.

366. "Flying Saucer Report Back in 1878 Found," *Dallas Morning News*, August 6, 1965.

367. FEUILLET, CLAUDE. "Plus fort que mille Atomes," *L'Express*, July 12, 1965.

368. SCHWEIGHAUSER, CHARLES A. "Super-race Visit Nonsense," *Saint Louis Globe-Democrat*, July 17–18, 1965.

369. DOUTHIT, PETER L. "UFO Phenomenon Given Close Study," *Fort Worth Star Telegram*, July 11, 1965.

370. "Those UFO's Have Been Around a Long Time," *Columbus Dispatch*, July 25, 1965.

371. "Saucers Genuine," *Sydney* (Australia) *Sun-Herald*, February 28, 1965.

372. "Study UFO," *Farmville* (Virginia) *Herald*, July 13, 1965.

373. SANDERSON, IVAN T. "Travelling Pinwheels of Tropic Waters," *Fate*, July, 1964, p. 42.

374. MINTO, WALLACE L. "What Lights the Mystery Wheels?" *Fate*, July, 1964, p. 53.

375. "Was it Flying Saucer at Bottom of Ocean?" *Las Cruces Sun-News*, July 6, 1965.

376. DELANAY, JOHN. *A Woman Clothed With the Sun*. Doubleday Image Series.

377. "The Case for Flying Saucers," *Australian Post*, April 15, 1965.

378. "Observation d'un Bolide Double à Vannes, le 3 janvier, 1898," from the observations of M. Georget,

Comptes Rendus. French Academy of Science, January 17, 1898.

379. ZASLAVSKAYA, N. A.; ZOTKIN, I. T.; and KIROVA, O. A. "Distribution of the Cosmic Spheres From the Region of the Tunguska Meteorite," *Soviet Physics Doklady,* IX, 5 (November, 1964), 333.

380. "Are Flying Saucers Linked With Mystery Signals?" *Lilydale* (Australia) *Express,* June 17, 1965.

381. Article on "foo-fighters" in *American Legion Magazine,* December, 1945.

382. FULLER, JOHN. *Incident at Exeter.* New York: Putnam, 1966.

383. "Engin Mystérieux en Lot-et-Garonne," *Nice-Matin,* August 3, 1965.

384. "Epidemie de Soucoupes volantes en Espagne," *Nice-Matin,* July 30, 1965.

385. "Mariner IV," *Paris-Normandie,* July 16, 1965.

386. "Encore une Soucoupe volante," *Nice-Matin,* July 12, 1965.

387. "Soucoupes volantes en Provence," *Le Provençal,* September 8, 1965.

388. "Phénomène etrange dans le Ciel corse," *Nice-Matin,* August 8, 1965.

389. "Une Sphere volante a fait une Halte de 45 minutes au-dessus de La Clape," *Midi-Libre,* August 5, 1965.

390. "Deux Nuits de suite les Evolutions d'une Soucoupe volante ont été observées par quatre Vigiles de La Clape," *Midi-Libre,* July 29, 1965.

391. "Platillos volantes—un Joven de Beasin vio el Lunes un extrano Objeto en el Firmamento," *Voz de Espana,* July 28, 1965.

392. "Interest Revived in Sightings by 'Saucer' Fans," *Oklahoma City Times,* July 22, 1965.

393. "Bright Objects in Sky Set Phones, Nerves Jingling," *Daily Oklahoman,* August 2, 1965.

394. VALLEE, J. F. "A New Look at Saucer Mysteries," *True,* September, 1965.

395. DOLE, S. H. *Habitable Planets for Man.* New York: Blaisdell, 1964.

396. REID, FRANK J. "The Luminous Portents of Earthquakes," *Fate,* November, 1965, p. 90.

397. HANLON, D. B. "Significance of the January 1965 Virginia Flap," *F.S.R.,* XII, 2 (March–April, 1966).

398. LORENZEN, C. "Great Western UFO Flap," *Fate,* November, 1965, p. 42.

399. VALLEE, JANINE, and VALLEE, JACQUES. *Les Phénomènes Insolites de l'Espace.* Paris: La Table Ronde, 1966.

400. *Unidentified Flying Objects: Hearing by Committee on Armed Services of the House of Representatives* (Eighty-ninth Congress, Second Session; No. 55), April 5, 1966, pp. 5991 ff.

INDEX

317

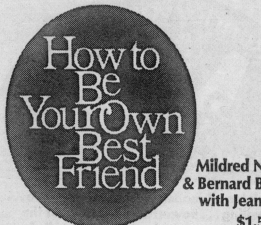